PHL

5406000054014

IN MEMORIAM

SO·THE·HEART·BE·RIGHT

Joanna Defrates

1945-2000

B/40/86

D1588041

This work originally appeared in February 1944 as a Pelican book. The present revised and enlarged edition is issued by arrangement with Penguin Books Ltd., the publishers of Pelican Books

PREHISTORIC BRITAIN

This work originally appeared in February 1944 as a Pelican book. The present revised and enlarged edition is issued by arrangement with Penguin Books Ltd., the publishers of Pelican Books

Crown Copyright reserved

Mulfra Quoit, Penzance, Cornwall. A partially collapsed megalithic tomb

Prehistoric Britain

JACQUETTA
&
CHRISTOPHER HAWKES

WITHDRAWN

THE BRITISH MUSEUM

THE PAUL HAMLYN LIBRARY

1949

Chatto and Windus

LONDON

PUBLISHED BY

Chatto & Windus

LONDON

✶

Clarke, Irwin & Co. Ltd

TORONTO

THE
BRITISH
MUSEUM

THE PAUL HAMLYN LIBRARY

936.
101
HAW

THIS EDITION FIRST PUBLISHED 1947
THIRD IMPRESSION 1949
PRODUCED IN COMPLETE CONFORMITY
WITH THE AUTHORIZED ECONOMY STANDARDS
PRINTED IN GREAT BRITAIN
ALL RIGHTS RESERVED

Foreword

IN a single century archæology has pushed the beginning of human history back some half-million years, and given it a perspective which was altogether lacking when knowledge was restricted to the comparatively short span of time covered by written records. Then, too, the material with which the prehistorian works is far more intimate than the documents of the historian. It is true that he lacks the romantic appeal of famous names, he cannot marshal an array of kings, heroes and law-givers, but instead he handles the actual things which helped men to pass their lives: the pots from which they ate and drank, the weapons with which they hunted or killed one another, their houses, their hearthstones and their graves. He is concerned with the lives and achievements of countless ordinary, anonymous people.

Archæology has enabled us to understand how, from the moment when primitive human creatures shaped the first tools, chapter after chapter has been added to the tale of man's accomplishments. He masters fire, he discovers a mechanical principle, he becomes an artist, he learns to farm, to weave, to shape pots, to sail boats, to make wheels, to cast bronze, to work iron, until imperceptibly we have reached the unfinished chapter of today. There is no break in this procession of events. For myself, I always see them as it were threaded on a taut line which stretches from the present near my eyes back and back into the distance of the past—a line which is in fact the historical time-sequence, the long line of the passing years. Because we are so conscious of this thread of time running through history, we have in this book held to it as a guide, following beside it for the tens of thousands of years that lead from eoliths to the Romans. A pedestrian method certainly, but one which keeps the vast complex story in good order and helps to convey the sense of continuity between the past, present and future of humanity, which is the underlying theme.

This book wishes to be no more than the briefest chronicle of the course of human history in the small but never unimportant corner of the world that we have come to know as the British Isles.

A word as to the manner of our collaboration. I have written

Chapters I–IV, the greater part of V, Chapter VII and the Topographical Appendix. My husband wrote certain parts of the Vth and the whole of the VIth chapter. More than that, his exacting scholar's eye scanned my text and allowed nothing dubious or inaccurate to pass. For this the reader will be more grateful than I was.

J. J. H.

Acknowledgements

WE wish to acknowledge permission given by the following institutions, authors and publishers for the reproduction of illustrations: Ashmolean Museum, Oxford (Pl. XI); British Museum (Pls. XIII, XV; Figs. 5, 7, 12-14, 16, 17, 23, which are official drawings by Mr. C. O. Waterhouse); Ministries of Education and Information (Front., Pls. I-X, XII, XVI; these photographs are by Mr. Walter Bird); Ministry of Works (Pl. XVIII); Air Ministry (Pl. XXII, Royal Air Force official photograph); National Museum of Wales (Pl. XIX i); Society of Antiquaries of London (Pls. XIX ii, XX i, XX ii, Fig. 25); Mrs. Burkitt (Fig. 1); Mrs. Burkitt and Prof. Childe (Fig. 2); Dr. Grahame Clark and Messrs. Methuen (Fig. 21); Dr. E. C. Curwen and the same (Fig. 6); Oxford University Press (Fig. 9); Royal Commission on Ancient Monuments (Fig. 24); Verulamium Museum, St. Albans (Fig. 26); Messrs. B. & N. Westwood & Sons (Pl. XVII); Figs. 4, 11, 15, 18 were specially drawn by Miss Irene Hawkins. Finally, we wish particularly to thank Professor Stuart Piggott for allowing us to use his unpublished reconstruction of the Haldon House (Fig. 3).

Table of Dates

THE reader will understand that the earlier these are, the less precise their accuracy becomes. Dates before about 10,000 B.C. are only rough indications; thence on to about 2000 B.C. they are (for Britain) simple approximations; thereafter, broadly speaking, they get gradually more and more accurate until exact historical dating begins with Cæsar's expeditions and the Roman conquest of the 1st century A.D.

Speaking generally, the basis of the earlier dates is geological (in part also astronomical); the later ones are for the most part based ultimately upon the known chronologies of contemporary Egypt, Mesopotamia, Greece, or Rome.

	B.C.
Palæolithic period, beginning	about 550,000
Aurignacian replaces Neanderthal Man	about 100,000
Palæolithic period giving place to ⎱	⎰ about 12,000–
Mesolithic period ⎰	⎱ 10,000
Maglemose culture flourishing: ⎱	about 6000
Britain becomes an island ⎰	
Dawn of civilization in the Near East	about 6000–5000
In Britain:—	
Neolithic period beginning	2500
Early Bronze Age: Beaker invasions	1900–1800
Early Bronze Age: Wessex invasion	soon after 1700
Middle Bronze Age: rise of Urn people beginning	1400
Late Bronze Age beginning	1000
Late Bronze Age: Deverel-Rimbury invasions	750
Early Iron Age beginning	500
Early Iron Age: La Tène invasions beginning	250
Early Iron Age: Belgic invasions in Kent	75
Julius Cæsar's expeditions	55 and 54
Early Iron Age: Belgic invasion of Commius	50
	A.D.
Cunobelin becomes king at Camulodunum (Colchester)	10
Roman conquest begins under Claudius	43

viii

Contents

Chapter		Page
	Prelude	1
1	The Palæolithic and Mesolithic Ages	3
2	The Neolithic Age	25
3	The Early and Middle Bronze Ages	51
4	The Late Bronze Age	85
5	The Early Iron Age	100
6	Britain and the Romans	120
7	Archæology	151
	Bibliography	181
	Appendix	185
	Index	274

Contents of Appendix

	Page
CLASSIFICATION OF FIELD MONUMENTS	185
I. SOUTH-EASTERN ENGLAND	187
(North Downs)	188
(Canterbury District)	190
(Dover—Hythe)	191
(South Downs)	192
II. WESSEX	197
(North Hampshire Downs)	198
(Central Hampshire)	199
(South Hampshire)	200
(Berkshire Downs)	201
(Wansdyke)	203
(Marlborough Downs)	203
(Salisbury Plain)	204
(Cranborne Chase)	207
(West Hampshire—Dorset)	211
III. THE SOUTH-WEST	213
(Bath—Bristol)	214
(Mendips and Quantocks)	215
(Exmoor)	217
(Bridport—Exeter)	219
(Dartmoor)	220
(Cornwall)	221
IV. THE COTSWOLDS	225
(North Oxfordshire)	226
(Northern Cotswolds)	227
(Western Cotswolds)	230
(Southern Cotswolds)	231
(Lydney to the Malverns)	233

Page

V. WALES   234

   (Monmouth and South Wales)   234
   (Black Mountains)   236
   (Pembrokeshire)   236
   (Central Wales)   237
   (North Wales and Anglesey)   238

VI. WEST MIDLANDS AND THE WELSH BORDER   240

   (Herefordshire)   241
   (Offa's Dyke)   242
   (Shropshire)   243
   (Cheshire)   244
   (Derbyshire)   244

VII. FROM THE CHILTERNS TO EAST ANGLIA   246

   (Chilterns)   246
   (Royston—Newmarket)   248
   (The Breckland)   249
   (Essex)   250

VIII. LINCOLNSHIRE AND YORKSHIRE   251

   (Lincolnshire Wolds)   252
   (Yorkshire Wolds)   253
   (North Yorkshire Moors)   255
   (West Riding—the Yorkshire Dales)   258

IX. NORTH LANCASHIRE: CUMBERLAND AND WESTMORELAND   261

   (Westmoreland)   261
   (Lake District)   262
   (Eden Valley)   262

X. DURHAM, THE ROMAN WALL AND NORTH-UMBERLAND   263

   (Durham)   263
   (The Roman Wall)   263
   (The Cheviots)   264

Page

XI. SCOTLAND   265

    (South of the Clyde and Forth)   266
    (North of the Clyde and Forth—to the Esk and
      Ardnamurchan)   268
    (The North-Central Region—from Esk and Ardna-
      murchan to Loch Broom and the Moray Firth,
      including the Hebrides)   269
    (North Scotland, the Orkneys and Shetlands)   271

List of Plates

Plate

Mulfra Quoit, Penzance, Cornwall.   A partially collapsed megalithic tomb *Frontispiece*

Facing page

1   Using a flint hoe   32

2   Casting a flat copper axe in an open mould   33

3   Maeshowe, Orkney.   Mound covering a megalithic passage-grave   48

4   Maeshowe, Orkney.   Runes carved by Vikings when sheltering in the passage-grave   49

5   Stonehenge trilithons   64

6   Stonehenge. The upright shows a tenon which fitted into a mortice-hole such as that visible in the fallen lintel-stone   65

7   Stennis, Orkney. Part of the stone circle, with surrounding bank and ditch   80

8   A line of Bronze Age round barrows   81

9   Skara Brae, Orkney. A house in the Bronze Age village   96

10   Skara Brae, Orkney.   A dresser made from stone slabs   97

11   Celtic fields on Fyfield Down, Wiltshire, from the air   112

12   Reconstruction of the Early Iron Age farmhouse of Little Woodbury, near Salisbury   113

13   Celtic art.   Sword with iron blade and bronze scabbard-mount, from the river Witham, near Lincoln   128

14   Celtic art.   Chamfrein, or bronze head armour for a horse, from Torrs, Kirkcudbright, Scotland   129

15   Celtic art.   Shield of cast bronze with red-enamelled studs from the river Thames at Battersea   144

16   Maiden Castle, Dorset.   The multiple ramparts   145

Plate   Facing page

17 Hadrian's Wall, looking east towards its ascent of Sewing-
      shields Crags, from the north gate of Housesteads Fort,
      Northumberland   160

18 The Roman works of Richborough Castle, Kent, from the
      air.   The outer wall and ditches are of the late "Saxon
      Shore" fort; within are the triple ditches of a slightly
      earlier fort, and the straight double ditch of the original
      invasion-base of Claudius   161

19 Excavation technique. i, Breach Farm, Glamorganshire;
      digging a round barrow by the quadrant method.
      ii, Maiden Castle; Roman temple overlying the storage
      pits of the Iron Age occupation   176

20 Excavation technique. Maiden Castle: (left) Section cut
      through the rampart and living-floors within; (below)
      Excavation of the east entrance by the grid method   177

21 Types of burial mound. The group of barrows at
      Winterbourne Cross-roads near Stonehenge (see key
      sketch opposite)   206

22 Types of fortification. Two Iron Age hill-forts in
      Dorset. Hod Hill (top), multiple-ramparted, with
      a Roman fort constructed in the lower corner; Hamble-
      don Hill (bottom), another multiple-ramparted type   207

List of Figures

Fig.		Page
1	Flint implements of the Palæolithic Age	11
2	Mesolithic bone harpoon	20
3	Isometric Reconstruction of Neolithic house on Haldon, Devon	31
4	Development of the handmill or quern. A, Neolithic. B, Bronze and Earliest Iron Ages	32
4	Development of the handmill or quern. C, Later Iron Age; and Roman Periods	33
5	Neolithic pottery. A, Windmill Hill type; B, Peterborough type	35
6	Neolithic flint-mine at Harrow Hill, Sussex, being cleared by modern excavators	38
7	Early Bronze Age pottery. A, B, beakers; C, food vessel; D, pygmy cup	53
8	Simplified Plan of Stonehenge	60
9	Jet bead necklace and gold necklet of the Early Bronze Age	67
10	Chalk-carved idol of the Early Bronze Age, from a round barrow at Folkton, Yorkshire	69
11	Reconstruction of a Bronze Age dug-out canoe	71
12	Middle and Late Bronze Ages, cremation urns	75
13	The development of the bronze spearhead	79
14	Method of shafting stone and bronze axes	81
15	Bronze cauldron of the Late Bronze Age	97
16	Iron Age Pottery. A, B, Hallstatt types; C, La Tène type; D, E, Belgic types	104
17	The Witham shield: outline diagram showing the boar	110

Fig.		Page
18	Reconstruction of the Glastonbury Lake Village	115
19	Carved wooden bowl from Glastonbury	117
20	Iron currency bars of the Early Iron Age	119
21	British coins: one of their Greek models on the extreme left	124
22	'The White Horse of Uffington'	126
23	The Desborough mirror, showing the engraved back	130
24	The Broch of Mousa, Shetland: sectional view showing the stairs and galleries in the walls of the stone tower	136
25	Celtic ornament showing Roman influence: embossed bronze panel with strip of enamel work, from Elmswell, Yorkshire	140
26	The Roman Farm at Lockleys, Welwyn. Reconstruction after excavation	141
27	Sectional diagram of the excavation at Peacock's Farm, Cambridgeshire	169
28	Section cut through a round barrow at Sutton, Glamorganshire	171
29	Composite section showing historical sequence at Camulodunum, Colchester	172
30	Key to Pl. XXI. The group of barrows at Winterbourne Cross-roads, near Stonehenge	206

PRELUDE

I BEGAN upon the first edition of this book in 1940 when, if one listened to the intellect alone, a German victory seemed almost certain. I was in fact preparing to write about the deepest roots of a civilization whose topmost shoots were perhaps soon to be hacked off. Seeking for a justification for this fiddle playing, I was able to suggest that although my subject was remote in time there was yet something topical in it. There was a sudden probability that the pattern of prehistoric events would be repeated, and that the repetition would be imposed upon one's own life. As this book will show, prehistorians have spent their learning and ingenuity on reconstructing continental invasions of Britain that took place thousands of years ago. In 1940 we expected to be eye-witnesses of another, and its victims.

It was amusing to see in how many ways the present promised to reflect the past; it was even reassuring—the feeling 'this has happened before' gave perspective to one's own fate. In the early summer of the year I was living in East Anglia where it was known that we were threatened by invasion from the Low Countries, North Germany and Scandinavia, just the regions from which the prehistoric invaders of our eastern coasts had usually come. What happened next? One by one I watched my acquaintance, openly or surreptitiously according to their natures, join in a westward migration, some to south-western England, many more to Wales. Irresistibly caught up, my small son and I found ourselves in Dorset, a unit in this mass movement to the west. How reminiscent it was of an earlier Germanic onslaught when the warlike and pagan Anglo-Saxons swept down on eastern Britain, and the Celts, pacific after the centuries of Roman rule, fled before them to seek safety among the western hills.

As the summer of 1940 advanced, German hordes were reported to be massing down the coasts of France, and the whole of southern England became uneasy. This again followed the prehistoric pattern, for throughout the Stone, Bronze and Iron Ages our southern shores had been invaded from France. In our particular western corner of Dorset we talked of the alarming nearness of Normandy and Brittany, of boats rumoured to be gathering at Cherbourg and Brest. I reminded myself how Dorset had known invasion from Brittany in Neolithic times, at the beginning of the Bronze Age and again in the Iron Age.

Finally there was Italy, the latest enemy. Letters from friends fled to Cornwall suggested that the Italians were threatening the safety of the south-western peninsula, while there were frequent rumours of Italian landings in Ireland. Here again prehistory could show analogues, for archæology has proved that those areas were always accessible to movements springing from the Mediterranean, for instance that which brought the Megalithic chieftains four thousand years ago. There could have been nothing unexpected in such repetitions of old patterns. Whatever may be true in the future it is clear that at that time not even aeroplanes had altered the control that geography exercises over human movements.

But now it all grows distant and unreal, quite as far from recall as the events of prehistory; I find it hard to believe that this body of mine took part in the great exodus from Paddington, that it had a place in the trains crowded with migrating families—those things might have happened at any time. Faint and impersonal though the memory now is, this opening digression has been allowed in order to give some idea of the natural routes by which settlers and conquerors have at all times approached the British Isles; Chapter One will immediately follow with some account of the nature of the country itself.

Chapter One

THE PALÆOLITHIC
AND MESOLITHIC AGES

To all except the most urbanized among us the physical nature of our country is of profound significance. The widely differing types of scenery that Britain can offer in so small a space have entered our consciousness at an early age, beginning perhaps with the first summer holidays that took us out of a familiar scene and into a strange one. No need for knowledge of geological formations to be aware of their powerful influence on the countryside they nourish. There is an instinctive appreciation of the difference between the dry, golden feeling of the sandy heaths, the pale, clear atmosphere of the chalk, the boundless, open-skyed freedom of fenlands, and the damp chill that strikes up from the heavy clay soil of the Midlands. They appeal to different temperaments and different moods. Yet, distinctive though these several kinds of country are, they have something in common, for all belong to the lowlands of southern, central and eastern England: an even greater contrast is to be found between these lowlands as a whole and the highlands of the west and north. Geologically the lowlands are young, and have the soft contours of youth, while the ancient rocks forming the highlands show the rugged features of a strong old age.

The line dividing these two worlds runs from east Devon to the southern boundary of Durham, but the highland zone is broken between the northern Welsh mountains and the Pennine Chain by the intrusion of the Midland Gap and the Cheshire Plain. North and west of that line one cannot be the same man that breathes south and east of it: the mountains, moorlands, swift streams, bogs, and their attendant trees, plants, birds and fishes work a transformation. Crossing it means more than crossing the Channel, for the highland zone is far more alien to the lowland than the latter is to the adjacent parts of northern France and Flanders.

If today we are still acutely conscious of these divisions within our country, early man had to be much more so. Centuries of cultivation have minimized the distinctions between the various regions of the lowland zone, while modern transport hurries one without effort across boundaries that were once formidable. On shanks' mare in a roadless land the traveller had a very different outlook. When man's ordering of the natural scene was unthought of or only just begun, he could not fail to be ever aware of the environment that was his master. What were the main geographical factors that limited prehistoric man's choice of movement and settlement? For the moment it is best to leave behind those more remote ages when Britain formed an unrecognizable part of the Continent, and deal only with the time when it had assumed approximately its present shape and temperate climate.

Consider first the forests. In prehistoric times no considerable progress was made in clearing the dense covering of oakwood and thorny undergrowth supported by the heavier and richer soils. This luxuriant growth, and the damp soil beneath, made great tracts of the lowlands, including much of the Midlands, impossible for human settlement and all but impenetrable.

In the days before drainage, marshland, too, was much more extensive; the East Anglian fens and the Vale of York formed the largest water-logged areas, but very many valley bottoms now pleasantly lined with green meadows were then swampy and hard to traverse.

It was only where soil was light and pervious, poor regions in the eyes of the modern farmer, that men were able to clear and settle the land. Hence the overwhelming concentration of prehistoric sites on chalk and limestone uplands, sandy soil, and the gravel of some valleys. For many people the great monuments of Stonehenge and Avebury, with the barrows and other satellites clustering round them, represent the essential core of all British antiquity. There is sound reason in this belief, however emotional its inspiration. The region in which they stand was all-important owing to its commanding geographical position. The physical map shows clearly how the Wiltshire Downlands form the nodal point of the lands suitable for prehistoric occupation. Not only does the chalk here reach its widest extent, but from it radiate all the principal chalk and limestone ranges of lowland Britain: the Mendips point towards the Bristol Channel; the Western Downs stretch far into Dorset; the Hampshire Downs, forking into the North and South Downs, reach the English Channel in Kent and Sussex; the Chiltern Hills linking with the East Anglian Heights penetrate to the North Sea; and finally the Cotswolds and Northampton Uplands finger northwards and make contact possible with the wide, habitable region of the Lincolnshire and Yorkshire Wolds. Equally important, the Wiltshire Downs are accessible by navigable rivers, most significantly by the Thames, which early formed a vital thoroughfare and whose gravel-filled valley was always favourable to settlement. Thus the whole of this wheel-like system had a kind of unity, and on its uplands men could rear their flocks and herds, their children and their crops, looking down on the forests that pushed up between the spokes, formidable and hostile, the haunt of bears, wolves, lynx, and perhaps of evil spirits.

Very different problems confronted would-be settlers in the highland country. There the upland ranges were shunned as boggy, windswept and generally inhospitable, the valley bottoms were blocked by oak forest, while then as now the extreme acidity of highland soil discouraged agriculture. Their choice was thus mainly limited to coastal belts such as that of eastern Scotland, where glaciers had left a more profitable soil, and to narrow coastal glens, peninsulas, and islands where well-drained ground was offered by the remains of old sea beaches. They could also take possession of the flanks of mountain valleys lying between the forested bottoms and the bleak crests above. There are signs that man could not afford entirely to ignore the high moorlands: probably he visited them during the summer when they could provide fair grazing for his beasts. Indeed, in the kinder climate of the south-

west, uplands such as Dartmoor and Exmoor could be permanently settled and were at times quite populous.

Another strong contrast with the lowlands. While there
we have found a general accessibility between all the habitable
territories, in the mountainous country, especially in western
Scotland and Wales, each little settled area tended to be cut off
from the next by almost impassable barriers.   To some extent,
however, the prehistoric communities escaped the isolation
that their land would have imposed by launching boats and
finding easier and swifter passage by sea than any mountain
trail could allow.   Nor did their craft always hug the shore:
there was often free intercourse across the Irish Sea between
south-west Scotland, north Wales, the Isle of Man and Ulster.
If Ireland falls outside our main survey, she can never be forgotten.   Inevitably her fate was closely linked with that of
the British highlands that reached out towards her even while
they walled her off from England and the Continent.

These, then, were the two great zones of Britain with their
contrasting pattern of human settlement. What was the relationship between them: the reaction of one upon the other?
Modern analogy has been used to show how the lowlands
were always prone to invasion from the opposing Continental
shores, and how each wave of immigrants tended to push
some of the older population into the hills.   The new impulse
might well itself reach the highlands, but attenuated and
transfigured.   Once there, it would be further modified alike
by a strong conservative tradition and by fresh external
influences.   For the highlands had their own contact with the
Continent along the Atlantic sea routes from Brittany to
Portugal, and thence with the Mediterranean both by sea round
the coast of the Iberian Peninsula and by land across its
neck.   They also had an all-important asset in their possession
of metal ores: gold in Ireland, tin in Cornwall, and copper in
Ireland, Cornwall, north Wales and western Scotland.   Thus
the highlands had distinctive ingredients to add to the British
stock-pot.

The curious, intricate outline of these islands perched on
the edge of Europe has from childhood become so strongly

engraved on our minds that it seems to have something of unalterable truth. In fact, of course, the British Isles are infinitely younger than man. Human beings of a kind have inhabited our world for at least half a million years: the chalk hills that stretched across the present line of the English Channel were not finally breached until quite recently, some eight thousand years ago, while much of the North Sea was still land at an even later date.

The map of Britain began to assume its present form during the last great geological epoch, that of the Pleistocene, which covers the period often called the Ice Age. This name is misleading, for it suggests an age of continuous cold, whereas in fact it was divided into distinct cold phases, probably at least four in number, with intervals when the European climate was sometimes much warmer than at present.

At the height of the cold conditions Scotland and a great part of England lay under vast ice-sheets and glaciers: the intervening spells saw the retreat of the ice towards the north and the spread of warmth-loving plants and animals in its wake. These glaciations remodelled the face of Britain. They caused changes in sea-level, the land standing sometimes higher and sometimes lower than today. Thus old land surfaces could become sea floors, and the deposits then formed on them re-emerge into the air as new land, while former shorelines might be left high and dry, sometimes far inland. Melting glaciers combined with these changes in level to reshape river valleys, filling them with gravel and channelling it into stepped terraces. The ice itself exercised tremendous power. It cut and moulded the northern mountains and valleys, and farther south laid down beneath it and around its edges the accumulated material torn up and pulverized during its slow journeying. In this way was formed the boulder clay which covers so much of the Midlands; outwash from the glaciers could also spread wide expanses of plateau gravels, and far beyond the actual extent of the ice, soil formation was affected by the freezing and thawing of winter and summer. When the sheet-ice and the glaciers had finally dispersed, these deposits remained to transform the countryside, control its future vegetation, and thus ultimately do much to dictate the lines of its human settlement.

When did creatures recognizably human first begin to play their part against this geological background? It is a hard question because recognition is itself so uncertain. In the long line of ape-like figures, which shall we select as the first of our human ancestors? Perhaps it is best so to distinguish the first creature to shape a tool. For the ability to do so is exclusively human—apes may use implements but never fashion them. They were man's substitute for the specialized horns, fangs and hoofs evolved by the beasts; although less efficient at first, they were to conquer in the end through their greater adaptability. Certainly tool-making is a more expedient criterion for the prehistorian to employ than bodily characteristics, for implements when made of stone will survive while almost all skeletal material perishes.

The idea of creating any tool artificially was entirely new—such a thing had never before happened in the world: naturally the earliest attempts would be very crude, and therefore difficult to identify. That is the position of eoliths. This name has been given to certain types of chipped flints that were first discovered in the plateau gravels on the North Downs of Kent, where geology may assign them to the Tertiary period, well before the beginning of the Ice Age. There is, however, nothing to show if the chipping is artificial or merely the product of natural forces—it does not follow any of the rules of later human workmanship.

It will probably always be disputed whether these eoliths do in fact represent the first fumbling attempts of man to arm for the infinitely long struggle between Nature and himself which stretched into the future over thousands of generations. But with the scene set for the Ice Age man steps well on to the stage and begins the play in which we ourselves are acting.

The phase of human history corresponding to the Pleistocene or Ice Age of geological time is known as the Palæolithic or Old Stone Age. It was at least a thousand times longer than the time that has elapsed since the Biblical Flood, yet the material progress achieved by Palæolithic man was slight indeed when compared with that made by the descendants of Noah. But there was progress: slowly as he learnt more of the character of the natural resources available, he improved his equipment, shaped his tools more skilfully, and adapted them to increasingly specialized tasks. Very early, too, he learnt to make use of one of Nature's most dramatic chemical processes—fire. Behind and impelling this process of material improvement was an all-important mental growth, which was to find an outlet in coherent speech. Speech, springing from the most rudimentary beginnings, became a vehicle for carrying the fruits of experience from generation to generation. As words became more numerous, sensitive and abstract, man's intellectual conceptions could grow more complex; it is difficult for us to follow them through the medium of stones and bones, but we get a sign when we find him furnishing the dead with tools and food as though anticipating an after-life, and they are more fully revealed by the end of the age, when he had become master of a highly accomplished art with a magical content.

Our contacts with the earliest Palæolithic men are confined to stone tools found incorporated in geological deposits and the rare discovery of actual skeletal remains; it is only later that a rather more complete and intimate picture can be drawn from the contents of cave dwellings. The earliest phases have been most successfully studied in the rich Pleistocene deposits that survive in East Anglia. These suggest that men were already shaping flints there well before the first onset of the ice, but it is not until the ensuing warmer interval that the evidence is unambiguous. But already by then two quite distinct methods of tool-making had been evolved that were to assume great importance in the future.

When confronted with the task of shaping a tool from a nodule of flint or other stone, successful results can be obtained either by chipping off the outside until the central core of the nodule emerges as the perfected implement, or by striking off a substantial flake and working that up into an implement. The core-tool will have both faces rounded and trimmed, while the other will probably have one flat face formed by the surface of the flake (Fig. 1, no. 2).

The distinction sounds slight enough, yet to primitive minds, generation after generation of which passed without thought of innovation, it would seem fundamental, and each specialized technique would be handed on unquestioningly from parent to child as an inevitable birthright. What is to us supremely significant is that these two traditions appear to have been evolved by two equally distinct human stocks, one of them ancestral to modern *homo sapiens*, the other a branch of the evolutionary tree that in Europe at least has failed to survive. They stand for a correlation between physical and cultural inheritance.

Their spatial relationship is also of interest, for while flake cultures are predominantly Eastern, extending right across Asia, the core cultures have an African bias: Europe, including Britain, forming the area of overlap between them. Thus from the earliest time our continent felt the benefit of a geographical position which allowed it to be enriched by two larger neighbours, Asia and Africa.

Much of Palæolithic history is concerned with the development and interactions of these two great groups. But they must be viewed against the ebbing and flowing of the Ice Age. For when the sun was triumphant Britain became a land attractive to life of all kinds, rich vegetation clothed the countryside, elephant and rhinoceros roved from the Thames valley to East Anglia, hippopotami floated in the rivers and wallowed in the swamps; when the ice had the victory, southern England alone remained habitable, and there vegetation was reduced to a low scrub, rivers froze and valleys were blocked with snow for many months, and only such hardy animals as mammoth, bison and reindeer could endure even the summer weather. And just as the big creatures replaced one another, so did the infinitely small: everywhere among leaves and grasses, in ponds and rivers, a host of tiny species were gradually superseded by others as the temperature changed, leaving their shells to record their fate, and therewith climatic history. Man also had to submit, almost as help-

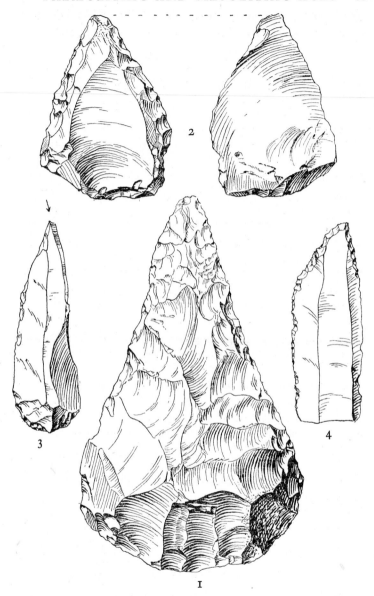

FIG. 1.—Flint implements of the Palæolithic Age.

lessly, for his elementary material equipment had as yet hardly begun to give him independence of his environment. The core-culture folk at the height of the cold phases seem, like the warmth-loving animals, to have retreated southward towards Africa, returning again with the milder weather. The flake peoples, on the other hand, with their more robust bodies and—one dare guess—hairier skins, may have been able to survive much closer to the edge of the ice. Each tradition shows its own cultural developments, and these have been named after sites where they are well represented—too often for the ease of our English tongues the chosen sites are French. The core culture which flourished during the first interglacial phase is the Abbevillian, already characterized by an implement always to remain the principal core form, a heavy, pear-shaped, all-purpose tool, rather meaninglessly known to archæology as the hand-axe (Fig. 1, no. 1). By the time England again became habitable this culture had been greatly improved into the Acheulian, whose hand-axes were more shapely, had sharper cutting edges, and owed their smoother finish to a new method of flaking with a wooden or bone bar in place of the hammer-stone. The Acheulian lasted through the greater part of Palæolithic times, the hand-axe tending to grow lighter and more elegant and the subsidiary tools more varied. It should be borne in mind that our area forms only a very small province of the Acheulian culture, for during the immensely long life it enjoyed its bearers were able to spread all over western and southern Europe, Africa, Palestine, and most of India.

Meanwhile the flake tradition also had its innovations: every ten thousand years or so it might produce a genius with a new idea for cultural improvement or change. Contemporary with the earliest Abbevillian was the Cromer flake culture, which rather before the return of the Acheulians after the second cold phase had given rise to the Clactonian. This was a culture which in time could show excellent flint work, largely in the form of pointed and sharp-edged tools made on heavy flakes and intended for all kinds of cutting and scraping, including the dressing of animal skins.

To the Clactonian and Acheulian traditions was presently added the Levalloisian; this became outstanding during the last interglacial, when it was responsible for beautifully finished points and scrapers which, by an ingenious new technique, were partially trimmed before the flake was struck from the parent core.

Abbevillian – Acheulian,   Cromerian – Clactonian – Levalloisian, what do these ponderous names, based on their flinty foundations, represent in terms of human living?   The economics of a very primitive food-gathering life must have demanded a small mobile group, probably united by ties of kinship (and, if we may believe Freud, already riddled with the Œdipus complex).   The men would have hunted game, while the women and children gathered everything that experience had taught them was edible of fruits, roots and grubs.   Probably when the climate was warm their diet would have been predominantly vegetarian: one can imagine how a week's gorging on elephant flesh might be followed by a long period when no meat was to be had.   In hunting the larger animals men must have used their cunning and ability for co-operative effort to devise traps and organize drives.

As to the personal appearance of these early hunters, we know nothing of what is usually implied by these words—hair, eyes and complexion can only be supplied by the imagination— but we have some valuable scraps of evidence as to the bony structure which they covered.   No remains likely to belong to a flake-tool maker have been found in this country, but we can turn to a contemporary who left a lower jaw to be incorporated in the Mauer sands near Heidelberg in Germany. This being must have been powerfully built and ape-like, for the jaw is chinless, but very heavy and armed with extraordinarily massive teeth.   Two vitally important English discoveries allow us to form a rather fuller idea of the core-culture people.   Possibly their oldest representative is the Piltdown Man of Sussex, who is known to have been living early in the Pleistocene period, although his precise antiquity is uncertain. His world-famous skull was found by gravel-diggers, who, mistaking it, as they said, for a coconut, had a shy at it before the precious fragments could be rescued by a local scientist. The bone is extraordinarily thick and the brain capacity small, but the high, unsimian forehead must have given its owner an unmistakably human appearance. It is now a widely held opinion that the jaw found at some little distance from the Piltdown cranium had nothing to do with it, but in fact had belonged to an ape.

The second great discovery was also due to the vigilance of an amateur archæologist. Patient watching of the quarries that are gradually biting into the mass of gravel laid down by the Pleistocene Thames had for many years yielded only animal bones and flints, but at last in 1935 part of a human skull came as a sudden reward. Its position in the Barnfield Pit at Swanscombe in association with fine hand-axes allows it to be recognized as the only quite certain representative of Acheulian man known to the world. The measurement of the two bones was followed with intense interest, which was heightened when it appeared how closely they resemble those of modern man. The Swanscombe skull, indeed, provides some of the best evidence for attributing the hand-axe cultures to our own direct ancestors.

In the earlier Palaeolithic ages which we have been considering, the core and flake traditions seem to have held aloof, each pursuing its own line of development; but in time they began to react upon each other, and in the third and last interglacial it seems that the Acheulian, Clactonian and Levalloisian traditions actually borrowed techniques and tool forms from one another. How far this implies also close social contacts between the two stocks is quite unknown, but it is not impossible to believe that they interbred.

One of the products of the stimulating interaction between the older traditions was a new flake culture, the Mousterian, which enjoyed its heyday during the final glaciation of the Ice Age. It is a familiar name owing to its association with Neanderthal man, that last descendant of the flake-tool makers whose very lack of charm seems to have made him the most popular of prehistoric figures. Everyone has read of his beetling brows, his prominent teeth, his chinlessness, his hairiness, and has seen them reproduced in pictures, even in bronze busts. There is an appeal in this ape-like being who yet had the skill of a man and some of his sentiments. His tools show excellent workmanship (Fig. 1, no. 2), and he has provided the earliest known instances of the careful burial and equipping of the dead.

The last cold phase was less intense than its predecessor and was broken up by slightly milder interludes. Nevertheless living must have been harsh enough in the tundra conditions prevailing beyond the limits of the ice, and although the tough Neanderthal physique was well adapted to endure them, it is not surprising that shelter against the worst rigours of winter was sought in caves. In Britain two were certainly inhabited at this time—Kent's Cavern near Torquay, and the Pin Hole in the Derbyshire limestone ravine of Creswell Crags—the oldest recognizable human dwellings in our country.

While Neanderthal man with his Mousterian flake culture was dominant in an ice-bound continent, where were the descendants of Swanscombe man? Were any still living in western Europe? This is an unsolved problem. The Mousterian often shows borrowings from Acheulian as well as Levalloisian sources, and therefore, although none of their skeletons is known, it is not inconceivable that some descendants of the hand-axe people may have maintained themselves side by side with their more simian contemporaries. However this may be, the late glacial times saw the complete triumph of our ancestral stock. With what now seems dramatic suddenness the beings whose appearance in a modern street would probably lead to their exhibition in Regent's Park were displaced by men who, if suitably clad, would hardly cause a stir at the Athenæum, still less at the Savage. In fact, of course, this dispossession must have been spread over many generations, but it is certainly true that everywhere in Europe the Mousterian and parallel flake cultures vanish completely, together with all traces of Neanderthal man, while his caves and hunting-grounds were taken over by men of modern type with a very different material culture. With the arrogance bred of our survival, it is very easy for us to see the Neanderthalers as low, brutish and altogether unworthy of continuance on this earth; but if history had gone otherwise, perhaps if the weather had been rather different, how readily they would have dismissed *homo sapiens* as a highbrow weakling fully deserving his extinction!

The late Palæolithic hunters had a much more delicate and specialized equipment than their predecessors, that is distinguished from the core and flake forms by the general name of 'blade' culture (Fig. 1, nos. 3 and 4). Their flint implements, all much smaller and lighter than anything usual before, were often made on narrow, parallel-sided flakes and blades, which enabled them to found the tradition of the cutting knife which has remained an essential human tool ever since. In addition, these people made flint chisels which helped them to master a new technique, the carving of bone, and in time to produce beautifully finished and elaborate forms such as multi-barbed harpoons and spear-throwers in this medium. The spear-thrower has a special significance. It is the first known instance of the use of a mechanical principle, that of the lever, for supplementing mere man-power. *Homo sapiens* had already started on that career of mechanic which has him in its grip today.

Another important accomplishment for which the earliest evidence dates from this period is the making of fire; man had made use of it from very early times, but now he knew how to create it for himself by striking flint against a natural metallic substance, such as iron pyrites. In the bitter weather wandering hunting-parties must have been saved many hardships and dangers by their ability to light camp-fires against the cold, darkness, and beasts of the night.

These great advances in man's equipment and powers enabled him to take full advantage of the ideal hunting conditions offered in late glacial Europe, where mammoth, reindeer, woolly rhinoceros, bison and horse throve on the steppe and tundra. In particularly favoured regions, such as south-west France and northern Spain, food supplies were now so easily obtained that the hunters had the economic security and leisure necessary to enable them for the first time to realize some of the spiritual potentialities of their humanity. Ritual, centred on hunting-magic and fertility cults, must have played a vital part in their lives, and to serve it they built up artistic schools that produced animal paintings, engravings and carvings hardly to be surpassed in their inspired naturalism. A desire and veneration for fertility seem to have found expression in statuettes of pregnant women that often show a wonderful control of form in their full, voluptuous lines. It is one of the most astonishing events in human history that in this, its first liberation, man's artistic impulse should have created works that still, after 20,000 years, convey genuine æsthetic pleasure, and which can be judged without condescension by any modern standards.

But these spiritual achievements were confined to the centres materially best endowed: that part of western Europe destined to become the British Isles was too remote, too ice-ridden, to support so high a standard of life. Probably the population never amounted to more than a few hundred souls, mainly absorbed in the quest for food. Caves in Derbyshire, north and south Wales, the Wye valley and the Mendips were occupied, but the majority only sporadically and for short periods; artistic content is extremely rare, and even flint and bone tools are generally poor and scanty.

In France an elaborate sequence of late Palæolithic blade cultures has been recognized, some introduced from farther east, some developed locally, but not all of them penetrated to our region. The first to do so was the Aurignacian, a culture originating in the Near East and spreading across Europe finally to reach Britain as a western outpost. The Aurignacians included skilled hunters and artists, and were excellent technicians in flint, trimming their tools with long, narrow flakes that gave an elegant fluted effect.

The next stray bands to arrive were Gravettians, a people with a rather more northerly range than their predecessors, who in south Russia and elsewhere had used their human wits to prey successfully upon the formidable mammoth herds and build up a way of life that was largely parasitic on these great

creatures. A long occupation of the Pin Hole Cave allows us
to watch the gradual evolution of their culture into a form
sufficiently distinct to warrant a name of its own, the Creswellian. This can be saluted as the first specifically British culture,
poor cousin though it is to its brilliantly successful French
counterpart, the Magdalenian, which saw Palæolithic skill and
artistry reach their highest perfection. A few examples of
the fine Magdalenian bone-work have been found in this
country, as far south as Kent's Cavern and as far north as the
West Riding, but we cannot guess if these were brought by
actual immigrants driven by circumstance from their own
more congenial territories, or whether, as valuable and sought-
after objects, they had been bartered from hand to hand.

The many skeletons unearthed from European caves (a
corpse in the home did not trouble and may even have encouraged these people) give a fair idea of the racial types of
the men responsible for the late Palæolithic blade cultures.
Already they were varied, but clear correlation cannot always
be established between racial and cultural divisions. There
were powerful and slight physiques, long and short faces,
while round skulls existed side by side with the dominant
long-head form.

Most of the late Palæolithic inhabitants of Britain belonged
to the Crô-Magnon race; tall, robust men with round but
strongly boned faces, and usually, though not invariably, long-
headed. Their most famous representative is the Red Lady
of Paviland who was excavated in South Wales by the great
Dean Buckland early in the nineteenth century. This discovery
should have won prominence as the first of a Palæolithic
cave burial, but Buckland was a Dean as well as a professor
of geology, and his theologian's conscience, mindful of the
creation of man in 4004 B.C., obliged him to dissociate the
human bones from those of the extinct animals among which
they lay, and attribute them to a lady living at about the time
of the Roman Conquest. His choice of names was no happier
than his chronology, for the Red Lady was in fact a young man
who had been ceremonially buried, together with his personal
ornaments and an elephant's head, under a covering of red

ochre. The use of this substance, known also on the Continent, gives a hint of the mentality of those responsible, for they may have conceived that its redness gave to ochre the life-giving power of blood.

The wealthy hunting societies of late glacial Europe might have maintained or even enriched their culture, or allowed it to stagnate and decline: they could hardly have advanced to a higher form of civilization, for the environment forbade it. But their future was not left in their own hands. Inexorably, although no doubt to them imperceptibly, the climate changed: summers grew longer and warmer, ice-sheets shrank and glaciers retreated. Enslaved to climate, plant and animal life had to change also. The mammoth, rhinoceros and reindeer in turn disappeared from western Europe, their going perhaps accelerated by the inroads of the human hunters themselves. On what had been open grassland or tundra with a scrub of dwarf birch and willow, forests spread, stocked with the appropriate forest animals—red deer, aurochs and wild pig. With the withdrawal or extinction of the great herds on which they had preyed, the economic basis of the hunting societies was cut away and their carefully adjusted culture made obsolete. This was one of the moments when early man was able to prove the full advantage of his self-made equipment over the biological specialization of the beasts; the reindeer found his coat intolerably hot and had to quit, man merely took his off and readjusted his habits.

The results of his labours were the Mesolithic cultures. These show two main trends in the adaptation of tool forms. One, already manifest in late Palæolithic developments such as the Creswellian, was the reduction of the size of flints to a 'microlithic' scale, accompanied no doubt by a freer use of the now abundant wood for hafting them, several together, as composite tools. This represented little more than a compromise between the old Palæolithic ideas and new needs. The other was the inventing of heavy wood-cutting tools to deal with that fresh factor and problem of the day, the forest. Armed with these axes, colonists were able to settle regions of northern Europe that had exchanged a covering of ice for one of trees, and there establish Forest cultures well adjusted to the changed conditions.

If these Mesolithic adaptations show no advance on Palæolithic cultural standards, but indeed in many ways, as in the loss of art, a sad decline, they did at least allow the old human stocks to survive in Europe and conserve a physical and material contribution for the future civilization that was to reach our continent from without.

Britain received three streams of Mesolithic immigration: the Forest culture known as the Maglemosian from the east, and two of the more purely microlithic cultures, the Tardenoisian and the Azilian, from the south and south-west. They were the first to follow the three lines of approach to this country whose use, as we have seen, was to become habitual.

Fig. 2.—Mesolithic bone harpoon.

The newcomers must have found already in possession a poor indigenous population descended from the late Palæolithic Creswellians. Indeed, these natives long contrived to maintain their independence, some of them migrating to Ireland thousands of years later.

The Maglemosians probably crossed the area now covered by the North Sea as fishers and fowlers, working their way over mere-studded fens, making use of dug-out canoes steered and propelled with broad-bladed wooden paddles. Such a canoe was found below the clays laid down by the river Tay at Perth, which allows Scotland to claim the oldest known boat in western Europe. On the way one of their number lost a precious bone prong from his fish-spear, which was only recovered some 10,000 years later, in 1931, when another fisherman found it in his net, trawled up from over 20 fathoms not many miles off the Norfolk coast (Fig. 2).

Once they reached the slightly higher ground that was soon to become the east coast of the British Isles, the Maglemosians occupied the river valleys and low plains suited to their way of life. The men must have hunted game and small fur-bearing animals, gone fowling for duck, geese, cranes, and many other birds, and fished extensively with pronged spears, barbless bone hooks and nets. The women's contribution of vegetable foods was augmented by the spread of trees and shrubs—hazel nuts in particular were relished—and they also would have been responsible for collecting the shell-fish that became an increasingly important element in the Mesolithic diet.

The Forest people's great contribution to the material culture of the age, their wood-cutting tools, were at first best represented by heavy core axes, but later an improved form made on a flake, and with a wide cutting edge, largely displaced them. These tools would have been used alike for felling timber and for such carpenter's jobs as hollowing out canoes and shaping paddles.

In short, the Maglemosians enjoyed a life tolerably well provided with material comfort, at least in the summer, but they did nothing to maintain the Palæolithic artistic traditions. Whether this was due to lack of economic plenty, and hence of leisure, or to a lack of genius, or the usual complicated balance between the two, we shall never know.

In comparison with these Forest people the Tardenoisians are shadowy figures. Their microlithic culture originated perhaps in north Africa, whence it was obliged to expand by the increasing desiccation which there followed the end of the Ice Age. They carried it over a wide area of western Europe, probably reaching Britain from north France and Belgium. We know them almost entirely from finds of their tiny flints made on the sandy lands to which their lack of wood-cutting tools restricted them. They were also able to make summer excursions to open uplands such as the Pennines, where a number of temporary camping sites furnished with rough hearths have been preserved below the peat beds. They were a neat-fingered people, for their microliths, although often measuring no more than half an inch long, are yet meticulously trimmed—sometimes into precise geometric shapes. The majority of these pygmy flints they must have set in wooden shafts to make arrows, darts and spears for hunting the small game and birds of their sandy territories. Dogs are now for the first time found attached to human settlements and were presumably used in the chase. The Tardenoisians can therefore claim to have originated the institution of the canine friend that has survived to become one of the most cherished and most hated of our national foibles.

The Azilians, who brought from the south of France a microlithic culture of Magdalenian descent no better adapted than the Tardenoisian to cope with forest conditions, found a different means of avoiding them in settling as strand-loopers along the coastal fringe. They were successful sea-fishermen, collected shell-fish, nuts and probably seabirds' eggs, went fowling, and hunted deer, boar and smaller animals. The best known of their settlements are all in south-west Scotland, two cave shelters near Oban, and a camping site on the island of Oronsay, but others must have existed along the shores of Wales and south-west England that have since been submerged by the sea. The debt of their culture to the Magdalenian is particularly evident in their most characteristic implement, a flat, rather feebly barbed bone harpoon which is clearly a degeneration from the elegant Palæolithic form.

Once established in Britain, these Mesolithic cultures began to influence one another and give rise to original insular developments. One of them was that of the Horsham people who used pygmy tools like those of the Tardenoisians, but had also adopted heavy axes in the Maglemosian tradition. They it was who have left us some of the oldest artificial dwellings known in this country: a little settlement clustered round the source of a spring at Farnham in Surrey. For shelter they had scooped the floors of their irregularly shaped huts well into the ground, roofing them with boughs and perhaps with sods.

The term insular which has just been applied to these developments of late Mesolithic times can now for the first time be justly employed. It was almost certainly during the Mesolithic period, and possibly about 6000 B.C., that England became separated from the Continent. Over the fenny country traversed by the early Maglemosians swept a rising North Sea. It is fitting that already in the opening phase of Britain's isolation we can watch this blending of cultures of diverse origin and their assumption of an unmistakable local character; it was a process often to be repeated during her future history. For Britain now acquired the peculiar powers of an island. Just as among the Galapagos Darwin found that island birds evolved a special plumage, we shall see that after crossing the Channel Continental cultures assume a distinctively British colouring.   Yet she escaped the peculiar danger of an island— stagnation through lack of stimulus.   Her exposed lowlands were always sufficiently near and hospitable to invite across the water both colonists and traders.

Before the end of Mesolithic times changes in climate followed, and were perhaps partly caused by, these changes in sea-level.   Since the end of the Ice Age Britain had enjoyed a climate of the 'continental' type—dry and with warm summers —but now the weather grew much wetter, south-west winds bringing rain and mist from the Atlantic.   The increasing moisture modified the nature of the forests, driving out the pines that had dominated them in early post-glacial days; instead, damp oak woods with abundant alder occupied all the heavy soils, and Britain assumed the character described at the beginning of this chapter, which must have lasted with no further essential change throughout the rest of prehistoric times.

The end of an epoch was at hand.   During the immense span of time since the birth of our first tool-making human, man had lived by taking the animals, fruits and plants which were spread before him on the face of the earth.   Certainly he had grown more successful, acquiring a store of knowledge and skill built up through thousands of years of bitter experience.   Yet he still lived very much as the fowls of the air. He had not thought either to sow or to reap.   The time for this was coming, and with it infinite possibilities for human enrichment.

Any modern visitor to Mesolithic Britain would hardly be able to guess that anything so momentous was astir.   He would see poor little groups of hunters and food-gatherers scattered round the fringes and in the clearings of the dripping forests. And watching the Azilian woman crouching among the rocks as she dislodges limpets with a stone, the Tardenoisian with his flint-tipped arrow lying in wait for a hare, or even the Maglemosian leaning over the prow of his canoe with a glistening fish thrashing between the prongs of his spear, he would not think that the foundations of his civilization were being laid. Nor were they by these people, or in this country, or indeed in Europe. It was in the East that new and propitious combinations of sun, soil, water, seeds and animal life were suggesting to men the possibility for revolutionary change.

Chapter Two

THE NEOLITHIC AGE

THE hunting life may be a good one: dangerous, certainly, but full of excitement and free from the monotony of routine existence. Given ideal conditions it may be so easy and leisurely that it allows men time and freedom of spirit to fill it with the joys of art and ritual. But the story already told of the catastrophic collapse of the Palæolithic hunting civilization caused by the changing climate at the end of the Ice Age illustrates its greatest weakness: the insecurity inherent in complete dependence on natural food supplies. When the spread of forests in western Europe deprived the great herds of their livelihood, and their disappearance in turn robbed man of his, he could save himself only by the adaptability that has always been his greatest strength. We have seen how the Mesolithic cultures, with their lowered standard of living, were the best answer he could make to this challenge. But the very different problems that were posed by the contemporary changes of climate in the East provoked a totally different response. It will never be known what part individual genius and initiative played in seizing the opportunities that were offered, but the outcome is well known: man began to escape his complete subservience to Nature, assert his will, and make her work for him.

Centres existed in the Middle East where animals and plants suitable for domestication by man flourished in conditions that prompted him to attempt it. The shifting of rain-belts across the world at the end of the Ice Age meant that while in western Europe the open grazing-grounds became wet and tree-ridden, in these more southerly zones they became, little by little, desiccated and desert. This withering of their food supply forced the animals to herd hungrily round the scattered oases, and there they would come into contact with human settlement. Thus it was natural enough that man should have the idea of exercising some control over the habits and movements of the herds that he daily saw about him. At first, no doubt, his authority was slight and his flocks lived in as nearly wild a state as the reindeer of the modern Lapp, but as the animals themselves grew more docile it increased, until with the practice of careful selective breeding man had gone far in his interference with nature.

If it was the hunting male who is likely to have been responsible for the domestication of animals, woman should probably be credited with the great parallel advance of this time—the cultivation of plants. It had always fallen to her to gather the wild vegetable foods, and when she had watched some forgotten handful of seeds sprout into new life, the notion of deliberate sowing might readily suggest itself. Here again selective propagation would in time improve the wild strains, and, granted sufficient rainfall, greatly increase their yield. We do not know which plants were the first to be cultivated, but cereals, and particularly wheat, certainly came to be the most important.

To all of us arable and pasture fields and grazing beasts are so familiar and essential a part of the countryside that it is hard to picture a world in which none such existed. Indeed, many of us go farther, and see the regular arrival of the wheaten loaf and the milk-bottle as belonging to the natural order of things. It is correspondingly difficult to think ourselves back into the lives of those who initiated the revolution that has ended in our baker's loaves and bottled milk. How would the adoption of stock-breeding and agriculture affect human living and its material progress? Obviously, while pastoralism would allow and in some circumstances encourage a degree of nomadism, mixed farming with agriculture would demand a much more settled way of life that was likely to lead to the establishment of village communities and an organized society. Perhaps this development affected the lives of women even more than of men: they could put down their babies in safety and have their hands and minds free to follow their practical creative bent. This new way of living gave fresh scope to inventiveness. The product of their liberated genius was the many domestic crafts, such as potting, weaving and fine basketry, which in simple societies they have continued to practise ever since.

This first great acceleration in material progress has been called the Neolithic Revolution, and it unquestionably had a deeper effect on the everyday life of men and women than any other episode in human history before the Industrial Revolution of the last centuries. And what an astounding acceleration it was! As far as we can judge, all the advances described— the invention of mixed farming and the new crafts—culminated within a single millennium, somewhere between 6000 and 5000 B.C.—a very brief span when set against the vast, uneventful stretches of Palæolithic time.

In the Middle East, where it began, this rapid progress was long hurried on by its own momentum. The surplus food which the new methods yielded beyond the mere subsistence of its producers not only caused a big rise in population, but made possible the support by society of increasingly skilled specialists in more and more numerous crafts. And to supply them with the needful materials a trading class was born to hunt the Near East and the Mediterranean for such rare and magical substances as malachite and obsidian and lapis lazuli, until, in time, the search was extended to metals. The discovery of the properties of copper, and then of its alloy with tin, bronze, had far-reaching economic, social and intellectual results. The ores were never obtainable in the early centres of civilization, but had to be searched out in remote mountains and carried long distances, and in response to such demands for transport came the invention of the wheeled cart and the sailing-ship. A host of new processes, many of them involving complicated chemical change, had to be devised and mastered—smelting, alloying, hammering and casting; in fact, man was becoming a scientist, however empirical his methods.

All these activities could not be conducted from the simple villages of the old Neolithic communities; the mutual interests of the specialists drew them together and urban life began— cities grew up as centres of manufacture and commerce. Nor did the surplus wealth of the Neolithic Revolution support only artisans and traders: it also went to maintain priests and kings. By 3000 B.C. many highly organized cities were flourishing in the alluvial plains of the Tigris and Euphrates and the Nile valley. One can picture the winding streets between the mud-brick houses of the citizens—perhaps a gem-cutter at work, or a potter spinning his wheel, weavers at their looms, a metallic tapping coming from the bronze-smith's anvil. There would be a market where country folk brought their produce—now increased by the invention of the man-driven plough to supersede the woman's hoe cultiva-tion. And, dominating all, the great palace or temple or combination of the two, where the ruler and his satellites held power through a judicious blending of secular with magico-religious sanctions.

These vital changes in human existence were accomplished in the East while western Europe was still in the possession of the primitive Mesolithic food-gatherers described in the first chapter. But, however slowly, the results of the Neolithic Revolution could not fail to spread outward until they reached even the distant shores of Britain. Several urges combined to force this expansion of Neolithic culture. One was the increase in population which caused a perpetual demand for *lebensraum*; another was the quest for new sources of raw materials which drove ambitious prospectors and traders to explore and settle farther and farther afield. A third and most important urge was that of the peasants, who were for ever in quest of the fresh land which their primitive agriculture was for ever exhausting.

By these means new centres of Neolithic settlement grew up in the Danube basin and along the Mediterranean, where in time they, too, became urbanized and developed their own elaborate civilizations. But the farther away from its source the Revolution spread the simpler its manifestations became, until in western Europe only mixed farming and the simplest crafts were introduced. The Iberian peninsula won some importance through its mineral wealth, and here alone in the west a few settlements were large enough almost to deserve the name of cities. It was from here, from Spain and Portugal, that we shall find parties of adventurers (p. 43) setting sail for the Atlantic coasts of Britain and Ireland. But these Iberian voyagers did not form the most substantial part of the Neolithic colonizers of this country. These rather were simple farming communities which, possibly originating in predynastic Egypt, had spread from the South of France northwards and westwards until groups of them began to cross the Channel to reach our southern and eastern shores. They were slightly built, dark people, with long, rather narrow heads and delicate features, members of that ancient Mediterranean race that today can be seen at its purest among the southern Italians. We can visualize how parties of such men, women and children pushed off in their small boats from various points along the Channel and North Sea coast, taking with them cargoes of cattle, sheep and seed corn. Probably the Channel was still considerably narrower than today, and our cliffs would beckon a land-hungry people with promise of conditions similar to those they had enjoyed on the chalk of northern France. Once across the sea, the newcomers seem to have spread rapidly over the upland system (p. 5), reaching the Lincolnshire Wolds, Yorkshire, lowland Scotland and presently even across to north-east Ireland.

Now for the first time cultivated plots appeared on English hillsides, and domestic flocks and herds grazed the uplands. Now for the first time also men banded together to construct settlements, and then tombs, on such a scale that their handiwork is still visible, the earliest marks of human activity that survive on the face of this country.

Nearly a dozen of the distinctive entrenched settlements of the Neolithic period have been detected in southern England, from Devon to Sussex, the great majority of them on the chalk downs. The largest of them, and the most fully excavated, crowns Windmill Hill above the great temple at Avebury in Wiltshire, and, in recognition of its importance, the name of this site has been given to the culture as a whole: thus archæologists speak, perhaps rather clumsily, of the Windmill Hill culture and Windmill Hill people. Another very interesting example of this kind of earthwork lies under the race-course on Whitehawk Hill above Brighton.

It is difficult to understand the purpose of the curious plan on which these oldest entrenchments were built. Several concentric rings of ditches and banks were dug with a considerable space between them, so that the area of the innermost enclosure may be less than a quarter of the total space encircled by the outermost ring. The ditches themselves were not continuous, but divided into short segments by solid causeways of undisturbed soil, a peculiar feature which has given these settlements the name of 'causewayed camps'. The material dug from the ditches was piled along the inner lip to form a bank that was sometimes crowned with a stockade. Why the extraordinary number of entrances which the causewayed plan implies? Homer ascribes to the Egyptian Thebes 'a hundred gates from each of which sally forth two hundred men', and it would be enlivening to transfer the scene to our English camps. But it is most improbable that simple farmers indulged in such military tactics; they are more likely to have made the entrances for the convenience of cowherds who wished to drive their cattle into the central area to keep them safe from marauding men and beasts. Certainly no trace of huts has ever been found in the central space, but instead the usual occupation litter of broken crockery, vegetable refuse, bones, dead dogs and the like lies in the ditches, suggesting that the inhabitants lived in the shelter of the entrenchments, penning the flocks and herds in their midst. Perhaps none of these camps was ever permanently occupied; they may well have been used only for one season of the year: the late summer, when the cattle and sheep had to be herded for branding and gelding.

In addition to the camps there must have been many isolated settlements dotted about the countryside, of which as yet only a few are known. On Haldon in Devon a fair-sized rectangular house with stone foundations has been uncovered (Fig. 3), while on the hill of Carn Brea in Cornwall are the remains of round stone huts which are probably but not certainly Neolithic. In the north of England quite a different type of dwelling existed at Ehenside Tarn in Cumberland, where

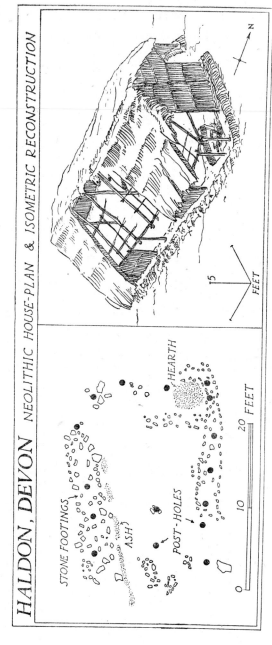

HALDON, DEVON NEOLITHIC HOUSE-PLAN & ISOMETRIC RECONSTRUCTION

Fig. 3.—Plan and Isometric Reconstruction of Neolithic house on Haldon, Devon.

Fig. 4.—Development of the handmill or quern.

A, Neolithic.

B, Bronze and Earliest Iron Ages.

Plate I

Crown Copyright reserved

Using a flint hoe

Plate II

Crown Copyright reserved

Casting a flat copper axe in an open mould

Windmill Hill people lived in some kind of waterside settlement, paddling canoes, and perhaps catching eels with wooden tridents.

Near by the settlement we can imagine the women establishing their small gardens and corn-plots on the sunnier slopes, bending low as they tilled them with flint or stone hoes (Pl. 1),

FIG. 4.—Development of the handmill or quern.
C, Later Iron Age; and Roman Periods.

with digging sticks or antler picks. Their principal cereal crop was wheat, of which they grew two rather poor varieties, club wheat and emmer. When the women had gathered their modest harvest, they ground the grain in the simplest of mills, a small stone rubbed round and round by hand upon a much larger one, which in time acquired a convenient hollow top (Fig. 4 A).

D

But of far greater importance to these people than their agriculture were the flocks and herds which the men tended and grazed on the hilltops and uncultivated slopes. Their cattle were fair-sized animals with wide-spreading horns, quite unlike the small shorthorn, *bos longifrons*, which was to be introduced in the Bronze Age, but possibly the descendants of a cross between this breed and the great wild ox, *bos primigenius*. The size of the herds was always limited by the wasteful necessity of slaughtering many head when grass failed in the autumn, a practice which lasted all through the Middle Ages, and could only be abandoned in the seventeenth century with the introduction of root-crops for winter feeding.

Pigs were commonly kept, and it may be supposed that they were often driven down into the forested valleys to root, and in season to fatten on acorns.

The herdsmen seem already to have used dogs to save their legs, a breed not unlike a long-legged fox terrier with small head and short back. They were evidently fed very largely on bones, for so rich were their droppings in calcium salts that they often hardened and survive for the diversion of visitors at present-day excavations.

Farm produce did not by any means entirely displace natural food supplies—men still went hunting, armed with bows and arrows tipped with fine, leaf-shaped flint heads, and brought back venison, birds and other small game to vary the round of beef, mutton and pork.

The domestic crafts practised by the Windmill Hill folk were simple and few—although it must never be forgotten that for every object that has survived the passage of four thousand years, scores made of perishable materials have disappeared without trace.

The women were exceptionally skilful potters, and their products make a worthy opening chapter to the long history of British ceramics. Working entirely by hand, they shaped round-bottomed bowls and jars, severely plain but usually well-proportioned and pleasing; the paste is often dark in colour, levigated with grits, and fine enough to allow quite thin walls and a well-smoothed, glossy surface (Fig. 5 A). They were always very sparing in their use of ornament, but occasionally would employ lines of pricks and incisions on shoulder or rim, or drag their finger-tips across the wet clay to produce a

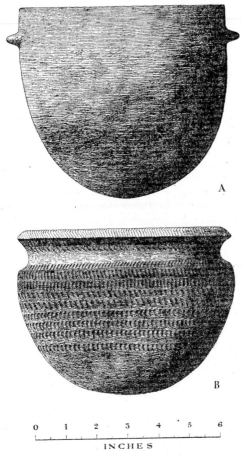

Fig. 5.—Neolithic pottery. A, Windmill Hill type; B, Peterborough type.

faintly fluted effect. Primitive potters are notoriously conservative, and little scope is left for individual taste—mothers would teach daughters their methods and designs, impressing upon them that theirs was the only right and proper way to make a pot, that any other would probably prove impossible and certainly unlucky. Nevertheless we do know of one Hampshire potter who, moved perhaps by a sudden whim or urge to assert herself, decorated a bowl by the imprint of a string of beads which we may imagine she took from her own neck.

In considering the reason for the rapid development of potting among Neolithic peoples, it is clear that with their flour pastes and milk their need for heat-proof and water-tight vessels was much more urgent than among the Palæolithic and Mesolithic hunters who could cook most of their foods by simple roasting on spits.

Primitive pottery forms are often derived from vessels made in other materials—baskets, gourds and the like—and the simple baggy shapes favoured by the Windmill Hill potters may well have been copied from leather vessels; thus, though none of their products has survived, we can infer that these people were accomplished leather workers. Whether skins were also used for clothing is uncertain. There is no evidence for weaving earlier than the Bronze Age in this country, yet we know that it was practised by the Continental kinsfolk of the Windmill Hill people, and it is most unlikely that they themselves had lost the art. They would hardly, however, have foregone the warmth of furs in winter time, and we may guess that some of their innumerable flint scrapers were used for cleaning and softening skins, which were then sewn with thongs threaded in bone needles.

Of Neolithic carpentry, again, very little survives, but the abundance of trees must have encouraged the use of wood. Shapely axe-hafts, clubs, paddles, a trident and the fragment of a wooden bowl from Ehenside Tarn give some slight idea of the mass of material that has perished elsewhere. No doubt also much more ambitious tasks were undertaken, such as the hollowing of boats and the dressing of timbers for house frames.

For many people the Neolithic period is rather drearily represented by the dusty rows of flints, sometimes of doubtful authenticity, which they have vaguely noticed in museum cases. Although this is an unfair conception due to the inde-structibility of flint and the devoted persistence of amateur flint collectors, there is no doubt that the output of small implements must have been very great. Simple types, such as the scrapers that bulk so largely in all these collections, could presumably have been made by every man for himself, but the very fine craftsmanship shown in some of the leaf-shaped arrowheads suggests that they were the work of specially skilled individuals. When we come to that most important part of Neolithic accoutrement, the heavy flint or stone axes (Fig. 14 A), adzes and picks, there is no longer any question that they were made by specialists who traded them among the peasant communities. They represent, in fact, the only essential import of these communities, the one gap in their economic self-sufficiency. This specialization was necessary not only because the shaping, grinding and polishing of such tools required much time and labour, but because their relatively large size and the need for strength demanded material that was not everywhere available.

The fine-grained stones that were particularly suitable had to be obtained from the Highland Zone, and at Graig Lwyd in north Wales a veritable factory has been discovered where the local rock was used in such quantities that a whole hill-side is strewn with the chippings and throw-outs of this ancient centre of British industry. The Graig Lwyd axes were evidently of good quality, for they found purchasers as far afield as south Wales, Wessex and even Essex.

Still more remarkable was the organization required for the large-scale manufacture of flint axes, involving as it did elaborate mining operations. In order to reach the big nodules of readily workable flint that lay bedded in the chalk of southern and eastern England, pits were sunk to a depth of as much as 50 feet, often with underground galleries to follow up and exploit the richest seams (Fig. 6). The principal flint-mining centres were along the South Downs, particularly in the Worthing region, and in Norfolk at the famous site of Grime's Graves; other centres were established in Wessex. Once a good seam had been struck, shaft after shaft was sunk until several hundred might be found in a single group, often with their galleries linked together to form a vast, intricate network far below the ground. Today such clusters show on the surface

Fig. 6.—Neolithic flint-mine at Harrow Hill, Sussex, being cleared by modern excavators.

as a confused jumble of bumps and hollows not unlike a disused bombing field.

Excavation among them has given us some of the most intimate and vivid pictures of Neolithic life. We can imagine how the miners formed a caste set somewhat apart from their fellows, even as miners are today, by the mysterious and dangerous nature of their profession, working unseen where ordinary people dare not go. Laboriously they dug their pits, working with shovels made from the shoulder-blades of domestic animals, and with picks, hammers and wedges of antler, then, the flint-bed reached, drove their galleries crouching or lying prone as they prised out the valuable nodules. The miners must have grown familiar with the maze of their subterranean burrows, but when they were long and dark they lit them with little chalk lamps: simple cups probably containing fat and floating wick. In some of the Sussex mines black patches on the roof still mark the places where these lamps burnt with a smoky flame that must have filled the galleries with strange, flickering shadows and a powerful smell.

The massive nodules, when at last they had been hoisted in baskets to the surface, were flaked into axes on the spot. Many workshops have been found, often in the shelter afforded by a partially filled shaft, where piles of flakes and wasters are proof of the mass production of a standardized tool-form.

A most dramatic find made recently at the bottom of one of the Grime's Graves pits leads on to the whole question of the magico-religious beliefs of Neolithic times. Enthroned on a ledge sat the chalk-carved image of a fat and pregnant woman, looking down on a very perfect chalk phallus and a great pile of deer-horn picks that had been laid as offerings at her feet. Here, in fact, was the shrine of a fertility cult, but one apparently intended to serve a curious and unexpected purpose. This particular shaft had failed to strike the usual rich flint-bed, and it seems reasonable to suppose that the shrine was set up to counteract the sterility of this pit and ensure the abundance of the next. But this was only one manifestation in the peculiar conditions of a mining community of a fertility cult that was generally practised among the Neolithic people— female figurines and phalli have been found at several causewayed camps and in a tomb, where presumably the rites were directed to more hopeful biological ends—the fecundity of men and beasts.

It is above all from tombs that we expect to gain insight into religious belief and practice. In all Near Eastern and Mediterranean centres of civilization, and particularly in Egypt, labour

and wealth were lavished on the dead to secure their content-
ment in the next world and hence goodwill towards their
survivors in this. Equally in Britain, with their humbler
resources, the Neolithic peasantry directed their greatest communal efforts to raising imposing tombs where generations
of their dead could be worthily lodged.

The mausoleum most fashionable among the Windmill Hill
people was the long barrow, an earthen mound or stone cairn
built on a monumental scale that must have demanded great
and well-organized labour. The stones piled into a long
cairn would be at least enough to build the average country
parish church. Many long barrows are from 200 to 300 feet
long and over 50 feet wide, and if nowadays they rarely stand
more than 8 feet in height, this is in part due to the levelling
processes of time.

The most familiar type of long barrow is the earthen one
which has no visible architectural features. As we know them
today (Pl. XXI), low, grassy, pear-shaped mounds lying among
the lesser fry of Bronze Age round barrows, their construction
looks simple enough, but when they were in commission many
had structures, since collapsed, which must have given them a
certain architectural quality. Such structures might include a
curving façade of stout timbers across the wider end and side
walls of turf or posts rising above deep flanking ditches. In
some of them, too, the larger end covered some form of wooden
chamber in which many bodies might be buried together.

The great majority of these earthen long barrows are to be
seen along the southern chalk from Sussex to Dorset, but there
are other interesting groups on the Yorkshire and Lincolnshire Wolds. A freakish example discovered below the Iron
Age camp at Maiden Castle in Dorset deserves special mention,
for it not only reached the fantastic length of nearly one-third
of a mile, but contained a dismembered corpse that had
evidently been jointed and had its skull split open to play the
central rôle at a ritual feast—probably with the intent that
the participants should absorb with his flesh something of the
dead man's qualities and might. But such customs cannot
have been very usual among our ancestors; burial in the barrows

was commonly by simple inhumation, the body being crouched, perhaps to represent the natural position of sleep, or possibly to recall the fœtal attitude in preparation for a rebirth after death. Sometimes, however, cremation was practised, most conspicuously in Yorkshire, where the long barrows were at times raised over specially designed trenches in which the corpses had been burnt on pyres of wood.

Another region famous for its long barrows is the Cotswold country, especially to the west, where along the steep scarp fronting the Severn a number are set on jutting headlands, where they can command superbly the great spreading expanse of the valley. These Cotswold barrows are not mere earthen mounds, like the majority in Sussex and Wessex; the local oolitic rock was available for the building of long cairns of neatly piled slabs, held in place with drystone walling and covering elaborate burial chambers formed with huge stone blocks or 'megaliths'. There was an essential difference in the use of this chambered type of tomb. The earthen form was a communal grave, in that it contained a number of bodies all interred simultaneously, but the stone chamber was a collective tomb intended for successive burials over a long period of time. Possibly the privilege of burial in these imposing monuments was limited to ruling families (all the skeletons in the chamber of one Wiltshire barrow showed a strong family likeness), a state of affairs that exists today, when the possession of a family vault is certainly an upper-class prerogative.

One of the best preserved and finest of these chambered long barrows is the charmingly named Hetty Pegler's Tump, near Uley, and a visit there is not soon forgotten. To enter one must stoop to pass below a massive lintel, supported on two upright blocks, into a gallery from which side cells open on either hand between towering pillars. And these few steps carry one from the familiar, brightly lit Cotswold scene into a strange cave world, with dark, shadowy entrances and a lingering ghostly presence in the air that may be felt only by the imagination but is none the less potent for that. Indeed, he would be a stone who in such an atmosphere is not tempted to materialize before him the men who once moved about in this cave of their own making, who cannot see a party of them coming through the low portal, staggering a little from the weight of the corpse which they are bearing to its sepulchre. Lifting it into one of the side-chambers, they must move aside the bones of earlier ancestors before they can deposit the body of their tribesman lying on its side with knees drawn up to chin. After celebrating the last rites and leaving with the body a few ornaments, and perhaps a bow and arrow and some pots holding food and drink, they withdraw, and carefully seal up the entrance behind them. So it will lie hidden until the day of the next funeral, but the site of the entrance remains a centre for ritual, where offerings may be laid and the ancestral spirits be propitiated or invoked.

Its ritual significance heightened the architectural importance of the portal, and when in some of the later Cotswold barrows the great central chamber was abandoned in favour of smaller cells let into the sides of the mound, the forecourt and portal were still set up, dummies leading nowhere, but providing a stage for the performance of the traditional rites.

The Cotswold barrows form only a part of a larger group of chambered long barrows centring round the Bristol Channel and the Severn. There are a number in south Wales, the best known being that called after St. Nicholas, not very far from Cardiff. There are also a few eastern outliers, including the most famous of the whole group, Wayland's Smithy, that lies so beautifully on the Berkshire Downs about a mile's walk along the great Ridgeway from the equally famous White Horse of Uffington. The popularity of this grave is due more to the romantic name of Wayland than to its own inherent interest; strange that a figure so essentially of the Iron Age as this legendary blacksmith, who would shoe your horse for a groat left on the roof of the smithy, should become attached to a tomb raised by a people who did not yet possess even bronze.

The Cotswold and related long barrows are not by any means the only megalithic tombs in Britain: there are hundreds, built in a variety of shapes and sizes, to be seen in the highland zone from Land's End to the Orkneys. The conspicuous manner in which they cluster along the coasts and round inland waterways with easy access from the sea suggests at once that they owed their inspiration to a maritime people who made the Atlantic and the Irish Sea their highway. Such a sea-going tradition was something so alien to the Windmill Hill peasant population that we must evidently look elsewhere for the originators of this Cyclopean architecture, and the direction to which we should turn is southwards, towards the more advanced civilizations of the Mediterranean.

The idea of building collective tombs with great stone slabs seems first to have been adopted in the western Mediterranean, where they were probably copied from similarly planned vaults hewn out of the solid rock. The mental conception underlying the idea is obscure: some have suggested that the tombs were intended as substitutes for natural caves, others that they were houses for the dead adapted from the houses of the living, others again have even ventured to recognize them as a rendering of the womb from which the spirits of the dead were to be reborn.

Whatever the explanation, it is certain that after about 2500 B.C. men were occupied in raising such monuments for their dead in Sicily, Sardinia, southern France, Spain and Portugal. From these centres the practice was carried to the distant lands of the west and north—to Brittany and our own coasts, and then onwards to the shores of the Baltic—until by 2000 B.C. it must have been possible to sail the hundreds of miles from southern Spain to Sweden finding along the whole route the coasts in possession of people sharing this cultural tradition in common. But there the uniformity stopped: it is unlikely that the megalith-building communities living in different regions would have been found to speak the same language, and they certainly did not have any common tradition for the manufacture of their tools, weapons and pottery. For it seems that the dissemination of megaliths can be likened to that of a religion, accomplished by a comparatively small number of 'missionaries' who made converts of, and came to dominate, the local populations of many lands. We can see these elaborate tombs as everywhere merely the solid and enduring setting for a ritual cult with its own powerful magic. Visual

proof of such a widespread cult is given by the curious symbolic patterns of magical significance that are carved on
many megaliths in Iberia, Brittany, Ireland and Wales, and
sometimes reproduced on sepulchral pottery. Doubtless such
missionaries were by no means so exclusively preoccupied with
holy things as the later Celtic saints, who followed much the
same routes to spread the Christian gospel and Christian architecture—their travels may have been very largely prompted
by economic motives. Nevertheless they owed their success
and their easy domination of native peoples to the supposed
magical power that went with their control of the megalithic
cult. In Britain they seem, for instance, to have had no
difficulty in establishing a control of some of the Windmill
Hill peasants, whose labour must have been employed for
moving and raising the great blocks and for collecting the tons
of stone that went into the covering cairns.

Just as Christian churches were built to many plans at
different times and among different sects—from the Orthodox
basilica and the Catholic cruciform cathedral to the pseudo-
romanesque Ebenezer and the tin chapel—so different groups
of megalith builders believed in the virtue of their own distinctive types of tomb. Two principal plans were followed
in western and northern Europe, the 'passage grave', in which
a circular or rectangular chamber roofed with slabs or corbelling
is approached through a narrow passage, and the 'long cist'
or 'covered gallery grave', which consists simply of a long,
parallel-sided burial chamber with no distinct passage-way.

Both these plans are found in the British Isles, together
with a host of variations from them, either in the direction of
greater elaboration, or, more commonly, of degeneration due
to lack of materials and labour or a decline in the zeal of the
faithful.

The most ambitious and successful architects were among the
followers of the passage-grave tradition whose labour and skill
have given us some of the most magnificent monuments of
our prehistory. Many of their greatest achievements are in
Ireland, where passage-grave territory stretched to the north-
west across central Ireland from the east coast, and of them all

the most justly famous is the tomb of New Grange in Co.
Meath. Here a huge circular cairn, 280 feet in diameter and
ringed with a circle of standing stones, conceals a beautifully
masoned megalithic grave no less than 80 feet long, its walls
and threshold enriched with an intricate medley of magical
carvings. But this is merely an outstanding example among
a number of remarkable Irish graves, which are sometimes
to be seen grouped together in cemeteries.

The school of megalithic art so well exemplified by the New
Grange carvings asks recognition as the first important non-
representational art of western Europe, and one which arose
in the service of religion. Although all its motifs were derived by gradual stylization from representations of men and
animals, they became at last almost entirely geometric. When
reproduced incoherently as scattered patterns without any
unity of composition, their purely symbolic purpose was
evidently uppermost in the mind of the designer, but when,
as at New Grange, there was some attempt at a general composition, the sculptor must have been genuinely concerned
with the visual effect of his work as decoration. It is an
art which cannot claim any great merit, which cannot for a
moment stand comparison with the naturalistic masterpieces
of the Palæolithic hunters; nevertheless at its best it achieved
a certain effectiveness, and merits some attention as the sole
expression to have survived of any serious decorative purpose
before the growth of the beautiful secular art of the Celts
nearly 2000 years later.

The men who introduced passage-grave architecture and
art seem to have reached Ireland from Portugal and south-
west Spain and to have brought with them an interest in trade
and metallurgy, including gold prospecting, which distinguished them from their more pedestrian contemporaries preoccupied with the production of food. From Ireland some
sailed for Scotland and, settling along the natural trade route
offered by the line of the Great Glen, in time established a
traffic in early copper implements—axes and halberds—then
for the first time becoming sought after in Britain. Others,
again, *en route* for Scandinavia, colonized the Western Isles

and more intensively the extreme north of Scotland and the Orkneys.

Maeshowe in those islands (Pl. III) is comparable in grandeur with New Grange, and is so similar in design that it must surely have been raised for a chiefly family coming from Ireland, or even from Spain itself. Had the grave goods survived, they could have given more certain information on this point, but it so happened that some 3000 years after the building of the tomb it was robbed by a band of Vikings who took shelter there. Perhaps benighted or caught by a storm on the bleak moorlands, they must have hastened to the great round artificial hill that dominated the flat landscape, and with mingled superstitious dread and bravado have groped along the 40 feet of passage-way to reach the spacious cruciform chamber, where perhaps no one had set foot since the last funerary procession withdrew some three millennia before. One can feel gratitude to these Norsemen for whiling away the time by cutting a runic record of their visit on the stones (Pl. IV), even while reviling them for the habit of plunder which prompted them to empty the grave of all trace of its original possessors.

The adherents to the rival megalithic sect of the covered gallery appear to have approached Britain from the south of France and the Pyrenees, whence their connexions can be traced even farther east in the peculiar 'Giants' Graves' of Sardinia. Sailing up the Irish Sea or round the west coast, they settled on either side of the narrows of the North Channel—in south-west Scotland, Ulster, and Man, where geographical conditions (p. 6) often dictated their splitting up into small communities, each farming a fertile valley or strip of coast. They did not strive after such ambitious architectural effects as the passage-grave people, and their tombs differ from passage graves in that they seem hardly to have been designed as buildings in which men could move freely about. Not only was the roof inclined to be low, but in many Scottish examples the cist was divided into small compartments by transverse slabs, over which it would only be possible to wriggle in a difficult and undignified manner.

Like the Cotswold chambered barrows, the covering mound was usually long in shape, and the centre of interest tended to be focused on a portal, which in the most elaborate examples was formed by two large uprights set at the centre of a semi-circular façade recessed in one end of the cairn. This forecourt, a more ornate version of the splayed entrance of the Cotswold chambered barrows, must have been planned for use, and it is not too fanciful to see it filled by a circle of dancers moving in some revolving figure, while offerings might be made at the portal to propitiate the ancestral spirits.

A tomb of this type on St. Kilda has been reported ; it is a profoundly romantic thought that 4000 years ago men and women should have reached and maintained themselves upon this island 50 miles out into the Atlantic, beyond even the Outer Hebrides—an island recently abandoned as too remote for human habitation. These were adventurers indeed, fearless of the sea, of the unknown, of utter isolation.

The long-cist people did not follow the passage-grave practice of decorating their tombs with sacred patterns, but instead sometimes engraved the same designs on their sepulchral pottery. This joint possession of a common symbolism shows the underlying unity of the megalithic belief, much as the symbols of the cross and chi-rho monogram could be used to demonstrate the common Christian doctrines shared by the Catholic and Orthodox Churches. Indeed, that they were not irreconcilably torn by sectarian bigotry is shown in areas such as the Hebrides, where the passage-grave and long-cist people met and so far united as to produce a hybrid architectural tradition which presumably reflects a parallel doctrinal compromise.

There remains a small megalithic group, of which Kit's Coty House is, by reason of its attractive name, the most familiar, isolated far from the main western centres of the Highland Zone in the Medway valley of Kent. These tombs had small, box-like chambers in long mounds enclosed by rectangular palings of upright stones, and are interesting because they were never directly connected with the main stream of the megalithic movement round the Atlantic and Irish Sea coasts, but were inspired by immigrants from across the North Sea, from the Low Countries and north-west Germany, where the so-called 'Huns' Beds' are very similar in design.

The Windmill Hill peasants, with their causewayed camps and long barrows, and the megalith-building chiefs who dominated them in the west, were the sections of Neolithic society that have left us monumental reminders of their existence. But there was a third people, destined to emerge and grow in importance during the coming millennium, whose less advanced economic and social organization prevented them from leaving any such striking monuments to call them to mind. These are the Peterborough people, largely descendants of the old Mesolithic inhabitants of Britain, who, while adopting certain Neolithic accomplishments such as potting, herding and simple husbandry, continued to follow the old mode of life as hunters and fishers. With the fair northern colouring which this ancestry would have given them, they must have differed strikingly from their more swarthy Mediterranean contemporaries. And at first they were able to hold themselves apart, for they were dominant in the east, while the Windmill Hill folk were mainly concentrated in the south and west, and preferred life in river valleys, by marshes and the sea-coast rather than on the hills beloved of the Windmill Hill uplanders. However, the two stocks naturally did encounter one another, particularly when after a time the Peterborough range extended farther westward. Their cultures are occasionally found mingled in Sussex and Wessex. They probably met, too, over trading ventures, for not only did the Peterborough people take some share in flint-mining, but it appears that they were the distributors, and probably also the manufacturers, of the Graig Lwyd axes from north Wales (p. 37). The adoption of distributive trading as a side-line by a hunting people is not altogether unexpected, as their few domestic ties would allow them the necessary mobility.

Very little is known of Peterborough settlements, doubtless because their houses tended to be impermanent and flimsy, and they had no conception of communal planning on the scale of a causewayed camp. The only known dwellings are

Plate III

Crown Copyright reserved

Maeshowe, Orkney. Mound covering a megalithic passage-grave

Plate IV

Crown Copyright reserved

Maeshowe, Orkney. Runes carved by Vikings when sheltering in the passage-grave round huts very much like those that sheltered their Mesolithic predecessors, with floors sunk a little into the ground and walled and roofed with small interwoven branches.

As potters the women were not highly skilled. They employed the 'coiled' method, by which long sausages of clay are laid in coils, then squeezed together and moulded with the fingers. In contrast with the Windmill Hill pottery, which at its best is so well made and unornate, the Peterborough woman favoured lavish ornament on coarse, clumsy and often ill-fired vessels, generally round-bottomed bowls, with a thick rim and deeply hollowed neck (Fig. 5 B). The ornament was produced by impressing the soft clay with twisted or whipped cord, the finger-nail, the serrated edge of a shell or the end of a small bird bone, and was scattered with more zest than discrimination over the entire surface of the pot. When, as we have seen, the Peterborough people encountered their neighbours, one of the tangible results was the adoption by the Windmill Hill potters of the idea of fairly free decoration, although they always used it with some restraint and applied it to their own superior wares.

Among Peterborough flint specialities the most interesting are arrow-heads with a broad cutting edge instead of a point, and the sickle, generally a parallel-sided blade slightly curved at the tip, specimens of which have been found with a lustre along the cutting edge that can only have been produced by friction against cornstalks.

It may be supposed that a relationship of mutual toleration mingled with mutual scorn existed between the Peterborough and Windmill Hill tribes in so far as they had any concern with one another. The uplanders would despise the valley-dwellers as poor irreligious natives with no idea of organized existence, its duties and advantages, while the valley folk might well feel that their contemporaries had sacrificed much of their freedom to a monotonous and restricted way of life, and much of the wealth thus won to an unprofitable and unnecessary pre-occupation with their dead.

It would be hard to over-stress the importance of the span

E

of British history covered by this chapter. A rural economy already containing the germs of ours of today was suddenly imposed from without on a primitive society that had changed very little for thousands of years. This Neolithic settlement was, in fact, the first of the long series of contacts between Britain and the higher civilizations of the Mediterranean which have played so stimulating a part in the development of our culture. It ranks in importance beside such later influences as those of the Roman Empire, the Christian Church and the Renaissance.

The ensuing Bronze and Iron Ages were to bring great advances in material achievement, but nothing so fundamental as this revolution from a food-hunting to a food-producing basis for society. The growth of metallurgy and the immense improvement in equipment which it permitted, and the commercial development which it demanded, were certainly important, but it was only from soil prepared by the Neolithic economy that this growth could ever have sprung.

Chapter Three

THE EARLY AND MIDDLE
BRONZE AGES

THE terms Stone Age, Bronze Age and Iron Age devised more than a hundred years ago have proved of lasting value, and their very simplicity has an appeal for the ear and the imagination. Yet they should be accepted only with discretion. It must not be supposed that everywhere and all at once men abandoned their stone tools and scorned to use anything but bronze, or forgot bronze as soon as the smelting of iron had been perfected. Even today, with our vastly accelerated rate of material progress, we can see overlaps between an old world and a new; electricity has still failed to displace the candle from many cottages, the tractor has by no means driven the horse-drawn plough off the fields, and by going only as far afield as the Hebrides one can see corn still being ground in a stone hand-quern. In all such instances primitive forms have survived the Industrial Revolution through a combination of distance from the urban centres of civilization with poverty, often strongly reinforced by individual conservatism. These factors have always operated, and it is not surprising that in days before organized production and distribution, and before advertising, the adoption of any innovation was slow indeed. Stone tools kept a place in man's equipment through the longer part of the Bronze Age, and the majority of the stray flint implements that are hopefully assigned to the Neolithic in a host of private and some public collections were really shaped after the introduction of metal.

We have already seen how copper was in free use in the East before even Neolithic culture reached Britain, and how the first interest in metallurgy in these islands seems to have been among the passage-grave people who had settled in the Highland Zone. With copper at hand in Ireland and in lesser quantities in Scotland, and one of the most important European sources of tin easily accessible in Cornwall, the smiths of the Highland Zone were favourably placed, and they were certainly at work casting copper and bronze implements well before metallurgy was practised in lowland England (Pl. II).

The adoption of metal tools in England was to be accelerated by an event of outstanding importance in our prehistory: the invasion of a fresh warrior race from the Continent. These people were not themselves great metallurgists, but they provided a ready and expanding new market for the Irish smiths, and for this reason their arrival from about 1900 B.C. is recognized as opening the British Early Bronze Age.

Archæological whim has attached all manner of labels to the prehistoric peoples whose own names have been lost for ever: it may choose a representative site such as Windmill Hill, but sometimes a particularly characteristic item in the people's equipment is selected. Thus these first Bronze Age invaders are known as Beaker Folk, from a highly distinctive type of pot in common use among them (Fig. 7 A, B).

Like Neanderthal Man, the Beaker Folk have been the subject of many word-portraits, in which their virility is emphasized with powerful adjectives. Their strong bones, muscularity, pronounced brows and determined chins have all been emphasized, perhaps over-emphasized, while special stress has very properly been laid on the round form of their skulls, which contrasts so strongly with the neat, long heads of their Neolithic predecessors.

The previous migrations of the Beaker Folk on the Continent are among the most remarkable to have been traced by archæology. It seems that the early cradle of the race was in inland Spain, where they were building their culture while the more advanced megalithic people (p. 45) occupied the surrounding coasts. When pressure from their neighbours provoked an expansion from their homeland, one wing followed the Atlantic coast route to Brittany and the Channel Islands, and it would seem to have been from here that the first wave of Beaker Folk sailed for Britain. Making their main landings round the mouth of the Avon and the Stour, they quickly overran the good lands of the Wessex chalk. But meanwhile yet larger numbers of Beaker people had been spreading east and north from Spain, colonizing the islands and shores of the western Mediterranean and thrusting through both east France and north Italy to the heart of Europe. Here in central Europe and

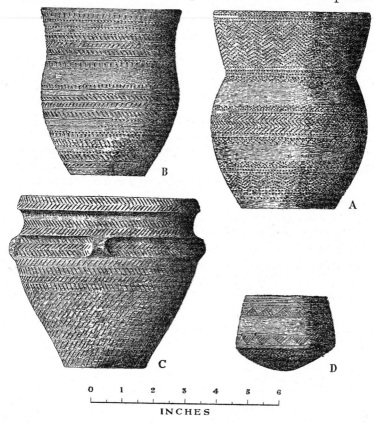

FIG. 7.—Early Bronze Age pottery. A, B, beakers; C, food vessel; D, pygmy cup.

the middle Rhine they encountered and mingled with an even more warlike stock, the Battle-Axe people, who had wielded this weapon to establish their race and their speech over wide territories from the Black Sea to the Baltic. In race these Battle-Axe warriors can be called 'Nordic', while their languages belonged to that great Aryan or Indo-European family from which all the main modern European tongues descend. It was men and women in whose veins these two streams of adventurous blood were united who sailed from the Low Countries across the Channel and the North Sea to reach our coasts all the way from Sussex and Kent to northern Scotland. They came in several groups, of which the last to arrive was the most numerous and powerful, and also that in which the Battle-Axe element was strongest.

Once arrived, these several waves of energetic conquerors soon occupied the greater part of Britain, ruthlessly dispossessing the Neolithic communities of their best pastures, and also no doubt of their herds, and sometimes of their women. Though largely ousted from the English lowlands, the Windmill Hill people survive as a physical strain in our population—that small, dark type common in the west and often mistakenly called 'Celtic'—but their culture was so thoroughly submerged that they disappeared from history, leaving only the slightest contributions to Bronze Age civilization.

The Peterborough people fared better, for with their different economy (p. 48) they had no need to compete directly with the newcomers for living space, and so survived to emerge triumphant after the force of the Beaker conquest was spent—much as the Anglo-Saxons reasserted themselves after the Norman Conquest.

But that force, while it lasted, was very great, and carried a few Beaker colonists even as far as Ireland in the west and the Orkneys in the north, although their numbers were too small to leave any strong mark on these farthest outposts. It is an astonishing migration this, astonishing that a race fostered in a Mediterranean country should be able to trek to central Europe and become familiar with the Continental conditions of the Danube and the Rhine before pushing on to the most distant Atlantic shores and to islands already looking towards the Arctic. And during all this time and over all this distance they maintained their own material culture so little changed that if four sherds of beaker pottery from Spain and Bohemia, from Holland and Scotland were ranged on the palm of one's hand it might be impossible to distinguish between them.

It is not surprising to find that this restless folk, perhaps largely nomadic, were herdsmen basically dependent on their cattle, although always with a lively interest in trade. Agriculture had a place of minor importance in their economy. For dwellings, tents were probably commonly used, but occasionally at least shallow circular or sub-rectangular pits were sunk into the ground and roofed perhaps with wattle, while it is likely that some of the familiar hut-circles that thrust through the Scottish and other moorland heather mark the stone foundations of Beaker dwellings.

With tools and weapons they were certainly better equipped than their predecessors, particularly in their possession of metal implements, few and simple though these were. Some of their equipment the first invaders may have brought with them from the Continent, but soon the Beaker Folk became the customers of the smiths of the Highland Zone, and particularly of the Irish smiths, from whom they purchased flat copper axes (Fig. 14 B), awls, and both tanged and riveted daggers made to their own design.

This metal equipment was reinforced by implements of flint and stone. Finely chipped, tanged flint daggers were frequent substitutes for the copper and bronze forms which they imitated, and a roughly circular flint knife with the cutting edge well ground and polished was also popular. The ordinary polished axe remained in full use, while in addition the strong eastern group of Beaker Folk showed their Battle-Axe inheritance by carrying a stone axe-hammer pierced with a shaft-hole, which is a simplified version of the more martial-looking continental forms.

All the Beaker people were archers, tipping their arrows with barbed flint heads and sometimes protecting their wrists from the sharp blow of the returning bow-string with stone guards: a Yorkshire warrior of wealth could afford the added ornament of gold nails to fix such a guard to its leather wristlet.

For fastening their dress they followed the prevalent, Mediterranean fashion for buttons, a low, conical form being usual, sometimes carved from glossy black Yorkshire jet incised with a cruciform design. Jet was also used for the simple rings that acted as belt-fasteners. How much one would like to know what type of clothing such belts and buttons secured.

It seems that both linen and woollen fabrics were worn, at least by a fortunate few, for their remains have been found in graves, and it can hardly be supposed that the dead would enjoy a monopoly of these luxuries. Some few of the well-to-do also were able to deck themselves with ornaments of Irish gold, and so for the first time in Britain display that shining yellow badge that in one form or another was ever to remain the coveted insignia of wealth and power.

In the manufacture of the distinctive pots after which this people has been named, the women showed very considerable skill, if little artistic sensibility. The paste is fine and hard, and in firing has often been allowed to oxidize to a pleasant reddish colour. Despite the really remarkable uniformity of beaker ware over its whole range, slight local variations could hardly fail to arise, and three main types were made by the different British groups. The high, expanding neck of one variety (Fig. 7 A) is due to influence from the ceramic traditions of the Battle-Axe people. The ornament, usually ranged in horizontal bands and limited to a few geometric patterns of rather niggling effect, was often in finely dotted lines produced by the imprint of a toothed implement, although cord impressions and simple incisions were also employed.

Were these vessels really beakers in the sense of being primarily designed for drinking? It is very probable that they were, and it has even been suggested that they were intended for some fermented drink, first brewed in the warm south, which helped the invaders to establish their mastery, rather as whisky has often opened the way for the less scrupulous white settlers in Africa and the Pacific, although the spiritual or magical power of alcohol may have been of greater importance.

If the Beaker Folk have left practically no domestic monuments, we are greatly indebted to them for those which they raised for sacred purposes. Although never lavishing the same excessive labour on their tombs as the Neolithic communities, funerary ritual was by no means neglected. The old idea of communal burial, however, had little appeal to these roving warriors, and their dead were buried singly, crouching with the knees so close to the chin that the corpses must have been trussed into position. With them they laid an equipment for the next world suitable to the wealth they had owned in this: perhaps a dagger, bows and arrows, and any ornaments that the men and women had worn during life, and in addition almost invariably they added a beaker which we can hope was left brimming with a drink potent to cheer the unknown road of death. (It is good to recollect that less than 50 years ago a Lincolnshire widow insisted on burying with him her husband's favourite beer mug.)

Very occasionally such burials might be grouped in flat cemeteries, but the traditional rite was the piling over the grave of a round mound or cairn in the shape of an inverted bowl. A number of the round barrows that are so often seen strung across the sky-lines of the chalk downs, and the round cairns that dot the moorlands (Pl. VIII), were raised over our Beaker ancestors. Sometimes the mounds cover a ring of posts that appear to represent a ritual house, occasionally they have been raised over an actual dwelling—presumably the dead man's own hut.

These barrows alone make a great contribution to the inheritance of our countryside, to the sights which in a passing moment may suddenly call the past to present life and fill us with a sense of ageless continuity. But still more should we thank the Beaker people for the foundation of two of our finest monuments: temples which as landmarks in our architectural history stand out in their period as Westminster Abbey or St. Paul's in theirs. Indeed, Avebury and Stonehenge are two of the most remarkable survivals from prehistoric times to be seen in western Europe. Avebury, near Marlborough, though less well known, is surely the more impressive of the two: it is almost incredible that a small population furnished with humble tools of wood, bone and stone should have the audacity to plan on such a magnificent scale. In its final form this temple comprised two pairs of concentric circles of huge stones weighing many tons apiece, standing side by side within a single stone circle, the largest of its kind in Europe, which was itself enclosed by a vast ring ditch embanked on its outer lip. The labour absorbed by this earthwork must have been immense. The chalk-cut ditch has a wide, flat bottom no less than 50 feet below the crest of the bank, and encloses an area of 28½ acres. Nor is this the whole design. Southward an avenue of pairs of stones, whose alternating tall slender and short squat shapes are thought to be male and female symbols, follows a slightly zigzag course down to the river Kennet, and thence to Overton Hill, where it terminates in another sacred enclosure known as the Sanctuary. Against the bases of two of the great stones in this avenue, and within the Sanctuary, the bodies of Beaker Folk had been buried in the usual crouched position.

The great antiquary Stukeley, who visited Avebury in the early eighteenth century, when it was much more nearly complete, records that a second avenue left the main circle to the south-west, but of this, if it ever existed, there is now little sign. Stukeley, whose early aptitude for realistic observation was overcome in later life by the growing romanticism of his century, contrived to see in the plan of Avebury the symbol of a snake, of which this south-western avenue was the tail and the Overton Sanctuary the head. Without following him into these extremes of romantic interpretation, we may legitimately allow the imagination some freedom in picturing the ceremonies for which this colossal temple was designed. We can suppose that on days of festival the uninitiated worshippers congregated on the bank to watch across the great gulf of the ditch the priests performing their mysteries on the sacred ground of the inner circles, much as a Roman audience watched gladiatorial shows from the tiered seats of an amphitheatre. What these mysteries were we shall never know; the sun certainly played some part, but did it serve only to fix the time of the festivals, or was it the actual object of their worship? There is other evidence for sun-cults in the Bronze Age, while the earth goddess and phallic fertility rites which preoccupied the mind of Neolithic man seem to have lost their hold. There was a shift of interest from the earth and the womb upwards to the sun and the heavens—well symbolized by the change from the dark, closed tomb to the open, sun-orientated temple as the principal architectural form. This change is exactly what known religious history would lead one to expect. It is typical of Indo-European religion that Zeus, a sky god, should rule the Greek pantheon. So it was the strong Indo-European element infused into our Beaker culture by the Battle-Axe warriors (p. 53) which gave its religion this skyward trend. We are witnessing the triumph of some more barbaric Zeus over the ancient Earth Mother dear to the Neolithic peasantry, the goddess whom they had brought with them from the centres of her fertile power in the Mediterranean and the Near East.

Everyone who has been to Avebury has also seen Silbury Hill. There it stands, less than a mile from the temple, in a slight circular hollow like a steamed pudding dished up for a giant. One hundred and thirty feet high, with a base covering more than five acres, it is the largest artificial mound in western Europe. From its appearance it might well be a huge barrow built over some outstanding Early Bronze Age celebrity, but a shaft sunk from top to bottom in the eighteenth century and a tunnel driven from ground-level in the nineteenth, followed by some recent trenching, have discovered virtually nothing. Its purpose and its age remain a riddle.

Stonehenge (Pls. V and VI) has always been the most visited of our prehistoric monuments; remember, for instance, the trouble and expense which Pepys endured to inspect it when on holiday in the west country, while a host of antiquaries and artists from Tudor times onwards have left us descriptions and delightful if inaccurate engravings. Yet it can never have been so magnificent as the complete Avebury, for despite the astonishing size of its stones the whole conception was far less bold—the entire sacred area being less than one-thirteenth as great. The easiest way to recall the complexities of Stonehenge is to approach it from without. It would be following in many prehistoric footsteps to mount up to it from the river Avon along the mile-and-a-half course of the 'avenue' enclosed between its two parallel banks and ditches, for this was a road which must often have been trodden when the temple was a living centre of religion. Led by the avenue to the north-east side of the monument, one crosses the low bank

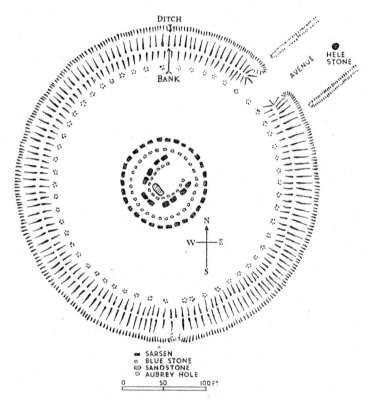

FIG. 8.—Simplified Plan of Stonehenge.

and ditch by its single entrance and, walking over the ring of empty socket-holes that has been uncovered just inside the bank, passes through the great outer circle of sarsen stones and that of 'bluestones' within, to find oneself entering between the arms of a double horseshoe, the outer one formed of five colossal trilithons, the inner of small 'bluestones'. And there, across the toe of this innermost bluestone horseshoe, lies the seeming centrepiece of the whole temple, the recumbent slab of the 'altar stone' on which popular imagination has offered up many bloody victims. Standing by this altar and looking back along the axis of the horseshoes to the 'Hele Stone' at the head of the avenue, one is facing the point where the sun will rise on midsummer day.

A pitch of architectural refinement was achieved at Stonehenge unparalleled in the prehistoric west. The transverse slabs which make a continuous architrave round the outermost sarsen ring are not only curved lengthwise to fit the circumference of the circle, but grow broader towards the top to compensate for the foreshortening when viewed from the ground. In addition, they, like the cross slabs of the trilithons, are secured by mortices hollowed out to fit over tenons projecting from the tops of the uprights (Pl. VI). All this detail becomes more remarkable when it is remembered that enormous patience must have been required to shape such stones with no better tool than a clumsy stone maul.

The bluestones, though dwarfed by the towering sarsens about them, are in fact no less remarkable. Geology has shown that they were brought here from Pembrokeshire, whence they were probably carried most of the way by sea. This journey of at least 200 miles gives insight alike into the unexpected possibilities of prehistoric transport and the great sanctity which must already in Wales have hallowed the bluestones to prompt such a prodigious undertaking.

It is a source of mortification to archæologists that the two monuments about which they are most often questioned, Stonehenge and Silbury Hill, are precisely those which have proved most difficult to interpret. In the case of Stonehenge this is partly due to the pre-scientific digging which its fame attracted. For instance, one recent excavator, on lifting a fallen slab in search of dating evidence, found instead a bottle of port wine generously laid down by an earlier investigator. However, despite such set-backs, certain facts are well established. The bank and ditch, together with the circle of empty sockets immediately within, are the earliest surviving features, and were the handiwork of the Beaker Folk. The sarsen horseshoe and ring were the next to be set up, apparently by the Wessex aristocracy, whose arrival from Brittany about 1700 B.C. will be related below (p. 70), and last of all the bluestones were put, evidently as part of the same scheme, in their present positions inside the sarsen ring, although they previously stood elsewhere on the site, in fact (as is now fairly certain) in the now empty sockets of the circle just inside the bank.   How long a period is covered by these additions and alterations to the fabric of the temple is hard to estimate precisely, but it is most likely that they were completed during the earlier part of the Bronze Age. What, then, of the Druids, those mysterious priests of the Celtic Iron Age with whose bearded and long-robed figures many of us have loved to people the great circles of Stonehenge?   The fountain-head for such picturesque ideas was in the imagination of Stukeley (Druids had an inevitable appeal to a Romantic), and for this reason it was long the pleasurable duty of the scientific mind to scorn and deny them.   Yet the discovery of undoubted Iron Age pottery on the site, and also (as will be seen later, p. 134) of Iron Age stone holes, has shaken such scepticism.   It is now possible and permissible to believe that there must have been a last phase when Stonehenge was administered by Celtic priests, although they had little share in its devising.   It seems, then, that Stukeley's hazards were really nearer the truth than he deserved.

These two great centres of worship, demanding such heavy labour and such feats of transport and engineering to build, must not be dismissed without thought of their social implications.   It is clear that the acceptance of such tasks implies an immense compelling power in religion, and possibly one fostered and directed by a strong priesthood.   But more than that, the ability to command such labour and the fact that the temples evidently served a considerable population and wide territories must mean some degree of social and political organization.   This is the counterpart of the cultural uniformity imposed upon Britain by the Beaker conquest, and is implicit also in the far-flung commercial contacts of the conquering overlords: their ability to obtain gold, copper and bronze from Ireland, Yorkshire jet, greenstone from Brittany.   Here is the liquidation for all time of the small, self-sufficient social units of the old Neolithic era.

Stonehenge and Avebury were not, of course, the only sacred buildings of their kind, but the outstanding examples of a quite numerous class. It appears that the ecclesiastical plan of the earthen bank and ditch enclosing wooden uprights found favour among the eastern Beaker groups coming from a stoneless country, while the stone circle was preferred by the invaders from Brittany, where there was not only suitable material, but a long-lived tradition for megalithic religious architecture. The two conventions meeting in Wessex could unite to produce the complex splendours of Avebury and Stonehenge.

A striking example of a temple in the eastern manner is Woodhenge, lying not far from Stonehenge, where the bank and ditch enclosed no fewer than six concentric ovals of posts, their long axis orientated on the midsummer sunrise. Here grim evidence was forthcoming of the savage demands made by primitive religion: buried on the axis of the innermost sanctuary was the skeleton of a baby whose head had been cleft open when it was offered as a sacrifice, probably at the dedication of the temple.

Another site where the eastern type of architecture is naturally found in its purest form is at Arminghall near Norwich. This monument must in its day have been most impressive, for within its double ditch was a horseshoe setting of gigantic oak trunks, sunk 7 feet into the ground and probably rising as much as 20 feet above it. Kindred embanked monuments can be seen at Gorsey Bigbury on the Mendips, the Stripple Stones in Cornwall, Arbor Low in Derbyshire, and even as far afield as Stennis in Orkney (Pl. VII); of these only the first is known to have been built by the Beaker Folk, but the probability is that they had some share in the inspiration of them all, and the raising of these temples throughout Britain is further proof of the widespread religious conformity that this people was able to impose. Their orthodoxy, however, inevitably became less in regions remote from their main settlements, as is shown by their actual use of the old megalithic collective tombs in the

Scottish Isles and their adaptation of a passage-grave tradition in the remarkable 'Recumbent Stone' circles of north-east Scotland. In these the stone uprights regularly increase in size towards one side, where the tallest pair flank a massive recumbent slab, in one instance as much as 17 feet long. They were not intended to serve wholly, or perhaps even primarily, as temples, but enclosed cremated burials under a small central cairn, sometimes furnished with a passage and kerb, all reminiscent of passage-grave traditions.

Those who are familiar with the moorlands of Cornwall, Somerset, Wales and the north of England will have seen simple circles of standing stones ranging in diameter from less than 50 feet to over 300 feet. Often it is not known when these were set up or by whom; some may be much later than Beaker times, but they should all fall within the limits of the Bronze Age. Perhaps the most fascinating thing about them is their names—Long Meg, the Nine and the Merry Maidens, the Hurlers and the Weddings, to quote a few—and the attendant folklore which tells how they are men and girls petrified for dancing and playing on the Sabbath, or wedding-parties and invading armies similarly turned to stone, and how they may return to life under the cover of darkness to dance again or drink at a near-by stream.

Before leaving the Early Bronze Age we can revert for a moment to purely secular matters. The ignorance of domestic life in this period which we have regretted in the case of the nomadic Beaker Folk is to some extent made good by the happy survival of an entire hamlet of the same age in the Orkneys. Its inhabitants were not themselves of true Beaker stock, but had probably been forced to quit the Continent to make way before the Beaker expansion. Kinsfolk of theirs were settled in many parts of Britain, particularly on the east coast, where they probably first landed, and in Wessex, but it so happens that it is only in the remote Orkneys that we can get any clear idea of their way of life. Here the most complete and best known of their settlements is Skara Brae, a village whose final fate was to be overwhelmed with drifting sand—sand which has preserved it from decay for thousands

Plate V

Crown Copyright reserved

Stonehenge trilithons

Plate VI

Crown Copyright reserved

Stonehenge. The upright shows a tenon which fitted into a mortice-hole such as that visible in the fallen lintel-stone of years. In the teeth of a harsh and inhospitable climate, a hardy group of colonists found it possible to form a settled community supported by herds of cows and sheep pastured on the open grassland, and by an abundant supply of shell-fish. Together these provided a staple diet which they could vary with venison, sea-birds and fish, although no trouble was taken to devise specialized implements for hunting or fishing.

Agriculture was not practised at all. They used no metal or foreign raw materials of any kind, and were as entirely self-supporting as any Neolithic community: an independent, intimate society, often cut off from the world by gales and rough seas, and concerned with little beyond the struggle for its own existence. As in such conditions there was no need for warfare, Skara Brae economy was quite free from the burden of armaments, and if life was hard, it was peaceful. The half-dozen houses and communal workshop were huddled together for mutual warmth and shelter, the narrow alley-ways between being roofed, and the whole cluster served by an efficient sewerage system of slab-lined drains.

A house consisted of a single, well-sized living-room (Pl. IX) and one or more side cells that probably served as store-rooms and privies. It is astonishingly good fortune to find in Britain houses largely intact after some 3500 years, but yet more fortunate that they should still contain much of their original furnishings (Pl. X). Wood being almost un-obtainable on these windswept islands, the villagers instead used the local flagstone to build furniture that was not only convenient but imperishable. So it is that we can recon-struct complete domestic interiors and feel something of their atmosphere. And they must have been pleasant enough homes. Imagine with what relief a woman returning in the early dusk of a northern winter afternoon, perhaps with hands cold and aching after collecting shell-fish, would have turned into the comparative shelter of the village alleys. Exchanging a word with a neighbour, she would duck through the low entrance of her hut until she could stand upright below her own roof and enjoy the warmth and familiar fragrance of the peat. Put-ting her limpets in a richly decorated pot on the stone dresser,

F

she could sit on the edge of one of the two box-beds, with
their mattresses of heather and skins, and warm her hands at
the central fire. Above the bed behind her head a small recess
in the wall would contain her special possessions, while
opposite, the store-room was readily accessible through a low
doorway. Altogether nearly as well-equipped and comfortable a dwelling as many inhabited in such remote regions up
to the last century. But the element of savagery was there,
and one instance would not be far to seek: hidden in the
foundations were the crouched bodies of two old women,
buried that their spirits might hold up the walls of the house.

Towards the end of the long life of the Skara Brae village a
few Beaker Folk crossed to the Orkneys in the most northerly
wavelet of the great tide of their invasion of Britain. This
tide had swept over the whole country, inundating the Neolithic landscape, but now it began to subside and some of the
old landmarks to reappear, although largely transformed as a
result of their submergence. The invaders had made a great
contribution to the age that was to follow, but as time went
by and they became assimilated with the remains of the old
population, their culture lost its narrow identity. Further-
more, the cultural uniformity which their forceful overlord-
ship had imposed broke down, and we find that at this point,
the end of the Early and the beginning of the Middle Bronze
Age, Britain is divided into two provinces, each with its own
history. While north of the Thames valley the various racial
elements that went to make up the Early Bronze Age population were left to intermarry, fuse and develop their blended
culture uninterrupted, south of it this process was given a
different complexion by a fresh invasion of Wessex from the
Continent.

In the northern province the Peterborough race reappears,
stiffened by a strong Beaker element and with a valuable
inheritance from the metallurgical and commercial interests
of the passage-grave people (p. 45). The product of this
mingling of races and their traditions was a distinctively
British growth awkwardly named the Food-Vessel culture.
The Food-Vessel province can itself be sub-divided into an

Irish and south-west Scottish, and a north-east British region with slightly divergent lines of development.

The habits of life which had come down to them both from their Peterborough and Beaker ancestors inclined the Food-Vessel people to a nomadic existence, winning their food supplies by stock-raising and hunting, while agriculture declined yet further in importance. But commerce certainly had its place in their economy, and prompted many of them to settle along the natural trade routes of Scotland and northern England, some of which had first been opened by the passage-grave people. Here they acted as middle-men and distributors between the Irish bronze- and goldsmiths and their customers in Britain and northern Europe, while the familiar Atlantic route from Ireland carried the same goods to western France and Iberia.

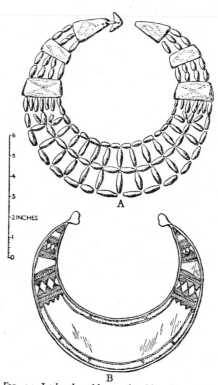

Fig. 9.—Jet bead necklace and gold necklet of the Early Bronze Age.

Ireland was becoming one of the chief mining and industrial centres of Early Bronze Age Europe, and the Food-Vessel traders drew their share of the profits. So successful were they that they were able to hang themselves, and more especially their womenfolk, with a variety of ostentatious ornaments. How many wealthy merchants since then have used the bosoms of their wives and daughters to display before the eyes of the world bright tokens of their own success! The height of fashion for Food-Vessel women were elaborate necklets of Yorkshire jet, crescentic in shape and built up from a number of ingeniously threaded beads and engraved plaques (Fig. 9 A). Never again until Victorian ladies jangled with a host of lockets, beads, brooches and bracelets were our native diamonds to enjoy such a vogue.

In Ireland this necklace was rendered in a still more sumptuous medium—a sheet-gold necklet of the same crescentic shape, and chased with designs imitating the lay-out of the jet plaques (Fig. 9 B). Such necklets, known to the pedantic as *lunulæ*, were exported to Denmark, north-western Germany and France as well as to the British market. Ear-rings of gold or bronze were also worn, of a sophisticated, basket-like pattern that was perhaps originally designed by Mediterranean goldsmiths who shaped similar rings to hang in the ears of the ladies of Troy and Egypt. Men as well as women may have worn the torques made from simple gold ribbon twisted into glittering spirals.

Stone still served for many tools and weapons, of which the most individual was an oval flint knife flaked all over one surface with a skill which proves that fine flint-knapping was not yet a lost art. Bronze implements at first show little advance on those already used by the Beaker Folk, being limited to flat axes, small daggers and halberds.

Potting was not highly accomplished. The women seem to have inherited from their Peterborough forebears an inability to fire their wares successfully, together with their rather clumsy 'coiled' technique (p. 49) and certain features from their designs—such as the hollow neck, broad, decorated rim, and love of unrestrained ornament (Fig. 7 B). This was particularly true in the Food-Vessel region centred in north-eastern England; in Ireland a lighter and more rounded form of bowl was usual, whose superior craftsmanship may have been due to knowledge handed down from the megalithic culture of the west.

In their religious ideas this people may have been influenced by those of the megalith-builders, and they employed a symbolism that is only a further stylization of that shown in passage-grave art (p. 45). This is manifest also in the most famous and curious cult objects of the time, the chalk-cut idols that were found under a round barrow at Folkton in eastern Yorkshire (Fig. 10). These squat, drum-shaped idols are carved with eye symbols and owl faces that would certainly have been understood by the megalithic people of Iberia and the western Mediterranean many centuries before. Yet there is little trace of megalithic ideas in the burial customs of the Food-Vessel societies. The dead were most often buried much as the

FIG. 10.—Chalk-carved idol of the Early Bronze Age, from a round barrow at Folkton, Yorkshire.

Beaker Folk had been, the bodies lying crouched under round barrows or cairns; although there might be several graves under one mound, they were essentially individual, and there is no implication of a communal rite. Another most interesting although less frequent practice was that of placing the corpse in a coffin hollowed out from an oak-trunk and sometimes shaped to resemble a boat. Here we have a reflection of the Egyptian idea of a passage by water to the next world, an idea which took firm root at this time also in Scandinavia, where it was to flower at last in the magnificent ship-burials of the Vikings. This conception would not be alien to the

Food-Vessel people, many of whom must have been habitual sailors adept at driving their dug-outs far overseas on their distant trading ventures. It must have been a man with such experiences behind him who was buried under the great cairn at Loose Howe in Yorkshire lying in a ritual boat (not unlike Fig. 11) covered by another inverted and with a smaller one riding like a dinghy by his side.

In addition to the food-vessel itself, stone and occasionally metal implements and ornaments, including the jet necklaces, were interred with the dead. One cannot but reflect on the emotions of a young woman of the day when she had to watch some coveted and perhaps irreplaceable ornament despatched to the next world with her grandmother.

While the Food-Vessel people were left to develop their culture and commerce in undisturbed possession of the country north of the Thames, Wessex was the scene of more dramatic events. The population there was a very similar ethnic hotch-potch of Beaker Folk and surviving Neolithic strains, but the process of their fusion and development was to be modified from without. In about 1700 B.C., once again, as at the opening of the Early Bronze Age, boats were crossing the Channel from Brittany bringing parties of well-armed warriors to annex the ever-desirable Wessex uplands. They were relatively few in number, but they succeeded in establishing a suzerainty over the native inhabitants, availing themselves of their labour, their wealth and their wives. Thus the descendants of the Beaker conquerors had to suffer the same fate which they had themselves meted out to the Neolithic peasantry a few generations earlier. With the essentials of life so easily provided, this new aristocracy was able to afford possessions far more varied and extravagant than anything known in Britain before. For their pleasure luxury goods were carried over great distances and from many quarters— the range of their trade connexions outstretched even those of the Food-Vessel people. Amber was brought from the Baltic, ornaments from central Europe, gold and bronze from Ireland, faience beads from Egypt. These gay blue beads

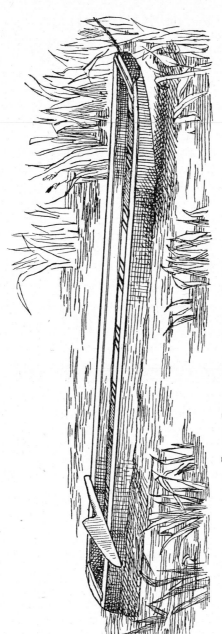

FIG. 11.—Reconstruction of a Bronze Age dug-out canoe.

were the first actual products of any Eastern civilization known to have reached this country (apparently through middlemen in the Ægean and central Europe), and it is not until the days of the Roman Empire 1500 years later that we know of any others. The fact that they could be imported in considerable numbers is, then, sufficient proof of the exceptional power and organization of the Wessex chieftains. Nor was Egypt the only civilized land with which they had contacts. Many details of design and technique in Wessex ornaments and weapons show that they were influenced by the craftsmanship of Greece, where the magnificent Mycenean civilization was now at its height. The ribbed gold cup from Rillaton in Cornwall recalls one from a rich grave at Mycenae itself, while one of the Cretan merchant princes ruling over the brilliant court of Knossos did not despise a gold-bound amber disc almost identical with pendants worn by his contemporaries in Wiltshire.

One of the advantages which secured the power of the new rulers was a greatly superior armament. They had daggers strengthened with a stout midrib and large enough to be formidable, and axes with flanged sides that at once increased their rigidity and allowed their hafting to be much more secure (Fig. 14 C). These new forms not only outclassed the old flat daggers and axes in effectiveness, their manufacture demanded a far more advanced technique of bronze founding that opened the way for future development. The simple, flat, open mould (Pl. II) would no longer suffice. For these shapes with relief on two faces a double mould filled through a gate was necessary.

Such new methods imply the presence of new men. The Wessex chiefs must have brought with them from Brittany a few skilled bronze-smiths, practised in double-mould casting and furnished with a repertory of designs that was ultimately drawn from central Europe. Smiths schooled in the Irish traditions, if their goods were not to be driven from the best markets, had soon to imitate the improved designs and methods of the newcomers, and the old inefficient implements fell out of use except in Ireland and the remote regions of northern

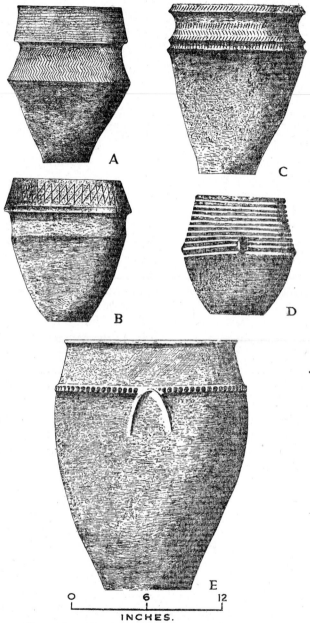

FIG. 12.—Middle and Late Bronze Ages, cremation urns.

population, who incorporated in them memories of Beaker and Peterborough wares.

The disc and bell barrows crowd round Stonehenge and Avebury in numbers which prove the continued sanctity of these great temples, and we have seen that the remodelling of Stonehenge into something like its present form was apparently ordained by the lords of the Wessex culture.

The heyday of the Wessex culture, together with the Food-Vessel period of the north, are recognized as forming the second half of our Early Bronze Age. But in fact the Wessex invasion might almost equally well be said to initiate the Middle Bronze Age. Certainly one period runs imperceptibly into the next with an unbroken continuity of culture. The full Middle Bronze Age is distinguished not by anything new, but by the gradual self-assertion and expansion of the native elements in the population.

Known as the Urn people, from the large cineraries which the women made for funerary use (above), they began this expansion in about 1400 B.C., and pushed on slowly but relent-lessly during the ensuing centuries of the Middle Bronze Age. At last their range was even wider than that of the Beaker Folk before them, for they not only crossed from Scotland to Ulster and effectively colonized the greater part of Ireland, but also settled regions in England such as north-east Yorkshire, Cheshire and the Pennines, which had hitherto been shunned for the poverty of their soil. A pastoral people themselves, they had no difficulty in mingling with the Food-Vessel societies, of whom they were, moreover, close blood relations (p. 70). So it was not by force of arms, but by peaceful penetration and absorption that they succeeded in dominating their new territories. But dominate they did: gradually the Food-Vessel culture gave way before them, though not without adding to the common inheritance.

Although their main food supplies came from their flocks and the hunting of wild game, the Urn people practised agri-culture, probably still simple hoe cultivation by the women. They even grew a new grain, barley, side by side with the wheats that had been known since Neolithic times. Some of the earliest surviving fields to be seen in Britain were probably first tilled by them—some small, irregular plots that survive on Dartmoor and the Cleveland Hills. On Dartmoor it is easy to detect how the women, as they turned the shallow soil with their hoes, gathered into heaps or threw to the edges of their plots the stones with which they were cluttered. Their homes stood near by, on the sites now marked by 'hut circles', groups of round stone houses with clustering beehive roofs, sometimes, as at Grimspound, ringed by a protective wall. Peat smoke drifting from the roofs and through the stone-lintelled doorways would come from a central fire like those which had burned a few centuries earlier far to the north at Skara Brae.

Houses and fields have survived on Dartmoor only because the stony soil has saved it from the plough: settlements of the Urn people on more fertile lands certainly existed, but have been obliterated by long ages of cultivation. Here and there, most notably in the Thames valley, the acute eyes of air observers and their cameras have detected and recorded the ghostly outlines of ring ditches, some of which may have enclosed groups of light huts or tents. And at Rams Hill on the Berkshire Downs is a ditched counterpart of the stone-walled steadings of the moors.

As well as grain, the women raised crops of flax for linen, while the wool from their sheep they wove into materials that were sometimes of extraordinary fineness. Such fabrics were, of course, intended ror clothes, and now for the first time we have some notion of prevalent fashions. No garments worn by British Urnfolk have survived, but a great deal is known of contemporary Danish costume, and dress on either side of the North Sea may well have had something in common. In Denmark oak coffins lying in waterlogged barrows have preserved for us suits of clothes complete in every detail. Men wore round woollen caps that must have been jauntily becoming, long cloaks hanging in full, graceful folds from their shoulders, and knee-length kirtles held up with woollen girdles. The women also had cloaks, but under them fashion demanded short-sleeved jackets, and skirts that could either be of woven cloth, long and formal, or a mere corded fringe just covering the knees. One lady increased the apparent abundance of her hair, which was of true Nordic fairness, by a pad concealed beneath it. The resulting bun was held in a net of intricately woven horsehair remarkably like the nets so fashionable in Victorian days and now enjoying a revival in the 1940's.

As for ornaments to enliven such clothes, the Urn people could not generally afford the lavish display of the Wessex chiefs. Nevertheless they did contrive to secure faience beads, and some of the leading families, those who owned the most head of cattle and sheep, were probably able to buy some of the wonderful gold work which is the pride of the Irish Middle Bronze Age. Most striking and opulent were the great torques made from four-flanged rods of gold twisted into glistening spirals and fastening with massive terminal hooks. These were traded not only to many parts of England, but by way of the south-western peninsula to Brittany and the Channel Isles. The most dramatic discovery was made at Grunty Fen in Cambridgeshire, when a peat-cutter, on removing a turf, saw something like a golden snake rise up from the dark soil. This was a torque which had been coiled up and buried for safety in some time of trouble well over 3000 years before.

With bronze implements the Urn people became increasingly well equipped. As the centuries passed undisturbed by foreign conquest, the British smiths used a body of skill and knowledge based on the old Irish traditions, but fertilized by the Continental ideas of the Wessex invaders, to create a very successful native school of metallurgy.

Starting with the dagger and the flanged axe, they gradually adapted them to meet fresh needs. To follow the history of these technical developments archæology resorts to one of its favourite methods, the typological study, which in this context means no more than arranging in their due order the various stages by which the groping craftsman makes an article more efficient, and perhaps at the same time more beautiful, or allows it to degenerate, and perhaps to become uglier. It is the same simple method which we all use instinctively when judging by eye the date of a motor-car, a wireless set or a tail-coat. Many people will still be able to recollect the evolution

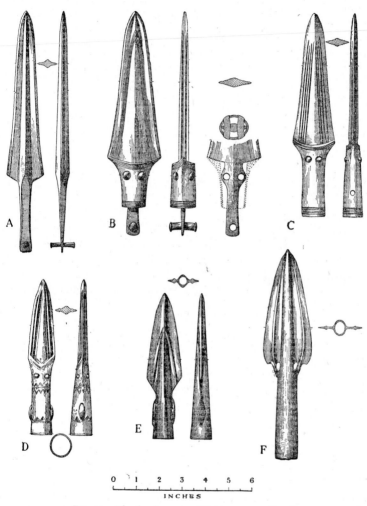

FIG. 13.—The development of the bronze spearhead.

of the modern double-decked bus with internal stairs from the old horse-bus with outside steps. In prehistoric times there are few more perfect sequences of this kind than that leading from the dagger to the socketed spear (Fig. 13). First a long tang was added to secure the dagger blade into the shaft of a spear (A), then a ferrule was found to be necessary to prevent the shaft from splitting (B), next it was thought better to make blade, ferrule and tang in one piece (C), finally the central tang was seen to be superfluous and was omitted, while loops were added to hold thongs for binding the head to the shaft (D-F). This process, which covered perhaps the first 250 years of the Middle Bronze Age, ended with a thoroughly serviceable weapon that also had a simple strength of line most agreeable to the eye. He would be an austere functionalist indeed who could object to the useless but pleasing pair of raised knobs on the socket imitating the rivet-heads (D) which in an earlier stage had served to secure the ferrule. On the other hand, when in a still later phase of development the side loops also became functionless and were cast higher and higher up the socket, until they became mere 'ornamental' openings in the blade of the spear, one should perhaps admit degeneration. This long story of the British socketed spear shows clearly how the typological method depends on man's natural conservatism, which prevents him from making any abrupt break with past forms—the same unchanging conservatism which today keeps a formal and functionless row of buttons on the cuffs of his coat. Without it archæology would often be at a loss.

The other new forms evolved at this time have less complicated histories. It is easy to see how a gradual increase in the length of the blade accompanied by a strengthening of the midrib would develop the dagger into the slender rapier, sometimes as much as 20-30 inches long, and an elegant weapon well adapted for sticking a man in the ribs. With the axe the problem to be solved was how best to secure it between the forks of its haft; this was achieved by raising the height of the flanges to prevent any up-and-down movement, and adding a ridge across the centre to hold the ends of the fork, and so stop the axe from pushing back and splitting its handle. In the fully evolved palstave (Fig. 14 D) the problem was well answered, although in form it was always rather uncouth, lack-

Plate VII

Crown Copyright reserved

Stennis, Orkney. Part of the stone circle, with surrounding bank and ditch

Plate VIII

Crown Copyright reserved

A line of Bronze Age round barrows

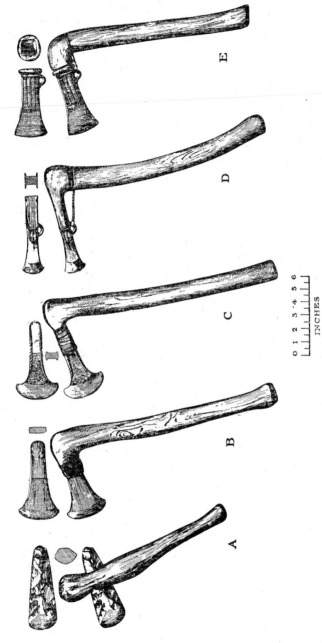

Fig. 14.—Method of shafting stone and bronze axes.

G

ing the fine lines of spearhead and rapier. For what purpose
were these offensive weapons intended? They may often have
been used in hunting, and the axe had many practical uses, but
there seems little doubt that they were primarily intended for
fighting. As the Middle Bronze Age was a period singularly
free from external dangers, one can well assume that the Urn
communities fought one another, for territory and for booty—
more particularly for cattle. Even so soon do we find man's
most precious raw materials, greatest skill and most advanced
scientific knowledge dedicated to killing his own species.

Once dead, either by this means or another, the Urn people
were almost invariably cremated, the bodies being burned on
great pyres of oak logs. Their ashes were then collected in the
large cineraries after which they are named (Fig. 12 A, B).
These great, clumsy and often ill-fashioned jars are in a sense an
enlarged variant of the Food Vessel adapted for funerary use.
The urns were sometimes ranged in cemeteries, but much
more frequently the old round-barrow usage was continued, the
principal cremation often in a central cist with the urns of
the less distinguished dead buried round it. Occasionally the
barrow has been piled round the structure of a ritual hut in a
manner reminiscent of the eastern Beaker Folk (p. 57). For
other funerals, again, the sanctuary of holy places of the past
was sought, the urns being buried in the precincts of stone
circles or megalithic tombs. One most remarkable site which
must have been a shrine in honour of two illustrious individuals
is at Bleasdale in Lancashire, where a pair of cremation urns
in a central pit were surrounded by a ring of massive oak posts,
a ditch with an entrance causeway, and a large outer circle of
posts linked with palisading.

Doctrine concerned with an after life would seem to have
changed considerably in the Middle Bronze Age. The regular
adoption of cremation is evidence for a less concrete conception of the fate of the physical body, a conception which is
again implied by a very great simplification in the equipping
of the dead. For the Urn burials are never accompanied by
an elaborate display of weapons and ornaments such as went

into the earth with the Wessex chiefs and the wealthier of the Beaker Folk. The gold torques, axes, spears and rapiers are never found in graves. A poor knife, a few beads, bone pins and belt-fasteners, occasionally a bronze razor that had probably served some ritual purpose, are the most that was left with the ashes. Evidently it was no longer considered necessary that a man should go into the next world in full pride of his earthly possessions.

This chapter has treated a stretch of British prehistory which has been conventionally and not inconveniently divided into two parts, the Early and the Middle Bronze Ages. But we have found these Ages to be so closely interlocked that the division is all but arbitrary. It is, in fact, more realistic to see the Bronze Age as opening with a time of movement, change and diversity which passes into one of slow settling-down, assimilation and uniformity. The first is a phase of impact on Britain from the Continent: the several invasions of the Skara Brae and Beaker peoples, followed rapidly in the south by the influx of the Wessex warriors. Then comes the calmer period after about 1500 B.C., when the various stocks old and new which had by then established themselves in the country united their blood and their traditions until, as the Urn people, they were able to spread an almost uniform culture throughout the British Isles. And this culture had time to grow insular, to develop a more distinctively British flavour than that of any previous prehistoric age. Undisturbed in these islands, the Urn communities had little concern with what went on across the sea. But, one wonders, did traders ever bring them news? Did they learn of the fall of the ancient and wealthy court of Knossos, destroyed in about 1400 B.C., probably by the Myceneans of mainland Greece? That all-important event, symbolized in Greek myth by the slaying of the Minotaur, can be said to mark the liberation of European civilization from its long dependence on the Orient. Or a generation later did they hear tell of the strange revolution led by the mystical young Egyptian pharaoh Akhenaten? How he built an entire new city where he could worship the one true god, paint, and dally with his lovely Nefertiti? That was a world far removed in spirit from the contemporary British scene, where a pastoral society was preoccupied with matters of stock-raising, hunting and inter-tribal feuds. They had little in common but the memory of a few blue beads. Perhaps the Urn people would have asked nothing more than to be allowed to forget the existence of all lands beyond the Channel except for the purposes of a quiet trade. But the Continent was inexorably there, and was rousing from its Middle Bronze Age quiescence.

Chapter Four

THE LATE BRONZE AGE

THE date 1000 B.C., when the British Late Bronze Age opens, is a good one at which to reflect on the racial pattern which was emerging on the Continent. For we are now on the edge of historic times. Soon it will begin to be possible to recognize peoples under their proper names. It is not always easy to remember that the very peoples whom we have met under the odd-sounding titles invented for them by archæology, after the birth and death of a few generations are those who emerge into the lighted strip of history bearing such familiar titles as Celts, Germans and Illyrians. The difficulty is to know how far back into prehistory we can legitimately push these identifications: how early, for instance, speak of Celts, when be more cautious with proto-Celts, and when the distance in time becomes too great for any name to be safely applied.

The broadest racial divisions of Europe have already been suggested in earlier chapters, and may be said to have held good from Neolithic times to the present day. These are the small, dark Mediterraneans in the south, the sturdy, round-headed Alpines along the mountain lands from the Balkans to Spain, and the tall, fair Nordics. But recognition of those subtle divisions, which are rather a question of common language and culture than of identity of blood, is much more difficult. As the Late Bronze and Iron Ages in western Europe are largely dominated by the Celts, one must ask 'Who were the Celts?' When they first began to play a part in history they are a people in process of expanding in many directions from their homelands in France and western Germany. And we know that the inhabitants of this region must have been largely descended from a mixture of Battle-Axe warriors, who were predominantly Nordic, and round-headed Beaker Folk from the south, on a solid substratum of Neolithic and ulti-

85

mately Mesolithic stocks; in fact, very much the same mixture which composed the Middle Bronze Age Urn societies in Britain. We need not doubt that the language these Urn people spoke as they drove their flocks and hunted their game from end to end of these islands must have been already recognizably Celtic.

But the Celticization of Britain was to be continued or intensified by a series of fresh invasions during the 1000 years covered by the Late Bronze and Iron Ages. These were caused by the expansion of two great Continental peoples. Away to the north of the Celtic lands Germanic tribes were breeding with their customary fecundity, while to the east of them, in central Europe, was a virile people of Illyrian stock, hardly less prolific. Almost simultaneously they began the drive for more living space, the Germans crossing the Elbe and ultimately thrusting down towards Holland, the Illyrians pushing westward until the effects of their pressure were felt across France as far as the Channel coasts. It was the Celtic tribes who had to absorb or give way before the impact of these western migrations. And Britain, as ever, stood open as a sanctuary for the victims of Continental upheaval.

About 1000 B.C. a few small groups of refugee Celts began their infiltration: some may have gone from north-west Germany to northern England and perhaps even on to Ireland, while others crossed from northern France to the Sussex coast.

One such party of refugees, probably representative of many others, established a farm in a lovely position on the South Downs, on Plumpton Plain, near Brighton. Here they made themselves a settled homestead, where they lived in round, thatched huts standing within earthen banks, linked by tracks with the cattle enclosures that lay near by. Round about the farm stretched a number of small, squarish cornfields, among the first of their kind to be tilled on British soil (p. 91). This little refugee community was evidently largely independent of the Urn people among whom it was planted, and maintained many of its Continental ways—the women, for instance, made much the same handled and incised pots which they had shaped from the clay of northern France. This was probably true of most of the colonists who reached Britain during these opening centuries of the Late Bronze Age: they made little impression on the Urn communities, whose pastoral and hunting life went on as before.

But their coming may have stimulated the one great development which distinguishes the beginning of the Late from the end of the Middle Bronze Age—a sudden adoption of many new bronze implements and a revolutionary change in the methods of the bronze industry itself. The metal was now becoming obtainable in larger and larger quantities as organization of the mining and transport of copper and tin improved. At the same time, the founders grew increasingly inventive, and devised ingenious new techniques in casting which allowed them to speed up their output and elaborate their designs. The bronze founders present an interesting social phenomenon. They formed themselves into a wealthy class almost independent of established society, a caste of itinerants who ranged wide regions in search of markets. It seems that there were no middlemen, these travelling smiths themselves making the implements they sold. They acted also as scrap-metal merchants, buying up their customers' broken or old-fashioned bronzes, probably taking them in part exchange for new types fresh from their own moulds.

Travellers in little-civilized lands are always liable to meet accidents, occasionally sudden death, so it is not surprising that throughout Europe and the British Isles the contents of the bronze-smiths' workbags are found today in many places where they have lain since they were lost in bogs, or from capsized boats, or were buried in an emergency and never reclaimed. Such collections usually include not only finished implements, but also solid lumps of metal that have been melted down in crucibles, odds and ends of scrap, and sometimes quantities of old implements fused together into a strange, distorted mass in preparation for melting and recasting.

Merchants who traded overseas brought the Urn people new ideas for the design of implements that had been thought out on the Continent. They could offer an axe with a wide socket which avoided the weak point always present in the forked haft of the older palstave (Fig. 14 E). Yet the latter remained in use throughout the period, perhaps because the weight in its solid blade made it more effective for hard cutting than the light socketed form. They also brought a laurel-leaf-shaped spearhead which was pegged or tied to its haft through a pair of holes in the socket. These were efficient enough weapons, but they always suffer from a cheap, mass-produced look, and have little of the beauty of line of the native side-looped spear. A much more significant new weapon which the itinerants could put into the hands of the Urn men was a fine double-edged sword, usually fitted with a leather scabbard ending in a long, tongue-shaped chape. Such swords differ from the older rapier which they displaced in being designed for slashing as well as stabbing blows. The changed manner of fighting which this design implies may well have imitated the practice of the refugees (p. 86), who would have been familiar with it in their Continental homes.

Another change for which these refugees were responsible concerns not fighting, but clothing. Whereas since Early Bronze Age times the people of Britain had generally followed the Mediterranean habit of buttoning themselves into their clothes, they now began to share the north European preference for large pins, a considerable variety of which were in fashion at this time.

Although these many new bronze forms were Continental in origin, like all foreign intrusions they soon assumed a distinctive British character. Native British craftsmen adapted the designs, and, backed by their good supplies of raw material from Cornwall and Ireland, were soon themselves exporting largely to the Continent, most freely to northern France.

In this way passed the first two centuries of our Late Bronze Age. While Greece was leaving the dark age following on the Trojan War, and was about to draw the first breath of classical civilization with the production of her austere archaic sculpture, and while Italy was cradling the strange Etruscan culture, we have seen that the pastoral Urn societies which had dominated Britain in the Middle Bronze Age continued much as before. They did little more than take full advantage of the improved equipment that was now on the market, and accept in their midst a few foreign refugees and merchants.

But in southern and south-east England their long period of undisturbed dominion was at last to be ended. The straggling immigrants of this first phase were the precursors of much more substantial Celtic invasions that began in the middle of the eighth century B.C. In the coming era the Continent was again and again to overflow on to our shores. Already in the eighth century the picture is sufficiently complicated. If some privileged being endowed with more than normal vision, exceptional patience and a long life could have watched from a lofty peak in the centre of England, he would have had to witness wave after wave of immigrants disembarking along the east and south coasts from Yorkshire to Land's End. Straining his eyes towards the Continent for an explanation of this exodus, he could see that its prime cause was the continued land-hunger of the Illyrian peoples, who had by now given something of their culture and race to the Celtic inhabitants of much of south and west Germany, parts of France and the western Alps. He could watch their pressure westwards expelling many of the inhabitants of Holland from their old territories, until, taking to their boats, they crossed the North Sea to our eastern coast.

Meanwhile, a scrutiny of the western Alps would show him a more dramatic scene. There, securely housed on platforms rising on piles from the margins of some of the loveliest lakes in Europe, were prosperous communities not only practising sound mixed farming, but also masters of an extensive industry. They were turning out cheap bronze goods for export on a prodigious scale. Axes, spears, swords, sickles, pins, bangles and a host of other objects useful and decorative came pouring from their foundries. But the observer would not fail to detect that their prosperity could not last, for a wetter climate was turning the water which had been their best protection into an immediate danger—the lakes were creeping up and threatening to flood the stilted villages. And beyond he would suddenly notice an even greater, though human, threat. Warrior tribes of south Germany had learnt from Italy and the South the use of iron, and now, in about 800 B.C., armed with powerful iron swords, they were sweeping down to complete the distress of the unhappy lake-dwellers. At last he could watch them abandoning their homes and come moving towards him, their cattle, sheep, pigs and dogs going with them. As they went, their advance set other Celtic tribes of western France in motion, and these, too, would presently be coming westward, crossing the Channel and sailing up our Wessex harbours, many of them using the excellent road into the interior afforded by the Stour-Avon estuaries at Christchurch. The lake-dwellers themselves he could follow as they steered a more northerly course across northern France until some of them went over the narrow seas to settle in Sussex and Kent, to sail up the Thames estuary and spread north into East Anglia. Some of those who chose the Thames estuary found that along its muddy banks it was possible to set up pile dwellings very much like those which they had left behind in the strangely different surroundings of their Alpine home-lands.

Thus the second half of the Late Bronze Age was certainly a time of many invasions, but as all the immigrants were racially akin, and akin also with the native Urn folk whom they found in possession, it was easy enough for them to settle down and form a nearly uniform culture throughout the English lowlands. Much of Yorkshire and the Highland Zone they never penetrated; there the Urn communities were left to follow their pastoral pursuits for several centuries longer.

These Late Bronze Age invaders have been supplied with the euphonious but cumbersome title of Deverel-Rimbury people, a double-barrel formed from two of their burial sites in Dorset. Their methods of life were considerably influenced by the central European Illyric strain in their ancestry, most significantly in a very great increase in the importance of agriculture. This renewed emphasis on the raising of cereal crops was an event of deep and lasting importance in British history.

In any attempt to trace an ordered evolution in our social and economic life, periods will be encountered when there were setbacks in the main stream of development. The most familiar is that of the Dark Ages, when the growth of urban life initiated by the Romans was delayed for many centuries by the Anglo-Saxon invasions. It is true also in a much more limited sense of the Early and Middle Bronze Ages. The Windmill Hill people of the Neolithic Age belong more surely to the line of development that was to lead to the peasantry of medieval and later times than do the restless, war-like, pastoral peoples who were their immediate successors. With the coming of the Deverel-Rimbury tribes this interrupted agricultural evolution was resumed, and indeed received a sharp fillip. For they brought a new device which greatly increased the scope of cultivation. The hoe gave place to the plough, and the woman to the ox—or, more accurately, to a pair of oxen. Crop-raising was no longer to be a side-line, a small-scale tillage of garden plots, an activity that was more truly horticultural than agricultural. With the introduction of the two-ox, man-driven plough the importance of the harvest greatly increased, as corn began to be grown in regular field systems. The fields were still of modest size, in shape and area very like the small, stone-walled enclosures that are their modern descendants in Cornwall and many parts of Ireland, squarish in outline and rarely covering more than a quarter of an acre. This form of lay-out is known as the Celtic Field System, to distinguish it from the Strip System of long, narrow fields especially characteristic of Anglo-Saxon and medieval husbandry. It is not difficult to recapture an impression of our chalk country when it was covered with such little fields, for in many places their faint outlines still linger on the turf. On a ploughed slope the earth will tend to creep down towards the bottom of the field and pile up along the lower edge, until each field is separated from the one below by a slightly ridged step, while it is divided from its neighbours on either side by standing balks and the earth cast up by the turning of the plough. Banks formed in this way often show as a faint network spread on the slopes of chalk hills (Pl. XI), most clearly when picked out in shadow by a newly-risen or a setting sun.

The small size and rectangular shape of such fields was well suited to the light Mediterranean type of plough with which they were tilled, a coulterless implement which could not turn a sod, but merely scratch the surface with its short, straight share.

It would be quite false to suppose that all Deverel-Rimbury farmers were exclusively preoccupied with their crops. In many areas stock-breeding was no less important. But the old, nomadic, pastoral life was no longer suitable: communities were tied to the ploughlands in which so much labour was invested, and could no longer range freely over the open hills. Instead, pastures belonging to settled families or clans would have to be enclosed, and in many parts of the country, most conspicuously in Sussex, Hampshire, Dorset and on Salisbury Plain, it is still possible to trace the boundaries of many such enclosures or 'ranches'. They often lay on the northern slopes of hills whose sunnier aspects were reserved for corn-fields, and each was enclosed by a chalk-cut ditch 5 feet deep, with a low bank on one or both sides. The white lines of these divisions must have gleamed conspicuously across the countryside, and it is likely that they generally came to be utilized as convenient drove roads when herds had to be moved from one district to another. Today the boundaries can often be followed for miles along the ridges, sometimes the ditch or bank showing clearly, sometimes dwindling to little more than a pale line marked by upcast chalk and flints where rabbits have burrowed more freely in the soft soil of the ditch.

In many parts of Europe early literature describes how land boundaries were first drawn with a plough, a rite whose sacred meaning was often emphasized by special ceremonies. In this manner Romulus marked the bounds of Rome. After the first ritual demarcation, the line would often, of course, be reinforced with a trench or a fence. It is therefore of special significance to notice that the form of the British enclosure ditches with their narrow bottoms and gradually splaying sides is very reminiscent of a magnified furrow. When tracing these earthworks one can believe with some confidence that their line was first trodden by a Bronze Age ploughman who, not much less than 3000 years ago, urged on his oxen to cut in the turf the first furrow of ownership. We can feel a certain pride, moreover, in knowing that they are probably the most ancient boundaries of their kind surviving in western Europe.

For the proper handling of their flocks and herds the Deverel-Rimbury people banked or ditched rectangular kraals some quarter to two acres in extent. Such places would provide shelter for lambing and calving, and perhaps in the autumn the whole clan might assemble there to help with rounding up, slaughtering of surplus stock and the salting of meat for the winter larder.

For their more permanent homes many of them owned small steadings very like those built by the first Late Bronze Age settlers on Plumpton Plain (p. 86). Not many miles west of this older farm a Deverel-Rimbury family established itself on the summit of New Barn Down above Worthing. There a hollowed track led one along the down between the neat array of small fields, then, turning sharply across the ridge, entered a rectangular farmyard, protected on one side by a bank and ditch and on the others by a fence set on a low bank. Inside the enclosure rose the conical, thatched roofs of some half-dozen circular huts and barns, ranged round a small, open yard. It was a compact, well-planned little farm, where life could be ordered and secure, one of many scattered over the uplands of southern England.

A very different type of dwelling was chosen by a wealthy Late Bronze Age group in the north of England. Possibly the choice was not a free one, but forced upon them to escape some danger, otherwise it is difficult to understand why such people should want to live in a narrow, dark and excessively damp cave overlooking the little Heathery Burn, near Stanhope in County Durham. They occupied it long enough to break a great amount of crockery and to eat a great amount of beef, mutton and game, throwing the fragments and the bones cheerfully on the floor. Their equipment was astonishingly rich, including quantities of socketed axes, spears, swords, tools and ornaments and even a mould and tongs for the practice of bronze founding. An elegant shouldered bucket or *situla* and a golden armlet and ring must have been even more strangely out of place in these dank and wild surroundings. So many and excellent were their possessions that one cannot fail to wonder if the cave were the temporary home of an exiled chief and his followers. This idea gains colour from the fact that the group certainly included a bronze-smith and probably brought with them a four-wheeled horse-drawn cart, both of which are likely to have been the prerogatives of a man of rank. If one may be permitted a momentary flight of fancy, one can see the party fleeing after some defeat, possibly at the hands of the first Iron Age invaders (p. 101), the leader accompanied by his retainers and his smith, forcing their way into these remote regions, the once proud chariot dragged with difficulty over rough, difficult country. And it is likely that their tenancy of the cave had an even more violent conclusion. Why were so many valuables abandoned on the floor, and why were the bones of at least three human beings found among them? It seems that some catastrophe, probably a sudden spate in the ravine, must have caught them unawares, thus ending in tragedy a story which we believe began in misfortune.

Still farther to the north a little Late Bronze Age settlement was established at Jarlshof in the Shetlands, where a few stone-built houses sheltered among the dunes close by Sumburgh Head. The villagers lived simply but efficiently, making the best use of whatever was to hand in a country so cold and exposed as these islands. They kept herds of shorthorn cattle and two breeds of sheep, cultivated their fields, and also hunted seals and went fowling and fishing. Their solidly built houses were of a curious plan, perhaps first devised in the Mediterranean and then introduced here by the Megalithic folk. From a central courtyard with a hearth opened four little side-chambers contained in the thickness of the wall, while opposite the entrance was a large alcove which could serve as a cattle stall. One ingenious householder tethered his cattle to a stall-ring fashioned from a whale's vertebra, and appears also to have collected cowdung for his fields—the first recorded instance of the use of manure by a British farmer.

At first the community was as nearly self-sufficing as their Early Bronze Age predecessors at Skara Brae, fashioning their implements from bone and the local slate and quartz, and even carving domestic pots out of soft rocks. But towards the end of the Late Bronze Age an event occurred which must have caused great excitement among the simple villagers and served to link them with the outside world. A bronze-smith suddenly arrived in the hamlet, set up his workshop in one of the courtyards, and began to mould swords, knives, pins and other articles that must have impressed the locals as representing the height of luxury and scientific wonder. We can suppose that the smith, on the contrary, felt himself wretchedly benighted, and often cursed an unjust fate which had deprived him of his more comfortable livelihood farther south. For he may well have been one of the victims of the blacksmiths and their new metal, whose arrival in Britain threatened many of the bronze-founders with unemployment (p. 98).

If Late Bronze Age domestic arrangements show some improvement in the social amenities, the varied abundance of goods obtainable by the end of the period must have meant a much greater advance in the standard of living—and of killing. To consider the latter art first. The new offensive weapons, the sword, spear and axe already described, as they came to be produced more cheaply and in larger quantities, must have reached an ever-widening section of the population. At the same time defensive armament was reinforced. Warriors could now protect themselves with round shields, either wooden with a bronze boss over the hand-grip, or all of bronze, the surface often enlivened by ring within ring of little *repoussé* knobs. Even horses might be armoured. One of the most magnificent objects surviving from this age is the great golden peytrel or horse's chest-piece that was found in a barrow at Mold in Flintshire. It is of fine sheet gold, mounted on bronze, and glitters with many rows of embossed designs that give a rich effect of light and shade.

Those invaders of south-east England who came from the Alpine lakes brought their own distinctive bronze types; their swords had parallel sides instead of bulging blades, and ended in a long, tapering, sinister-looking point, while their axes were a peculiar winged elaboration of the flanged palstave form.

But improvement was not restricted to weapons of war: men and women were also infinitely better equipped for their peaceful callings. Specialized tools were ready to the hand of the craftsman: socketed gouges and chisels for the carpenter, hammers, tracers, punches, tongs and miniature anvils for the bronze- and gold-smiths. To reap his increasing corn crops, the field worker could use a well-designed socketed sickle, while for the wealthy housewife cooking facilities were vastly improved by the introduction of sheet-bronze cauldrons (Fig. 15). In these great, fat, round-bellied vessels, fitted with ring handles for hanging them over the flames, food could be seethed and stewed in an appetizing manner hitherto impossible. Their design was copied by the Irish smiths from the Mediterranean, where such cauldrons are already mentioned in Homeric verse. From Ireland they were imported as luxuries into Britain, a fact recalled by the tale in the Mabinogion that tells how a certain British king was the proud owner of one which had been brought over to him by an Irishman, 'a huge, reddish-yellow-haired man, coming up from the lake with a cauldron on his back'. Everywhere their possession was recognised as a certain mark of rank and wealth.

A second type of bronze vessel then in fashion, the *situla*, a high-shouldered bucket far more elegant and formal in taste than the portly cauldron, was an original Italian design that came to be widely imitated in western Europe.

Other domestic crafts to advance their methods in the Late Bronze Age were spinning and weaving. For the first time there is evidence that spindles for twisting the yarn were weighted with round 'whorls' to increase their spin, while some form of upright loom was adopted in which the warp threads were held taut by cylindrical clay weights.

Improved weaving must have led to better clothes, and with them many ornaments were worn. Gold was still freely imported from Ireland.

In contrast with this wealth of goods for the living, the

Plate IX

Crown Copyright reserved

Skara Brae, Orkney. A house in the Bronze Age village

Plate X

Crown Copyright reserved

Skara Brae, Orkney. A dresser made from stone slabs

dead were more poorly provided than at any other time in
our prehistory, and there is an almost complete absence of new
religious monuments of any kind.   This need not mean that
the Deverel-Rimbury people were stern rationalists, that a
wave of agnosticism swept Britain in the Late Bronze Age;
their religious tenets may even have been more spiritual and

FIG. 15.—Bronze cauldron of the Late Bronze Age.

less superstitious than those held at other times, but certainly
their beliefs did not impel them to great labours in the building
of temples or tombs, or to great sacrifices for the enrichment
of their dead.   They had inherited from central Europe the
custom of cremation burial in large cemeteries or 'urnfields'.
The true central European urnfield had no grave-mounds,
but in the west the old Battle-Axe warrior tradition was still
sufficiently alive for low saucer-shaped barrows often to be
raised over the cremations, or for the urns to be buried in the

flanks of older tumuli. In Britain this persistence of the
barrow idea was particularly strong in Wessex. No durable
possessions went with the ashes into these cineraries, and the
urns themselves, even at their most ornate, can show no more
than plain lugs, flutings, or bands of clay corrugated with the
impressions of the potter's finger-tips (Fig. 12 D, E). Indeed,
of all the dreary sights to be seen in our museums, none is more
inevitably dreary than the contents of an average large Deverel-
Rimbury cemetery: row upon row of barrel-shaped or cylindrical urns, dark in paste, often lopsided and ill-fired. Yet
their very number, so wearying to the eye, has a special
importance for it signifies the very great growth in population
which better agriculture made possible by increasing food
supplies. By the end of the Late Bronze Age southern
England was more thickly settled than ever before.

After 1300 years the British Bronze Age was reaching its
close. While in the north many of the old Urn Folk were
still semi-nomadic pastoralists, the south was rich in settled
hamlets and steadings surrounded by their arable fields and
grazing grounds. Cheap bronze had made good tools and
weapons available to many, and the merchants who supplied
them waxed in wealth and importance. There was better
farming and craftsmanship, better clothes, more food and
better cooking. Altogether a sufficiently prosperous land.
Nor was the coming of the new age of iron to make any
profound change in its structure. The bronze workers were
naturally the hardest hit. These proud inheritors of a craft
which in Britain had well over a millennium of tradition behind
it had either to adapt themselves or succumb. In the Lowland
Zone iron was gradually to displace bronze for the manufacture of tools and weapons, so that the founders were faced
with the choice of learning to work iron, casting only the
ornaments and fittings that continued to be made in the more
beautiful old metal, or retreating to trade on a humbler scale
in the Highland Zone, where bronze long held its own. We
have already encountered one such impoverished merchant
driven to seek his living at Jarlshof.

It was not that iron was at first greatly superior to bronze—

indeed, it was little harder and in appearance far more uncouth —but that it was plentiful. Much of the bronze-smiths' power had depended on their knowledge and control of the sources of two raw materials: copper, which was far from common, and tin, which was even rarer. But with iron there was no need for such elaborate organization—ores could be found in abundance and in many places. Once its smelting was understood, once furnaces could be brought to a sufficient heat, iron could be produced far more cheaply and readily than bronze. Its adoption in Britain, therefore, really only intensified a social process already begun in the Late Bronze Age—the putting of good tools and weapons within the reach of the many instead of the few.

Iron had been used by man very long before it was first brought to Britain. In Mesopotamia and Egypt it was occasionally used as early as 3000–2500 B.C. But it was the Hittites of Asia Minor who first began to work it on a large commercial scale, trading it freely among their neighbours in the eastern Mediterranean, and it was from them that the craft first reached Europe, where it became known to the Greeks by the end of the second millennium. The warriors with iron swords whom we have seen driving out the Alpine Lake-dwellers in about 800 B.C. (p. 89) were sharers in the first widespread European iron-using civilization, that of Hallstatt, which originated in central Europe, but soon spread among the Celtic tribes of the west. At about this time the worsening of the climate which had flooded the lake villages began to have a serious effect on the farming communities of northern Europe. Threatened with famine, many were obliged to migrate southward, and it was mainly this cause, combined with a universal growth in population due to the development of agriculture, which sent further groups of Celts across the Channel, bearers of a late version of the Hallstatt culture. So it was that the first true British Iron Age began in southern England in the fifth century B.C.

Chapter Five

THE EARLY IRON AGE

ALTHOUGH the use of iron was not general in Britain before the immigrations that began in the fifth century B.C., the vigorous Hallstatt civilization of central Europe, with its groups of restless swordsmen, did not fail to make itself felt at an earlier date. Already by the sixth century adventurers with knowledge of Hallstatt ways were percolating into these islands armed with swords that were usually made of bronze, yet followed the design of the iron weapon. Such pioneering groups exerted some influence on the Late Bronze population, and in particular we find the native bronze-smiths casting modified versions of their Hallstatt swords.

Some of them even arrived possessed of iron implements, and taught the smiths how to forge iron. One among them whom we may treat as representative of the rest was a warrior who seems to have sailed from western France to establish himself in south Wales on the fertile land of the Glamorgan Plain. Native hillsmen in the Black Mountains, envious of his property, organized a sally down to the Plain and looted his household. But as they were retreating triumphantly back towards their own fastnesses some alarm made them throw their booty into the mountain lake Llyn Fawr, where it was destined to lie for some two thousand five hundred years. The prize had been a rich one. It included two of the precious bronze cauldrons, which bobbed some little way across the surface of the lake before becoming water-logged and sinking. Then there were spearheads and axes of the ordinary Late Bronze type, but the chief had also owned a Hallstatt bronze razor and a sickle made of iron. The sickle had evidently been wrought by a native craftsman faithful to his traditional bronze patterns, however ill-suited to the new metal. Most remarkable of all was a great iron sword which, though native in some of its details, in form and size and in the curious winged chape which adorned its scabbard, exactly resembled the weapon carried by the Hallstatt swordsmen of the Continent.

Settlers of this kind who used iron implements, and had the blacksmiths to forge them, acted as heralds of the true Iron Age which began in the fifth century B.C., when changes of climate and land shortage drove large numbers of fresh invaders to our shores. These came in several groups, landing all round our eastern and southern coasts, just as their precursors had done in the Late Bronze Age. The eastern seaboard received colonists from the Low Countries, among whom Hallstatt civilization was already much diluted, so far had they lived from its greatest centres. For this reason they were readily able to fuse with a British Bronze Age population with which they had much in common, and so build up a culture in which old traditions mingled with new. It was otherwise in Wessex, where Celts from northern France imposed a more advanced Hallstatt culture which took comparatively little from that of the old Deverel-Rimbury people.

If in much of the south of Britain this transition from the last Bronze to the first Iron Age was clear cut, while in the east it was blurred, in neither did it very greatly change the habits of life developed during the previous centuries. The backbone of society continued to be the yeoman cultivator, who could turn warrior at will, and there is still little evidence for a disproportionately wealthy exploiting class.

This was the fifth century. While in Greece the poets, philosophers and sculptors of Periclean Athens were working for the enrichment of a beautiful and highly organized city state, Britain thus remained a simple agricultural land with lonely farmsteads and at most a few small villages. When looking down on the scatter of post-holes and pits marking the site of one of these modest Celtic farmsteads, it takes an effort to realize that without any very incredible chances its original owner might have found himself in classical Greece and watched the building of the Parthenon.

An Iron Age farm that well represents for us the kind of simple home achieved by the well-to-do members of the Wessex population stood at Little Woodbury, on the chalk downs overlooking the Avon valley a mile or so from the place where the spire of Salisbury cathedral was to rise some fifteen hundred years later. The farmer and his household (which may have included some of the live stock) lived in a spacious round house (Pl. XII) standing in a circular fenced compound among the minor buildings and equipment of the farmyard. The busiest time to visit such a settlement would be the autumn. Then one could see the heads of corn carefully reaped with small sickles and hung on lines stretched between pairs of wooden posts. When the sun and wind had dried them, the grain would be winnowed in shallow depressions in the chalk, then divided into two parts, the larger for winter food, the smaller to be reserved as seed for the coming season. This seed corn, on which the hopes of the next season depended, had very special care, being stored in little square granaries, well ventilated and raised above the dampness of the ground. The other part of the crop, that which was intended for food, was dried in clay ovens to prevent germination before being poured for storage into deep, chalk-cut pits, roofed over and lined with basketry or skins. As grain-stores, these pits had a short life, for after a few years they became infected with moulds and had to be abandoned: they were then commonly converted into rubbish-tips and filled with ashes, bones and all manner of domestic litter. During the course of some three centuries no fewer than three hundred and sixty such pits were sunk in the compound at Woodbury.

A household of this kind would be able to cultivate about 15 acres of arable, of which only one-half or one-third would be sown in any one year, while the downland grass offered good pasture for flocks of a small breed of sheep and a herd of shorthorn cattle. Below in the wooded valley pigs could find a living, and the farmer bring variety to his table by hunting red deer and other smaller game.

Farm equipment included the two-ox plough, perhaps now sometimes shod with iron, iron sickles, and querns for grinding flour by rubbing a smaller stone to and fro on a larger one.

Cloth was more than ever in demand, and the women must often have been seen sitting outside the house spinning yarn with the help of simple bone, pottery, or stone spindle whorls, or inside weaving at their looms with a line of triangular clay weights dangling from the warp threads. To separate and control these threads and to press down the woof they used well-made bone combs with long, decorated handles. Unhappily we shall probably never know the colour or designs of the fabrics cut from these Iron Age looms, nor much about the style of the clothes for which they were intended.

The craft of potting, too, achieved a much higher standard than anything known in Britain before. Now for the first time there is the sharp distinction to which we have since grown accustomed between the 'best' service and the coarser kitchen ware. The fine crockery included shapely and thin-walled bowls (Fig. 16 B), some with simple geometric decoration cut on a glossy red surface. This attractive red colouring was obtained by dipping the pots in the iron oxide known as hæmatite to form a coating which was afterwards highly polished in imitation of bronze. One can imagine such bowls ranged on a shelf in an Iron Age farmhouse warmly lit by the fire and looking almost as attractive as a dresser full of old lustre.

The manufacture of such pieces demanded a special skill and knowledge which could hardly belong to the ordinary housewife. It was, in fact, carried on by experts, who seem to have traded their wares over quite wide areas. The simple cooking utensils, on the other hand, were made at home out of the local clays, although the women often imitated in this crude medium the elegant form of the bronze *situla* (p. 96).

Iron seems to have been used only sparingly, or at least was carefully husbanded, for little is ever found in the early settlements: a few knives, pins, rings or other small objects being the most that remain.

Not all the Early Iron Age population can have lived in isolated farms such as Little Woodbury. Their dwellings sometimes clustered together on lower ground in groups that can fairly be called villages, a probable site of such a village being that at All Cannings Cross in Wiltshire. But these clusters were not nearly so common as we used to suppose when every grain-store was believed to represent a 'pit-dwelling', so

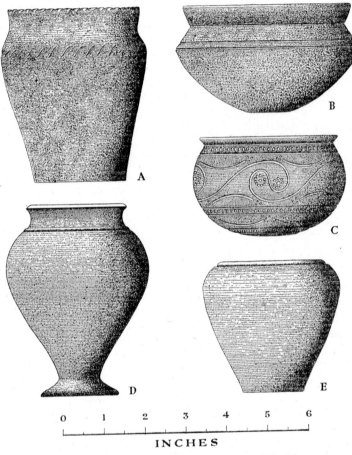

FIG. 16.—Iron Age Pottery. A, B, Hallstatt types; C, La Tène type; D, E, Belgic types.

that Little Woodbury would have been mistaken for a village of over three hundred houses! On this subject archæologists have waged a stubborn battle. Clearly the imaginative appeal of the pit-dwelling is very great: there is something of the romantic savage in the picture of our ancestors passing their lives crouched in holes ten feet below the ground. So great, indeed, is it that for long its supporters were blind to the evident truth that no human being could linger over a fire in such a pit and emerge alive, cold reason, however, has been accepted in the end and pit-dwellers have dropped from our history; instead it is recognized that these peasants had a practical means for storing the winter food necessary to support their increasing numbers.

As well as open villages there were strongholds on many hills, especially among the chalk downs of the south. The defences were slight enough at first—often a wooden palisade following the contours of the hilltop. Such places were probably intended primarily as temporary refuges for times of danger, even if farmers may sometimes have chosen to settle more permanently within their protective walls. Though unambitious in structure, these refuges already indicate a fair-sized social group united for its own security. And before long there were happenings which made such defence an imperative necessity.

While the Hallstatt Celts were quietly digging themselves into British soil, the expansion of the Celtic peoples had been causing widespread disturbance on the Continent. In the fourth century before Christ Celts had crossed the Alps, conquered territory in Italy and sacked Rome; by the third they were pushing farther eastward, fighting the Macedonians, assailing Delphi and even crossing into Asia Minor, where they were to settle and become the 'foolish Galatians' of St. Paul. Nor, as we have just hinted, did the West escape. In this same century their warrior bands crossed the Channel and caused panic among the population of Britain. With them into Britain they brought a culture that can no longer be called Hallstatt. Already when the first Hallstatt settlers were arriving in this country their kinsfolk in eastern France and south Germany were building up a new culture, that known as La Tène, which came to represent the height of early Celtic achievement. The Celts of these regions were helped to make this development from their old Hallstatt civilization by the stimulating contacts which they were receiving from the Mediterranean—particularly from the Etruscans of Italy and the prosperous Greek colonists of Marseilles. The Celts sent south such goods as backward peoples can usually supply to their more advanced neighbours, slaves and raw materials, above all metals, furs and amber from farther north. In exchange they imported a Mediterranean product for which they had developed a passionate desire: wine. With this wine came all the equipment for its proper enjoyment, fine bronze and pottery vessels for its carriage, storage, mixing and drinking. Chiefs might afford a whole table service of bronze wine vessels, many of which would be embellished with the stylized plant designs of classical convention. In this manner such patterns came before the eyes of the Celtic artist-craftsmen who were presently fired to adopt them as foundations for their own work. So that it has truly been said that 'La Tène art may largely have owed its existence to Celtic thirst'.

But no barbarian could merely imitate a Greek. The Celts soon transformed these borrowed conventions, with others that reached them from the Scythians of south-eastern Europe, into something inimitably their own; the orderly human spirit of classical taste fled before the free, flamboyant, visionary spirit which now inspired barbarian genius, to yield at last one of the most masterly abstract arts which Europe has known.

These good wines and lovely objects were for the gratification of a wealthy warrior aristocracy, for men such as those whose richly furnished graves are known by the Middle Rhine and in the Marne region of France. There they lay below covering mounds, buried in full pomp with lavishly ornamented sword and helmet, with their wine-flagons and their fighting chariots. It seems that it was about 250 B.C. that numbers of such warriors began, as we have seen, to cross to Britain, sailing probably from the mouth of the Seine, and to introduce for the first time the La Tène culture which was to bear its final and most mature fruits in these islands.

The consternation which their coming provoked among

the British peasants was not without practical results. In a way not altogether unfamiliar to us today the inhabitants began hastily to throw up defence works; farmers such as the owners of Woodbury dug ditches round their homesteads and strengthened their fences, while hilltops were crowned with quite formidable forts, sometimes replacing the older palisaded strongholds (p. 105). Hardly less familiar landmarks than the long and round barrows are these 'camps' which crown so many of our hills, their defences following the natural contours. Probably many of the earliest were put up at this time in the third century before Christ against the inroads of La Tène warriors from northern France. Their building was a formidable effort, even more formidable than their present appearance suggests. Today, though impressive in scale, they look simple enough: a single turf-covered bank sloping gradually into a mild, grassy ditch: from a distance no more than a tiny nick in the profile of the hill. But this form is the outcome of collapse and decay. Picture them as they were when new-built and ready for defence. The attacker was first confronted with a steep-sided ditch cut deep into the chalk; beyond lay a narrow strip of level ground under direct fire from the ramparts, which presented an almost sheer wall of timbers or coursed turf or stone secured by stout uprights. Against the back of this revetment the chalk bank was piled, its top making a protected rampart walk for the defenders. At the weakest point in the circuit, the entrance, the rampart might swing inwards so that the wooden gates stood inset at the end of a funnel-like entry which could be raked by cross-fire.

One can imagine the scene so well—the dead white of the newly dug chalk, the raw feel and smell of the fresh timber, the wood-chippings scattered on the trampled ground.

So sudden and short were the onsets of danger that these early forts were often abandoned unfinished, and few were occupied for long. The determined and organized resistance to aggression which they represent discouraged the La Tène raiders and prevented them from settling in any force on the southern chalk. Groups of them did settle here and there, certainly in Sussex round the great fort of Cissbury near Worthing, and in places in Wessex and east Kent, and these brought perceptible changes into the old Hallstatt traditions, but no wholly La Tène type of society was established. Other groups seem to have penetrated beyond the Thames—into East Anglia, for example—establishing their power over the Hallstatt peasantry. Here must be the origin of the royal line of the Iceni which was to end bloodily and heroically in the great queen Boudicca.

In Scotland a rather more substantial colonization took place when, in the third century B.C., La Tène invaders overcame a native population still mainly living in a belated Bronze Age. Landing in the east, they soon spread right across the country to its Atlantic coasts. They it was who built the so-called vitrified forts of Scotland, such as those well known at Castle Law near Abernethy and Finavon in Angus. It has recently been shown by practical experiment that this vitrification or fusing of the rock of which they are built was not deliberate. The forts were in fact originally built by the curious method which Cæsar found in use among the Gauls: stone facings were bonded together with vertical and horizontal timbers, and more wood went into the rubble core. When such a building was set on fire, accidentally or by an enemy, the timbers burnt away, and their sockets made such efficient flues that enough heat was generated to melt and fuse the stones. The final but unintentional product was a vitrified fort.

But it was in eastern Yorkshire and Lincolnshire that the newcomers established their most characteristic colonies. There La Tène chiefs ruled their followers and the native population with an absolutism that allowed them to maintain more of their Continental habits and standards. The tribe to settle east Yorkshire was that of the Parisi, who still held that territory when Ptolemy was writing four centuries later. Coming as they did from northern France, we can safely recognize them as an offshoot of the people whose name has been so conspicuously preserved in that of the French capital. It is an amusing thought that such an historical link should exist between the Parisian and the Yorkshire tyke.

In this north-eastern region, more than any other, society fell into a highly aristocratic pattern, recalling that of the Early Bronze Age. Wealth and power were concentrated in the hands of a small minority who formed a world of relative luxury. In that world it seems that women could occupy a high and honourable place.

Much thought was given to personal appearance. The men wore cloaks or plaids fastened at the shoulder with safety-pin brooches sometimes studded with coral, and hung wrists and ankles with bronze or jet bangles. With wealth and leisure the amiable vice of vanity could be cultivated, and we find La Tène women sophisticated enough to employ polished metal hand-mirrors in making their toilet (Fig. 23).

The chiefs' weapons were of the finest. They carried iron-bladed daggers, the bronze hilt often in the form of a manikin with splayed arms and legs, and short iron swords sheathed in bronze scabbards that might be richly chased with La Tène designs. For defence they had oval wooden shields with ornamental mountings in bronze, and perhaps occasionally helmets.

These heroes no longer had to go into battle on foot, but drove in the two-wheeled chariots which the Celts had adopted from the Etruscans of Italy. The chariots were wooden, and had spoked, iron-tyred wheels standing between two feet six and three feet high. By Cæsar's time at least, they opened forwards to allow the warrior to dart recklessly down the shaft-pole between the pair of horses when he wished better to reach an adversary or cast a javelin. From snaffle-bits of surprisingly modern design the reins passed through decorated bronze terret rings into the hands of the charioteer, whose duty it was to manœuvre the vehicle for his warrior master.

When admiring the beauty of La Tène weapons and trappings, it is well to remember that the resplendent aristocrats under whose patronage they were made probably passed their everyday lives in squalor. Their houses were of the simplest—round huts lacking in domestic amenities. It was in part this combination of lavish personal display with graceless living that the Greeks and Romans despised in their barbarian neighbours.

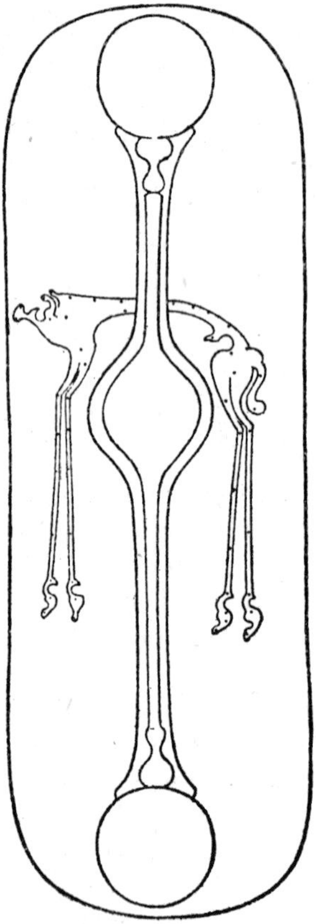

In an aristocratic society of this type it is not surprising to find a return to elaborate and expensive funerary rites. The dead were laid in pits below small, round barrows, fully clad and decked with ornaments, and, just as in France, they might be accompanied by their war chariots, sometimes complete, more often dismantled. It was only a very great man who could hope to be furnished with horses; normally they were too valuable for sacrifice, and their harness alone went into the grave. Very frequently large joints of pork or whole pigs were buried, and even the humbler graves were supplied with a leg standing in an earthenware jar. This custom probably implies more than a strong preference for pork; as game highly prized by a hunting aristocracy, the boar had a special prestige—a religious significance even greater than that now enjoyed in this country by the fox. Accordingly we find pigs portrayed by Celtic artists in a manner suggesting special honours, the most remarkable examples being the strange attenuated creature that straddles the Witham shield (Fig. 17) and the spirited little bronze beast from Hounslow that probably once crested some warrior's helmet.

FIG. 17.—The Witham shield: outline diagram showing the boar.

The greatest contribution to history made by this north-eastern La Tène colony was in the work of its artists. During the centuries which followed its foundation they more than any of their contemporaries were responsible for the growth of a British school of decorative art which is one of the outstanding episodes in the story of our civilization.

Their achievement has mainly to be judged from the metalwork which has survived where a mass of lovely but perishable things must have disappeared. But it is enough to show that these artists happily combined the surest sense of plastic form with an equal mastery of decorative design in the flat. Their plastic skill is admirably shown in the horse-bits already mentioned: one feels that æsthetically the craftsman who conceived them could do no wrong. In surface decoration the earliest style is still based on renderings of classical plant forms, but these were conceived in a Celtic freedom that developed towards a pure geometric style, a style of dynamic pattern, the poise of which only stiffened into a duller and more formal symmetry when touched by the influence of Rome.

One of the loveliest individual masterpieces of the early designers is the sword dredged from the river Witham (Pl. XIII). The bronze scabbard mount curls up and over in curves as free and unpredictable as a sea-wave. Another most dramatic piece designed a little later is the Torrs chamfrein or horse's head-armour (Pl. XIV), an object which both in its form and in the decoration of its surface is extraordinarily striking and forceful. Though much later in date, the fine bronze mirrors from Birdlip and Desborough (Fig. 23) are evidently part of the same flow of genius, as is also that great national treasure the Battersea shield (Pl. XV), but we shall find that here fresh currents are augmenting the stream (p. 129). This later phase, which led to the final one when British La Tène art was first debased and then suppressed by the alien traditions of Rome, belongs more properly to the last chapter.

Meanwhile, and long before our Celtic art had reached the advanced stage to which we have now followed it, another region of Britain was receiving La Tène immigrants. The motives which took them from west France to south-western

England seem to have been rather different from those operating elsewhere. Here in the south-west it was not only to plunder and seize land that they came; they were pursuing trade, even if it was at the sword's point. The tin of west Cornwall had been a major factor in the Bronze Age economics of western Europe, and now once more this peninsula was invaded by warrior traders who saw that its control would bring them wealth. Here we get the first glimpse of recorded British geography. The daring Greek explorer Pytheas visited Cornwall in about 325 B.C., and to him is ascribed the famous account of how its people mined and smelted the tin and brought it across in waggons at low tide to the island of Ictis, whence Continental merchants took it by ship to the west French coast, and so overland to the mouth of the Rhône and the markets of Mediterranean civilization. Unless the coast-line has changed, Ictis is most likely to be St. Michael's Mount, and the trade evidently supported a large mining population in the tin-bearing regions round about and kept them in touch with the Continent.

Conquest and exploitation here meant a rich prize for the La Tène adventurers, and since the earlier inhabitants were not warlike, and probably but little advanced beyond the material level of the Late Bronze Age, the prize may have been easily won. But to secure their hold the invading leaders needed fortified strongholds. We have already seen how the descendants of the Hallstatt people in Wessex and elsewhere built hill-forts against the La Tène invaders of the third century B.C. The same thing may have been tried here and there against our south-western invaders, but the strongholds which they built for their own security, though standing likewise on hill or upland sites, are forts of a distinctive type, with a strictly circular ground-plan. In west Cornwall such stone-walled ring-forts as Chun Castle are prominent features of the landscape, and often stand above a contemporary hamlet, much as a medieval baron's castle at once protects and overawes its village.

The hamlets here were also distinctive. A typical one, dominated by the fort of Castle-an-Dinas was that of

Plate XI

Celtic fields on Fyfield Down, Wiltshire, from the air

Plate XII

Crown Copyright reserved

Reconstruction of the Early Iron Age farmhouse of Little Woodbury, near Salisbury

Chysauster, south-west of St. Ives, which lasted from late in this period into Roman times. It had at least eight houses, built on the courtyard plan (p. 94), flanking a cobbled street: these were surrounded by garden plots and small arable fields, and the inhabitants were not only cultivators, but also miners and smelters of tin. Both fort and village dwellers made and used the subterranean galleries which the Cornish know as fogous. These were apparently hiding-places against attack, and, whatever their origin, they go with the forts to show that violence and warfare now loomed large in all men's lives.

Farther east, in Cornwall, there were fewer fogous, but more ring-forts, such as Castle Dore near Fowey, within which the inhabitants dwelt in timber-built round huts. Farther east again, this south-western culture came closer to the main stream of British civilization, and fort-building drew more on the older contour-plan tradition described above (p. 107), issuing presently in imposing new developments.

By the beginning of the first century B.C. the increasingly warlike character of Celtic civilization was in this corner of Britain enhanced by the rise of a new weapon, the sling. With this simple loop of leather, a man could hurl a smooth pebble or a baked clay bullet with great force at comparatively long range, to smite his enemy as David smote Goliath, and organized companies of slingers could play as deadly a part in battle as riflemen in modern warfare. The art of the sling came probably along the tin route from the western Mediterranean, where for example Balearic slingers were so famous, and the development of the art of fortification to suit it was apparently begun by the Veneti, the coastal people of Brittany who plied most of the cross-Channel trade with south-western Britain. The main feature was to multiply the number of your lines of defence, to set the greatest possible distance between yourself inside them and the attacking enemy outside. This multiplication of ramparts was, it seems, first applied to the 'cliff castles' with which these people fortified the promontories of their rocky coast, and the application was perhaps first generally made when all ancient France or Gaul was invaded by the wild Cimbric and Teutonic tribes from northern

I

Europe, just before 100 B.C. Similar cliff castles, evidently the work of these same Veneti or their British associates, stand thick along the coasts of Cornwall, and the principle of multiple ramparts, suited to sling warfare, was also extended inland, for ring-forts and soon also for hilltop fortresses of larger size, contour-planned in the older native tradition (Pl. XXII).

The result was a gradual spread of hill-fortification on a great scale, from the south-west northward and eastward, wherever aggression or colonization by the south-westerners, or imitation of them by other tribes, carried the new sling warfare. Neither at first made much headway in Wessex; the famous Maiden Castle near Dorchester (Pl. XVI), originally a moderate-sized fort of the older native type, was early in this phase enlarged, but with only a single ditch and rampart, and by the Wessex natives, not the south-western aggressors.

It was from Cornwall and Devon coastwise along the Bristol Channel that the new art of war spread mainly. Some groups of trading colonists were probably going this way already, for example to Bredon Hill fort, on the edge of the Cotswolds, but more followed and on both sides of the Severn. The iron of the Forest of Dean was probably one of their major objectives, and there was coastal settlement farther west in Wales, while others began to move northward into the country of the Marches. Presently all this quarter of Britain was by warfare, trade, and migration linked together in a loose cultural unity, of which the forts serve as an abiding sign.

But by far the most remarkable centres of La Tène culture which are known in this region are protected not by fortification, but by water—the Somerset lake-villages of Meare and Glastonbury. These were settled later than the first invasions into Cornwall, and it may well be that further immigrants from Brittany, to be noticed later (p. 128), had a share in their foundation, or at least development; but their excavation has given us an exceptionally full picture of the life of the period. The Glastonbury village (Fig. 18), lying about a mile north of the modern town, is the better known. It was excellently placed for trade, being connected by the Mendips

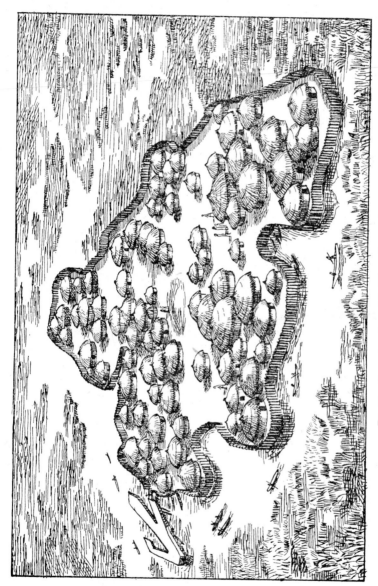

FIG. 18.—Reconstruction of the Glastonbury Lake Village.

with the main upland system of British trackways, and within coastwise reach of the Cornish tin exporters, as well as in direct touch southward with the shores of the Channel. For the security which the stormy times demanded, the founders of the village chose a piece of marshy ground that probably became completely flooded in winter and spring. Well equipped with iron billhooks, they hacked down the growth of alder and willow which cumbered the site, and then, with immense labour, went on to build up an artificial island on the ground they had cleared. Its main bulk was a bed of horizontal logs, close-packed and sometimes as much as 4 feet in thickness, but it was made yet more substantial with clay, stones, brushwood, and bracken, much of which had to be carted from a distance. To prevent it from spreading, they bounded their island with a stout palisade of vertical timbers driven well down into the marsh, the tops projecting to form a strong fence.

At the height of its prosperity this man-made island exceeded 10,000 square yards in extent, and on it stood some sixty round huts with wattled sides, trodden clay floors, and roofs thatched with reeds. Each house had a stone or clay hearth in the centre of the floor, and some had paved doorsteps, while cobbled alley-ways led between them. The village would first appear to the visitor as a huddle of thatched roofs rising among the thickets of alders and willows; carts are bringing produce from the higher ground where the villagers keep their beasts and cultivate corn and vegetables, while dug-out canoes moored at a landing-stage are ready for fowling expeditions among the many waterways, or for longer trading excursions. Inside its protecting wall, the village itself is full of life and activity—a compact stronghold of humanity isolated among the swamps. Duck and coot can be heard calling and splashing among reeds where herons and cranes stand motionless; occasionally a bittern sounds its uncanny, booming call; and there, top-heavy, comical, and grotesquely beautiful, a family of pelicans is sailing down the open waterway. The villagers naturally avail themselves of all this wild life over their fence to add delicious variety to their meals: they enjoy wildfowl of many kinds, especially duck, and also such freshwater fish as perch, roach, and trout.

Indeed, in all ways their industry and enterprise gave them a high standard of life. Carpenters were highly skilled and ambitious. Their accomplishments ranged from the heavy work of constructing platforms and houses, and of hollowing canoes, through cart-building and beautiful wheelwright's work, to such delicate operations as the lathe-turning of wooden vessels (Fig. 19) and the carving of ladles and graceful

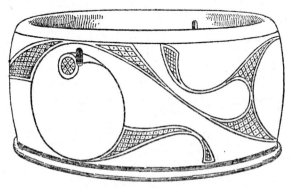

FIG. 19.—Carved wooden bowl from Glastonbury.

handles for iron implements. This iron equipment was itself varied and efficient. Blacksmiths' designs have changed little through the centuries, and Glastonbury sickles and bill-hooks hardly differ from those used to trim our own hedges and ditches, while neat little saws, as well as chisels and gouges, were forged for the carpenters. Bronze still had many uses. A sheet-bronze bowl ornamented with large hollow rivet-heads is one of the prides of Glastonbury town, where somewhat tinny reproductions can be bought as souvenirs— an honour which would surely have surprised and delighted its one-time owners. Among more domestic crafts, weaving was much practised; the same long-handled combs were popular as those used by the women of the earlier Iron Age, but an improvement of method is shown by the trim little bone bobbins which carried the yarn in wooden shuttles.

Another important labour-saving device—invented long since in the East—was the rotary quern for grinding corn (Fig. 4). For nearly two thousand years, ever since the introduction of cereals for food in Neolithic times, housewives had been content to make their flour by pushing one stone to and fro over another. Now they had only to turn a handle to revolve an upper stone pivoted in the nether one.

The Glastonbury people—perhaps it was again the women —were excellent potters. Their products are famous among all our prehistoric wares for the rich La Tène decoration which was engraved on smoothly-rounded bowls (like Fig. 16 C) or fat, comfortable-looking pots rather like Chinese ginger-jars. The incised patterns are often both ingenious and pleasing, though a certain stiffness is introduced by the frequent use of compasses in laying out the designs—a matter to which we shall return below (p. 129). When the wheel principle was in use not only for vehicles and for querns, but even for turning wooden vessels, it is surprising to find that the fast-turning potter's wheel was apparently still unknown. The Glastonbury villagers have perhaps been made to sound excessively industrious; but they were not above gambling, with dice to throw from carefully carved boxes. Probably the strongest impression one gets from the village is that the art which had formerly been enjoyed only by the Celtic aristocracy had here spread, simplified in form but still admirable in taste, to the common people and their everyday works and surroundings.

Their general standard of culture was perhaps unusually high, for they were evidently a trading community, importing Cornish tin, lead from Mendip, Dorset shale, glass beads and amber from the Continent, and, probably mainly from the Forest of Dean, quantities of iron, which went not only to make tools, weapons, and useful appliances of many kinds, but to furnish the medium of commerce itself—that is, a currency. This took the form of long, flat iron bars (Fig. 20), pinched up at one end, perhaps derived from the roughouts for sword-blades, but standardized in weight. They must have been very cumbersome to handle, but are found here and over a wide area in the south-west of Britain, further evidence of its unity of culture, and of its outside connexions also, since they extend into Wessex, the Thames valley, and the Midlands. The way across the Midland forests was marked by the belt of Jurassic rock-subsoil which makes a corridor of open country from the Cotswolds over into Lincolnshire, and there is an important ring-fort on this line at Hunsbury near Northampton, where the local ironstone was worked and a variety of remains shows a culture very like that of the Somerset villages,

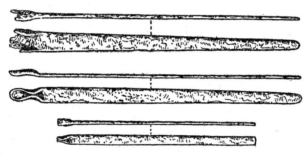

Fig. 20.—Iron currency bars of the Early Iron Age.

though it began earlier and did not survive as late. This way went the main connexions with the north, where the Parisian and other La Tène peoples were still flourishing, their more distant venturers now even reaching the north of Ireland.

And the other way went the connexions with the Continent across the western end of the Channel, where the sailing-galleys of the Veneti plied between Britain and Brittany. Though an iron anchor and its chain are known from a fort near Poole Harbour, actual remains of those galleys have never yet been found. But their description has come down to us, written by the man who brought their power to an end. That man was Julius Cæsar, the Roman conqueror of Gaul, who in 56 B.C. met the defiance of the tribes of Brittany in a great sea battle off their coast, and utterly destroyed their assembled fleet. The next year he addressed himself to the invasion of Britain.

Chapter Six

BRITAIN AND THE ROMANS

IT may seem strange to the English reader, for whom going abroad has usually meant Dover to Calais, that the broad Atlantic end of the Channel should ever have served for a main crossing between his island and the Continent. But this Brittany crossing was, of course, part of the ancient Atlantic sea-route, and it connected the metal-bearing west with the easiest ancient way to the markets of the Mediterranean, past the mouth of the Loire and across south-west France. On the other hand, the Straits of Dover, until near the end of prehistoric times, lay between regions not particularly wealthy or important in themselves, and not particularly connected with the more distant centres of European civilization. Only when occasional major folk-movements broke into the sequestered northern corner of France did they bear any distinguished traffic. But as the Iron Age wore on, major folk-movements became more frequent and more formidable; in particular, while the Mediterranean civilization that became the Roman Empire was spreading from the south, the Germanic peoples had begun to press down from the north. Their climate had been getting colder and wetter, and, with better farming and the introduction of iron, their population bigger and their armament stronger. One of their outlets was across the Rhine in this direction.

As early as Hallstatt times, their pressure this way had been one of the causes of Celtic migration to Britain, and by the time the Cimbric and Teutonic tribes mentioned in the last chapter broke through into Gaul and beyond, there had been much Germanic infiltration among the Celts of the Low Countries, and a mixed Celtic population of similar Germanic tinge had succeeded to the older La Tène culture of the Marne (p. 106). These peoples were called Belgæ, and at the beginning of the first century B.C. they had spread west to cover most of the country between the lower Rhine and the lower Seine with their own latter-day version of La Tène civilization. The lands directly across the Straits from Britain were thus drawn into that civilization much more fully than before, and their population increased. At the same time German aggression moved south and grew stronger. Presently the Celtic tribe of the Helvetii, pressed between the upper Rhine and the Swiss Alps, could bear it no longer, and determined to migrate in a body towards the west. Their departure would have left a great breach for German entry into Gaul; and it is at this point, in 58 B.C., that Julius Cæsar arrives upon the scene.

The growing power of the Romans had some time before annexed what is now the south of France, and Cæsar's object now was not only to keep the Germans out, but to annex the whole country for Rome. Ultimately he succeeded. We have already seen how in the course of his famous campaigns he conquered the Veneti of Brittany. But the Belgæ in the north-east had given him much hard fighting in the previous year, and he had not been at this long before he found that they were being helped from Britain, where, just across the Straits of Dover, they had kinsmen of their own, who had migrated thither less than a generation before. The Belgæ, in fact, had overflowed into south-eastern Britain, and had made the lands they had settled provinces of Belgic culture.

Remains of this Belgic culture have often been discovered. The Belgæ, like the Germans, cremated their dead, and they buried the ashes in shapely urns, usually pear-shaped and often with a pedestal foot (Fig. 16 D), which are sometimes found grouped in cemeteries or urnfields. The best known are in Kent, where they settled first: Swarling, near Canterbury, and Aylesford on the Medway. In most graves the urn was accompanied by other pots, no doubt to hold funeral offerings of food and drink, and sometimes by bronze or even silver brooches, shaped like a large and ornate safety-pin. At Aylesford there were also bronze vessels—a pan and wine-jugs—from Italy, and a great wooden bucket bound and handled in bronze, with two unearthly-faced human heads frowning above the rim, and designs beaten out on the upper band, including strange, leafy-tailed horse-monsters. Here we have a fresh instalment of La Tène art from Gaul; yet it is not for such isolated treasures that the Belgæ are most notable, but rather for their more efficient and better-equipped mastery of the arts of everyday life.

They made pottery on the true potter's wheel; their iron-work, of which there will be more to say presently, was superlative, as was their woodwork also, and in addition to warlike and domestic gear they made new heavy types of plough, some heavy and perhaps with wheels in front, armed with a big iron coulter to cut the sod and mould-boards to turn it. Whereas the old, light, two-ox plough could only scratch a superficial furrow even in easy soils, these new ploughs enabled comparatively heavy ground to be tilled, which could first be cleared of timber with iron axes; and so there began something of a revolution in British agriculture and land settlement. Thus, while the scattered farmsteads in which they mainly lived were still primitive as dwellings— simple round or oval huts for the most part—their produce nourished a thriving population. And Belgic fighting strength carried still farther the dominance of warfare over Iron Age life. They fought on foot, on horseback, and from chariots, and though they had not developed the same art of multiple fortification as the western peoples, they could make formid-able hill-forts enough, on woodland sites for choice, with defences often relying especially on a steep and wide main ditch. And in twenty years from their first coming they had spread from Kent to the Thames, and from the Thames deep into northern Hertfordshire.

Cæsar's judgment of the situation was that the security of a conquered Gaul demanded a conquered Britain. Accordingly, in August 55 B.C. he made a start by crossing from Boulogne with some 10,000 men, to explore, and, if all went well, to force obedience at least on the Belgæ of eastern Kent. But all did not go well: his fleet was damaged by a stormy high tide on the beach near Deal, and the local tribes with their chariots and horsemen gave his army some very sharp en-counters. He therefore got the expedition back to Gaul as soon as he could, and prepared for a larger one next year. Elaborate preparations were made, and about midsummer he crossed again, with a much larger force; he struck inland at once, and stormed the Belgic hill-fort of Bigbury near Canterbury—but only to learn that his fleet had once more been damaged by a storm. While it was being repaired, the Kentish tribes allied themselves with the leading Belgic chieftain beyond the Thames in Hertfordshire. This was Cassivellaunus, an aggressive leader, against whom Cæsar's assistance had already been sought by one of the non-Belgic tribes, the Trinovantes, who lived in Essex. Cassivellaunus knew he could not withstand the Roman legions in a pitched battle, but by skilful mobile warfare he harassed their advance over Kent, and again after they had crossed the Thames and reached the Trinovantes. At last Cæsar found and stormed his hill-fort capital at Wheathampstead; but even then the Romans had to beat off a fresh onslaught by his Kentish allies on their naval base. By early autumn he came to terms; but though Cæsar imposed on him an annual tribute, and a promise to leave the Trinovantes alone, the great Roman general retired to Gaul aware that Britain had not really been conquered at all. The fame of Cassivellaunus' resistance lived on ever afterwards in British story, but Cæsar soon found that to conquer Gaul itself he needed several more years of bitter fighting, while he had only marked down Britain for conquest in the future.

Cæsar's account of his invasions and of Britain generally, given us in his famous *Commentaries*, is the earliest surviving piece of written history concerned with our island. But he did not get beyond one corner of it, and by setting what he has told us against a background of modern knowledge, we can fill out his picture in many ways. It is clear that through the Belgic colonization, the corner which he visited had for the first time become the most powerful and most civilized, as civilization then went. It is clear also that the non-Belgic inhabitants hated and feared the Belgæ, and opposed their expansion. The Trinovantes were even glad to take sides with Cæsar against Cassivellaunus, and between Wheathampstead, their enemy's capital fortress, and St. Albans, where his successors presently settled, a great Belgic boundary ditch may still be seen, along the valley known as Beech Bottom. To dig this 100 feet wide and over 30 feet deep as they did, the intruders must indeed have been uneasy at first in their adopted land. The Wheathampstead fortress ditch is even bigger, and the tale of hostilities between the Belgæ and their neighbours is not confined to Hertfordshire.

In Kent their southern flank ran along the wooded fringes of the Weald, and here the inhabitants protected themselves against them by building large hill-forts like Oldbury Camp

FIG. 21.—British coins: one of their Greek models on the extreme left.

near Ightham. These inhabitants were largely an offshoot of the earlier La Tène immigrants into Sussex, whose expansion over the Wealden forest was no doubt connected with its important deposits of iron ore. There is evidence that the Kentish Belgæ also worked Wealden iron, while, as we shall see, their fellows north of the Thames ultimately reached the ironstone region of Northants and Oxfordshire. From the ores thus won, reduced in clay-built furnaces, the Belgic smiths forged their weapons of war, their chariot- and harness-fittings, their implements of forestry and farming, and the furnishings of their chieftains' hearths. These last were superb iron firedogs rising at either end to the likeness of a knob-horned ox-head, which display a true artist's feeling for fitness of design in wrought metal. But the westerners' iron bar currency, which they met with in the Thames valley and beyond, they did not make, for they brought with them from Gaul what was perhaps the most momentous of all the inventions adopted by La Tène from Mediterranean civilization—coinage.

Celtic coinage on the Continent was imitated from Greek, and in central Gaul was first minted in the second century B.C. Early in the next century gold coins of the Belgic Gauls began to circulate in south-east Britain, first those of the Bellovaci (from the district where Beauvais still preserved their tribal name), and then, starting in Kent, where the earliest Belgic colonists settled, those of the Atrebates (from the district of Arras). Such Gaulish types may sometimes have been actually minted over here, and the first distinguishably British coins took their type from an Atrebatic model. The designs of both faces look quite extraordinarily meaningless, until one sees them and their Gaulish models side by side with the Greek type from which they were ultimately derived (Fig. 21). This was the standard gold coin of the famous King Philip of Macedonia (the father of Alexander the Great), and it has on one side the head of the god Apollo wearing a laurel wreath, and on the other a driven chariot with two horses. The successive Celtic imitators, to whom the whole idea was strange, reduced both designs in time to uncouth patterns, the head perishing in a maze of blobs crossed by a sort of herring-bone version of the wreath, and the chariot and pair broken up into another maze of blobs, in which one can just see the dismembered skeleton of what was once a horse. But gradually after that the head design was worked out in Britain into a regular cross-pattern, based on the old wreath. And the never quite forgotten horse on the other side was suddenly created afresh, prancing in a weird but animated life. The famous White Horse of Uffington (Fig. 22) is probably a gigantic rendering of the same new form of strange, half-supernatural creature, cut in the chalk of the Berkshire Downs by a people who boasted him as a tribal or religious emblem. And that brings us back to our main story. For this people were for the most part fresh Belgic settlers from Gaul, who, when Cæsar was at last victorious there, would not submit to Roman rule, but took refuge in Britain instead.

Cæsar in both his expeditions had used the services of the king of the Atrebates, whose name was Comm or Commius. He was a person of some standing not only in Gaul, but in Britain, where we have seen his people's coinage circulating in Kent. Later he turned against Cæsar, and when the Gaulish resistance was broken he fled to Britain, with shiploads of followers. This was about 50 B.C., and in due course coins

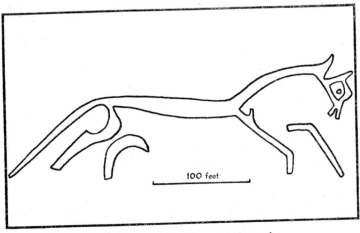

100 feet

FIG. 22.—'The White Horse of Uffington.'

inscribed with the name of Commius are found in Britain; not indeed in Kent, where one would not expect him after his association with the hated Roman, but farther west. There, between the west Sussex coast and the middle Thames, they follow after those with the new type of horse from Gaul just mentioned, and also after a local version of the coinage of his own tribe, the Atrebates. It looks as if Atrebatic and other refugees from Gaul settled in these regions in various tribal groups—the new horse on the coins was perhaps contributed by Remi from the district of Reims—which Commius eventually made into a single kingdom.

Like their relatives in the south-east, these people were not only stout warriors: they introduced improved farming and other peaceful arts, and their coins replaced the old native currency of iron bars. Their pottery was made on the wheel, and it is by this that the remains of their settlements are most easily recognized. But, unlike the south-eastern Belgæ, they came as survivors of a culture broken by the conquest of their homes, and thus it is natural to find its potters' art reduced among them to a much-diminished range, the commonest type of vessel being a simple bowl or jar with a plain beading for a rim (Fig. 16 E). Such bowls were also used as urns for burying the ashes of their cremated dead.

Commius seems to have died about 20 B.C., and by then the new Belgic lands probably stretched into Wessex as far west as the river Test, which has its mouth in Southampton Water. They included the Isle of Wight, but the chief harbour was by Chichester, where the first landings had probably been, thirty years before. Whether or no they made the series of defensive ditches (compare p. 133) to be seen near here, it must have been the Belgæ who brought the native occupation to a sudden end at the old hill-fort of the Trundle, overlooking Goodwood racecourse on the downs above. Then farther inland they had wrecked the native fort on St. Catharine's Hill above Winchester by fire, and taken for their own the native settlements on the neighbouring downs, as they did the virgin site of Winchester itself. Apart from a few fortified capitals, the Belgæ needed hill-strongholds themselves only in the frontier lands where they fought continually with the natives to extend their territory.

The natives for their part, built or renewed hill-forts of their own against them. In Wessex the strong forts characteristic of this time begin just west of the line where the circulation of the Belgic coins described above leaves off, the line of the river Test, whose steep-sided, marsh-bottomed valley cuts a frontier like a curving trough across the chalk downs of Hampshire. Their defences are variously planned, but most of them have multiple ramparts and ditches, such as we have already seen introduced into the south-west by the Veneti from Brittany, and some a have more or less circular plan like the south-western ring-forts. Where such works are renewals of abandoned earlier forts, they may form a strong citadel inside the old rampart, as at Bury Hill and Danebury near Andover, or else, as at Yarnbury Castle north-west of Salisbury, an enlarged circuit surrounding it. The farther one goes west, the longer the inhabitants were able to withstand Belgic encroachment, and the more imposing are the forts. The grandest of all is the renowned Maiden Castle in Dorset, where the earlier fort, already enlarged (p. 114), was now transformed (Pl. XVI): the new multiple works brought its size to close on 100 acres, and the inner rampart, towering at least 50 feet above the bottom of its fronting ditch, was massively built in chalk and earth and clay and limestone masonry, the limestone laboriously brought from outcrops over two miles away. The entrance defences were as complex as they were formidable, and the 45 acres of the space within made now no mere occasional camp of refuge, but a permanently inhabited township, the capital of the nameless chief whose will raised this stupendous fortress.

His domain was 70 miles westward from the first footholds of the Belgæ on the Chichester coast, and they did not reach and conquer it for some seventy years. The military architecture which served to hinder them so long was probably first brought to central Dorset by more western folk from Gaul, perhaps the fighting remnant of the Breton Veneti themselves, when Cæsar had broken their power across the Channel in 56 B.C. Like their relations earlier in Cornwall and along the Severn Sea, they were warrior adventurers, and with their swords and spears and deadly sling-stones they forced themselves by conquest upon the natives, and secured their hold in these great forts, just as the Norman conquerors of later England did in their castles. Under their rule, the farming life of the countryside went on virtually unaltered, and the round houses and granary store-pits of the traditional sort were still made much as before. But they did introduce a new kind of pottery to the lingering Hallstatt tradition, bowls and jars with a bead-rim rather like the Belgic, but of simpler form, and made without the potter's wheel, often with loop handles sunk in the body on either side.

Plate XIII

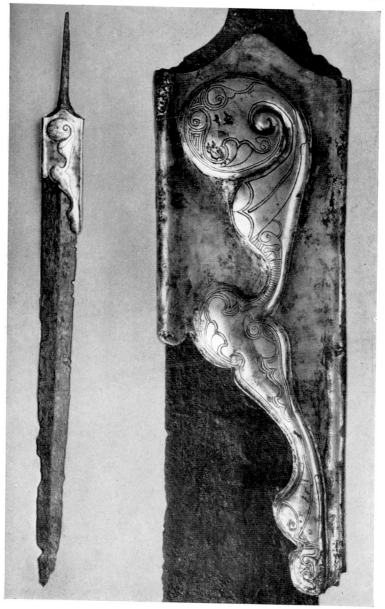

Celtic art. Sword with iron blade and bronze scabbard-mount,
from the river Witham, near Lincoln

Plate XIV

Celtic art. Chamfrein, or bronze head armour for a horse, from Torrs, Kircudbright, Scotland

These territories shared in the general south-western circuit of trade and metal-working, and they used the iron bar-currency, but later took to coinage modelled on the Belgic. By then the neighbouring Dobuni, as the people of the Cotswolds and the lower Severn were called, had begun to issue coins bearing the names of kings, with designs based on Belgic models, and the Iceni of the eastern counties, and the Brigantes centred in western Yorkshire, had done the same. The coins of the Dorset people were uninscribed, but we know that their tribal name was the Durotriges.

The warriors from Brittany who ruled them, and the Belgæ farther east who finally conquered them, were not the only groups of people to be driven across from Gaul in these times. There were also minor groups, and these included immigrants who had something of their own to contribute to the growth of the old La Tène style into a distinctively British Celtic art.

The scribing of geometrical forms of La Tène design on pottery with compasses, helped out by small circle-stamps, was practised in Brittany before Cæsar's conquest, and rather similar designs, like Fig. 16 C, were now brought over to the Glastonbury lake-village and other places, notably in East Sussex, Surrey and parts of Kent. Their influence probably helped the development of the curving La Tène scroll-patterns into a purely geometrical style. In this style, on pottery and still more strikingly on bronze-work, we find the unfaltering curves and circles of such designs set off by hatching with the look of basketry—though it was more probably inspired by the stitchery of gay textiles, which themselves, of course, have perished. The best-established schools of fine bronze-work in Britain were in the northern and eastern territories, where the La Tène style had been implanted by the Parisi and their like (p. 108), but this geometric tendency was furthered from the south, and the results appear in various regions, especially along the connecting line across the Midlands (p. 119) between south-west and north-east.

They appear on ornamented sword-scabbards, as found at Hunsbury (p. 119) and in Somerset near the Meare lake-village, and on a number of smaller things, but most perfectly on the

K

bronze mirrors which we spoke of in the last chapter. Their engraved backs show a varied range of these ingenious

FIG. 23.—The Desborough mirror, showing the engraved back.

spreading curve-patterns, but the most successful are those from Desborough in the Midlands (Fig. 23) and Birdlip at the

Cotswold edge above Gloucester, in which symmetry keeps the design from straggling without spoiling its grace. As time went on, symmetry became more and more sought after, and it is not hard to see in this the first-fruits of a new influence in British art, the classical influence of Rome. For Gaul was now a Roman province, and in the last twenty years before Christ renewed contacts across the Channel began to bring that influence in. One can admire it, rendered in skilfully cast relief, in the taut, springy formality of our great masterpiece, the shield found in the Thames at Battersea (Pl. XV). But in some of the mirrors it is less admirable, and the nature of its effects can be judged particularly well in the school of ornament centred among the Belgæ, which specialized not in line-drawing on metal so much as in enamel-work. In earlier times enamel had been an attached embellishment on metal-work, like the coral which it imitated, but the Belgic craftsmen poured it molten into prepared spaces in their designs, at first in roundels of various kinds like those on the Battersea shield, and then in hollowed-out fields in the ornamental surface itself. Their enamel colour was red, which contrasted showily with the yellow of the bronze; but the effect of Roman influence on their designs was to make them more tidy and correct-looking, like that of the harness-mount from Polden Hill on the Somerset edge of western Belgic territory, and in the end fussy or merely clever.

But we have not yet reached the last years of British independence to which those pieces belong. For two full generations from about 20 B.C. the power of the Belgic kingdoms in the south of Britain grew, and rivalry and conflict sharpened, especially between that founded by Commius south of the Thames and that of the successors of Cassivellaunus north of it. Commius had three sons, and their history can be made out in some sort from their coins, which can be arranged in order of age in their various districts, and almost from the outset show the influence of Roman models. The dominion of Cassivellaunus in Hertfordshire descended to a king named Tasciovanus; his coinage, showing the same influence in its own way, was minted mainly at Verulamium, the settlement by St. Albans where he had his chief capital.   The terms imposed by Cæsar were a dead letter now, and he soon resumed aggression against the Trinovantes, which reached its goal when he died about A.D. 10.   For his son at once attacked their king (who took refuge with the Roman emperor Augustus) and annexed their capital and lands.   The capital was named Camulodunum, where now is Colchester in north-east Essex, and the son, who became the greatest of the British kings, was named Cunobelin—the Cymbeline of Shakespeare's play.

   This act of conquest had far-reaching consequences.   The Trinovantes had already received Belgic culture and settlers from Kent, and when Cunobelin combined their territory with all his father's dominions he was master of a large and solid kingdom.   By about A.D. 25 he had added to it all Kent, and carried his frontier on the north and west to the edge of the Fens and across Northants and Oxfordshire to the Thames, which divided him from the rival kingdom of the house of Commius.   At first sight his capital far away in Essex seems an odd choice, but the Colne estuary made Colchester a port, and under him it quickly attracted trade with the Roman Empire across the Narrow Seas.   It was now, too, that the first small trading-station was established, probably by Roman merchants, on the site of London.   A great military disaster in A.D. 9 had broken the Romans' plan of conquering Germany, and for their merchants the growth of commerce with Cunobelin's Britain could partly offset the loss of German markets. The Britons exported corn and cattle, metals and also slaves— the captives of their wars, whose iron shackles have several times been found—and received as imports luxuries such as glass and fine pottery, which prepared their material culture for its predestined end—absorption in the Roman Empire itself.

   These foreign goods—red-glazed pottery from Italy and its imitations from Belgic Gaul, the great jars which held southern wine, and ornaments such as brooches and the like—have been found in plenty in the central area of Cunobelin's capital, which lay just outside modern Colchester looking on to the river; the native products, pottery above all, were profoundly affected by their example, and on this mounting material civilization the British king grew rich. And on the excellent coinage which he minted, in gold, silver and bronze, the designs show a positive invasion of Britain by Roman art. The full extent of Camulodunum was immense, though its inhabited areas were scattered, and it was defended on the landward side by line upon line of great dykes of earthwork, much of which may still be seen. Near one of these, at Lexden, was a cemetery of many graves, and here stands a huge barrow, which has been excavated and found to contain a mass of furnishings for the splendour of the dead. There seems to have been a great funeral bier of wood and iron, with lavish ornaments of enamel-studded bronze; the many bronze objects include statuettes in almost wholly classical style, and there was actually a silver portrait-medallion of the Roman Emperor Augustus, made from a coin. This may, indeed, well be the sepulchre of Cunobelin himself.

Exactly what religious beliefs were bound up with such funeral rites is difficult to say, but it appears here, as in many Celtic graves, particularly on the Continent, that grave-goods had been damaged so that they too should be accounted dead, and thus be available for their owner's use beyond the grave. As we have seen, the bodies of the dead were now cremated, and it was certainly the disembodied soul of a man which was held immortal: its passage at death into a new and different body was part of the doctrine taught by the powerful Celtic priesthood of both Gaul and Britain, the order of the Druids. Cæsar and other writers have left an account of the Druids which has appealed greatly to people's imagination, and at one time almost every prehistoric monument was thought to be 'Druidical'. Actually their human burnt-offerings, their blood-sacrifices, their divination, their philosophy and their power as teachers and judges are difficult to place in a modern account of ancient Britain, mainly because the religious monuments of the Iron Age, when they flourished, are so little known. It seems probable that their lore combined traditions coming from a wide range of origins: the cutting of the mistletoe on the sacred oak, for example, was a German as well as a

Celtic ceremony, though the golden sickle they are said to have used was perhaps directly descended from the sickles of the Bronze Age in Britain and Gaul. But their development as an organized priesthood seems confined to these western lands, and probably has at least some of its roots in the religious life of the Bronze Age. We have seen that in that life elements brought in by the Beaker and other invaders blended with the mysterious cults of the megalith-builders (p. 63). Thus, while it is quite wrong to think of Stonehenge as properly a 'Druids' Temple', it appears that the Druids did use Stonehenge, for, as has already been pointed out (p. 62), outside the stone circles there emplacements for two more circles have been found, which seem to be additions made at some time in the Iron Age. And near Frilford in Berkshire remains of a little Iron Age sanctuary have lately been excavated which looks very like a shrunken and distorted version of an Early Bronze Age 'henge': on the other hand an Iron Age enclosure found on Heath Row airport proved to contain a square wooden building with a central chamber surrounded by a kind of veranda, in plan exactly like the stone-built temples which were raised in south-eastern Britain in Roman times. Perhaps, then, this form of temple was newly devised in the Iron Age. Druidism, in fact, in the details of its institutions, probably differed in different parts of the country. But it was beyond much doubt compounded with ancient elements which the whole land, for all its multitude of gods and goblins, held to some extent in common. And thus it must have been something of a unifying force among the Britons, in an age when local tribes and cultures, invading or invaded, were making such a welter of strife with one another.

The strife was not confined to the frontiers between the Belgæ and their neighbours. We have already seen how Cunobelin extended his kingdom by war. Later he seems to have sent his sons with expeditions across the Thames, to carve out princedoms from the lands of the house of Commius. Another expedition had started westwards across north Oxfordshire, where Belgic dyke-building is again in evidence in Blenheim Park, to reach the Cotswolds at Bourton-on-the-

Water.   And the Belgæ south of the Thames were also striking west, reaching now beyond Maiden Castle to Hembury Fort in Devon, assailing the Glastonbury lake-village, and probably climbing the Mendips and the hills past Bath and Bristol.   The great stone-walled fort of Worlebury at Weston-super-Mare has yielded many skulls and bones from a massacre, and at Bredon Hill fort, on the far edge of the Cotswolds, the main entrance of about this time has been found choked with the grisly remains of another, in which the victims' bodies had been hacked to pieces and their heads lined up on the gate to burn and crash with it to the ground.   And the tremendous hill-forts beyond the Severn, through Herefordshire and all up the Marches of Wales, were built and rebuilt, sometimes on a colossal scale, in a way which shows clearly enough that the Iron Age of Britain had become truly an age of iron.

Migrations of peoples in the west went far.   Along much of the west of Scotland there are signs that people now were coming up from the south, though indeed beyond a few bone weaving-tools and the like there is little for us now to re-cognize them by, except the small, strong ring-forts of their chiefs, underground galleries like the Cornish fogou (p. 113), and structures developed from the Cornish courtyard house, which they seemingly brought with them.   But those in the far north inspired the growth of the circular, sometimes towering, stone structures known as brochs (Fig. 24), with stairs and chambers in the thickness of their walls, and an open court within—their whole design proclaiming them the strongholds of a people bred to raiding and fighting by sea and land. Probably more of such migrations affected Ireland too. Though their material remains are as yet lacking, the oldest epic tales of Irish literature reach back to this age, and tell of a world as full of the noise of battle as it is full of mystery and magic.

Fighting was, indeed, an accepted part of men's lives in the ancient world, in civilized Greece no less than in barbaric Britain.   But to both there came a time when war became more than an occasional affair between high-spirited neigh-bours, and threatened to grow into a perpetual curse.   That time came when the pattern of society became too unbalanced for the normal tenor of peace to be maintained, so that war ceased to be a local adjustment of forces, and began to throw the pattern still farther out of balance. New forces were at work, which the old simple forms of society could not control. The Greek city states could never for long unite, and the civilization they had done so much to create came to demand

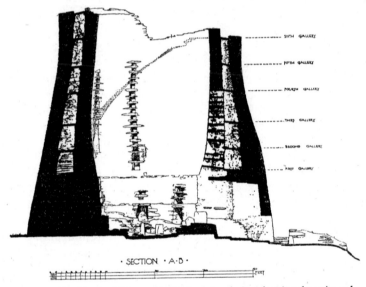

FIG. 24.—The Broch of Mousa, Shetland: sectional view showing the stairs and galleries in the walls of the stone tower.

their merging in something bigger. At long last that something turned into the Roman Empire, and now it was the Roman Empire that came to merge in itself the tribal disunion of Britain.

The Belgic kingdoms had certainly succeeded in merging lesser tribes, and Cunobelin's was something approaching a national state. But it was the creation of one man, and both the force and the wealth which made the Belgic power rested on their culture's borrowings from the higher civilization overseas. It was not long before the higher civilization was ready to call for the payment of its debts. Cæsar had under-rated his task, and had come and gone too soon; but close on a hundred years later the Roman Empire judged that the time was ripe. Soon after A.D. 40 Cunobelin was dead, and his kingdom in turmoil. From his successors' violence the last of the sons of Commius fled to Rome, and the new emperor Claudius saw that the situation demanded a response. Britain was disunited, and her wealth, which private enterprise had shown to be profitable, was ready for direct action to exploit. The policy of annexation, which frontier problems elsewhere had kept for so long postponed, could now be launched at last; and an end put to the dangerous independence of an island so much a part of Celtic Europe, and so plainly needed for complete Roman mastery of the West. The Empire could afford the legions: men, ships, munitions, money would be capital well invested; and Claudius, for his own reasons, wanted the laurels of a conquest.

He got them. In the year 43 a strong Roman army, in three divisions, landed on the coast of Kent. At the passage of the Medway, Cunobelin's sons were decisively beaten; and when, after a halt on the Thames, the Emperor him-self arrived for the march on their capital, Camulodunum fell without a blow. Tribal disunion brought other sur-renders also; and the threefold advance of the next few years, west, north-west and north, had friendly territory both on its left flank in Sussex and its right in East Anglia. West-ward, the Wessex hill-forts—including Maiden Castle—were stormed; and in 47 the first frontier-line was drawn, from Devon to the Humber, with all the Belgic lands overrun behind it, and the vales of Severn and Trent in front. From this it was not far to the mountains of the Highland Zone, first of Wales, and then of the north; but there, as the whole tale of Prehistoric Britain has led us to expect, the advance ran into trouble and slowed up.

The tribes of Wales fought fiercely, and remained uncon-quered when their leader Caratacus (Caradoc), Cunobelin's surviving son from the Belgic south-east, was defeated in 51 and forced on into the north. The queen of the Brigantes there betrayed him to the Romans; but the Brigantian patriots rallied to her husband, and remained unconquered too. Moreover, when in 61 the north-western army thrust in between, to reach the Irish Sea and crush the stronghold of Druid religion in Anglesey, the south-east burst out in the famous revolt of the Icenian Boudicca, which cost the Romans a legion and three towns before it could be beaten. The material and moral damage took long to repair. Only in the 70's could the northern war be resumed, and the Welsh one at length wound up. But then, from 79 to 85, the great governor Agricola drove north in campaign after campaign, passed the Forth-Clyde isthmus, and reached the gate of the Scottish Highlands. In a single battle he broke the gathered clans of the northern Britons, and his fleet sailed on to cow the broch-folk (p. 135) in the fastnesses of Caithness and Orkney. Britain seemed to him as good as conquered from end to end. Yet Rome, after his recall, had not the force to turn his successes in Scotland to permanent account. There was trouble; and then, at last, a big forced retreat. About 120, the emperor Hadrian had to come over to take matters in hand. He clearly saw that dealing with Scotland would now be a slow business, and that it needed first, not only a firm rear in Brigantia, but a firm front where the retreat had ended—the strategic line between Tyneside and the Solway. And so was built Hadrian's Wall (Pl. XVII). South of it lay the Province of Britannia: north of it was Prehistoric Britain still.

How had the Province been developing meanwhile? From the first, Roman trade and money had poured in: Britain was an expanding market, especially for manufactured goods, such as the red-glazed 'Samian' pottery of Roman Gaul, and the conquerors' new-built roads and harbours served trade no less well than the army and government. With these communications, the first Roman towns arose: London above all, her estuary for the first time linked by roads with the hinterland; a new Verulamium, close by the old (p. 131); and a new Camulodunum (pp. 132, 137) at Colchester, in the form of a colony of army veterans. These were the towns Boudicca sacked—unwalled collections of wooden buildings, save for

Claudius's stone cult-temple at Colchester, but thriving centres none the less; Chichester, capital of the early 'friendly state' of Sussex, was probably another, with another stone temple built to Roman gods. The Icenian 'state' (pp. 108, 129) in East Anglia was more aloof: for example, till its rebellion and extinction, it kept alive the native arts in metal and enamelling. But native taste, along with native independence, soon withered (p. 131) in all the south, leaving traces only in the minor arts of the Province. It withered more slowly in Wales, and not without new glory; in the north more slowly still, and, thanks to a more creative handling of Roman forms, with still greater glory—seen in the beautiful bronze panel found in 1938 at Elmswell in East Yorkshire (Fig. 25), no less than in the more famous gilt brooch, of the later first century, found at Aesica (Great Chesters on Hadrian's Wall), or the often handsome Brigantian 'trumpet'-brooches, of the earlier second century, which the south could only poorly imitate. In Scotland, some native art lived later, but with little of the old feeling for grace in metalwork.

Metals to the Romans were a much valued prize of conquest. All minerals belonged to the State, and mining in Britain went on throughout the occupation. Cornish tin, indeed (p. 112), was long neglected for Spanish; but the lead of Mendip, and of Shropshire and North Wales, Derbyshire and West Yorkshire, began to be worked as soon as these regions were under firm control. Silver, too, was extracted from it by special smelting; and the one possible British gold-mine, near Dolaucothy in Carmarthenshire, was found and exploited in the second century. Copper was mined in North Wales and Shropshire, and probably in Brigantia too; as for iron, it was worked especially in the Sussex Weald, the Forest of Dean and the Midlands, and elsewhere, including the north. There was also some mining for salt, and some (mainly local) use of outcrop coal. But the major profits of all this mining left the country, and went to the Imperial exchequer. The Province was expected to pay for itself without them. And the basis of its internal solvency—as in all provinces and ultimately in all ancient civilization—was expected to be the land.

Fig. 25.—Celtic ornament showing Roman influence: embossed bronze panel with strip of enamel work, from Elmswell, Yorkshire.

Where land was already in native cultivation, there may have been changes of tenure, but there was probably not much change in the cultivation system. For example, on the Wessex and Sussex chalk, the small, squarish fields remained but little different from what they had been in the Late Bronze and Early Iron Ages (pp. 91, 102), and similar fields are found elsewhere, *e.g.* in the north. Moreover, the tillers of such fields continued in great measure to inhabit farmsteads or villages essentially of prehistoric type. Meanwhile, the wealthier sort

Fig. 26.—The Roman Farm at Lockleys, Welwyn. Reconstruction after excavation.

of native soon began to invest in a house and farmstead built in the Roman manner, at first often of wood (Fig. 26), but more and more of stone, and always of rectangular plan, with partitioned rooms and sometimes baths and central heating. These are the familiar 'Roman villas' of our maps. And their estates, moderate or large, and mostly on richer soils, were doubtless thus better farmed in the long strip-divided fields which are implied by their heavy ploughs. But these ploughs and fields had come in before the Romans, with the Belgæ (pp. 122, 126). So, while in Roman Britain the better sort of house-building was revolutionized, farming was for the most part simply continued, adapted, and extended from pre-Roman practice. The Romans presumably reckoned that, as the population gradually increased with the suppression of tribal warfare (pp. 124, 134), prosperity would increase with the cultivation of new and better land.   Certainly many villa estates prospered on this, for instance around the Cotswolds; and in the Fens a great new agricultural area was created by Government engineering and drainage.   The 'Roman peace' was a blessing genuine enough.   And it brought not only material progress, but Latin literacy, and things of the mind.   But it was expensive.

In particular, it meant the creation of numerous towns.   To the Romans, as to the Greeks, the town was the real focus of civilization, and their plan for civilizing Britain was to convert the old native tribes into units of local government, each with a newly created town as centre.   Thus the Cantii of Kent had Canterbury; the Durotriges of Dorset had Dorchester—superseding Maiden Castle (p. 128); the Midland Coritani had Leicester.   There were also smaller towns, such as Rochester or Brough-on-Humber, centres of smaller districts, and of course the larger towns: London, the financial and soon probably the general official capital, and ultimately no less than four colonies of army veterans, Colchester, Gloucester, Lincoln and York.   These all had lands of their own, divided up among the colonists, and everywhere no doubt some town-dwellers worked suburban lands; but the towns were in the main markets, centres of industry, and social and administrative centres.   The tribal councils were encouraged to put up walls and imposing public buildings, first by progressive governors like Agricola, and then by Hadrian himself, to whom for example the council of the Cornovii, in 130, dedicated the new forum (market building and administrative 'basilica') of their chief town, at Wroxeter near Shrewsbury.   Town walls, often first of wood and earthwork, had by then begun to be built or rebuilt in stone, with fine gateways, as at Colchester, London, Lincoln and soon Verulamium—which also had a theatre.   There were public baths, too, and temples—at the 'spa' at Bath the two were conjoined; and shops and many good town houses, largely of stone likewise.

Thus civilization grew.   But so did costs. The country

could perhaps have supported the towns, had that been all. But it had also to support the army. Till late in Agricola's governorship, Britain had four legions, and afterwards three; and it also had numerous auxiliary regiments, foot and horse, which were disposed over the hill-country of Wales and the north in permanent forts, connected by roads in a strategic network. These at first were of earth and timber, like their more temporary predecessors in the south and Midlands; but about A.D. 100 they began to be rebuilt in stone, matching the great base-fortresses of the three legions, at Caerleon in Monmouthshire, Chester and York. The 17 forts of Hadrian's Wall were similar; and each mile of it had a smaller 'milecastle' and two turrets, regularly spaced. The natives, for their part, in all this Highland country, their major hill-forts dismantled, lived scattered in homesteads or huddled villages, differing little if at all from the prehistoric. But north of the Wall, in Northumberland and southern Scotland, they were scattered very densely, and in settlements more prevalently fortified, often small but strong ring-forts (p. 135) of earth or stone, with larger hill-forts occasionally among them. Here we are back in Prehistoric Britain outright. And it was these people, and those beyond them, who had wiped out Agricola's northern conquests and forced the building of the Wall: they were the enemy; it was for them that the Province had to maintain so great an army, and such great frontier works. The business of reducing them might be slow, but it had got to go on.

The next emperor, Antoninus Pius, decided that it should go on faster. So, about 140, the Romans moved north once more. They advanced their frontier to the waist of Scotland, the narrow isthmus between the Forth and Clyde, already once fortified by Agricola. Here a new Wall was built, with 19 forts along it, and some forward garrisons beyond. It was linked, by fort-protected roads and by sea, with Hadrian's system, at first depleted but soon restored to considerable strength, behind it. The natives between the Walls were thinned by deportations to the Continent, and the Romans set about consolidating their winnings. The reckoning doubtless was that the rear and middle areas would now be pacified, as Wales had been, and the front in due course sustain further offensives, following Agricola's trail towards Highland Scotland. But the reckoning was wrong. In the years about 156 not only the Antonine winnings, but Brigantia as far south as the hills of Derbyshire, rose in revolt against the over-stretched-out garrison. There was a serious crisis, and fresh trouble shortly after. The burden of military expenditure was not eased but worsened: the expected fruits of northern conquest were becoming sour grapes. Then, about 181, the northern Wall was pierced and an army defeated. With heavy fighting, the defeat was retrieved. But retrieving the Forth–Clyde frontier was another matter. It had to be abandoned. And the re-occupation that was probably intended never came. For now, in 193–6, there was civil war within the Roman Empire, and Albinus, the governor of Britain, stripped the Province of troops to fight a personal battle for the Imperial power. He lost. And meanwhile the northern tribes poured in, and systematically destroyed everything in their path as far south as York and Chester. They were bought off, and restoration followed; but Hadrian's Wall was its limit.

The new emperor was Septimius Severus, a soldier and a hard realist. He must have seen it was no good attempting any longer to annex Scotland: it simply was not worth while. What he had to attempt now was to guarantee security to Hadrian's frontier, so that the Roman investment in Britain behind it should be worth while. And this could be done in just one way: by smiting the tribes in Scotland with such slaughter and destruction that they would cease to be a menace. With that achieved, repair and reorganization of Hadrian's Wall and its supports could do the rest. Severus concentrated a great field-army and a fleet, with great supply stocks at their bases, and struck north. In repeated campaigns—we still cannot trace them in detail—he hit and hit at his enemy, storming and harrying in every part of Scotland he could reach; and in 211, exhausted and back at York, he died wanting still more done. But his son judged his work to be enough. With the Wall in order, forts built or rebuilt and their gar-

Plate XV

Celtic art. Shield of cast bronze with red-enamelled
studs from the river Thames at Battersea

Plate XVI

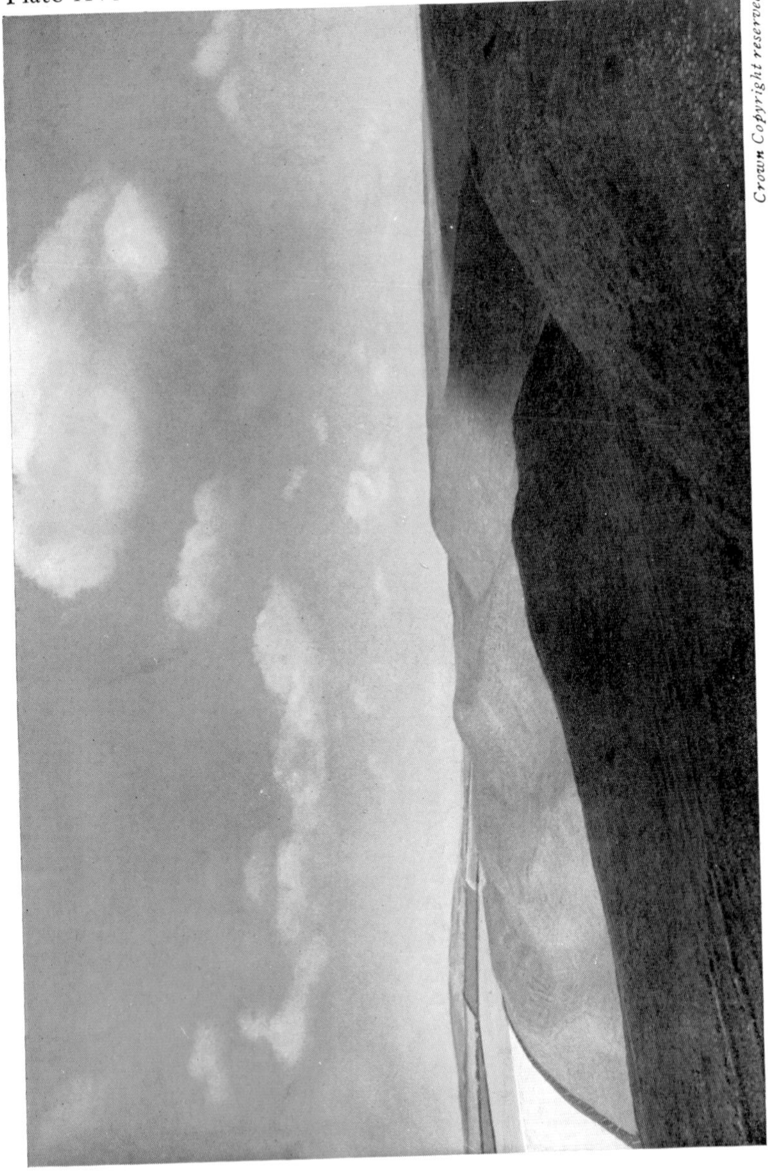

Crown Copyright reserved

Maiden Castle, Dorset. The multiple ramparts

risons settled permanently on the land, light troops patrolling up to Cheviot and Tweed, and this desolation beyond, Britain would be safe. And for a long time it was so. The disasters which shook the Empire later in that century, in the East and from across the Rhine, were not repeated here. All the same, safety had been obtained only through dropping the old Imperial scheme of annexing the whole of the island. And the question now was whether the Roman part of Britain could after all make good.

As we have seen, the main centres of Roman civilization, away from the military districts, were the towns. Their heyday of prosperity was reached in the time of Antoninus, in the middle second century. After that, decline set in; for the reason, broadly speaking, that the town economy spent more money than it made. Merchants and manufacturers and retailers made money, of course; but the towns really lived upon the country, for, directly or indirectly, their business and their civilized life and buildings and amenities depended upon the profits of the land. The people in them who really counted were the upper class, which included of course officials and merchants in the bigger and economically stronger cities, but consisted in the main of the wealthier and most Romanized Britons, largely, no doubt, descended from Iron Age chiefs and tribal aristocracies. They were also the principal owners of villas (p. 141) in the country; and both their country and town houses were built for lives of good bourgeois comfort: paintings on fine plaster walls, tessellated pavement floors, the hypocaust central-heating system for rooms and baths (like our 'Turkish' baths), and so on. We have seen how they also spent money on public buildings in the towns; by Severus' time, the decline was damping this down. Yet Severus, here as all over the Empire, needed these people as the economic mainstay of the State, and especially of the army, on which all depended. He made them help rebuild Hadrian's Wall, and in some cases renew their own town walls, and he taxed their communities hard—his successors, harder still. So the provincial economy was very properly driven back more upon the country. Only the soil could make it solvent.

L

The increase and growth of villas, recognized by archæology both in this and the century following, can only mean more work done accordingly upon the land. But it was on the land, and in rural life as a whole, that there was most in common between Roman Britain and Prehistoric (p. 141). Thus, while the villas themselves now tend to look more and more Roman—the richer ones almost magnificently so—the activity that they represent was a truer development from prehistoric life than that of the prematurely blooming towns. The simple old homesteads and villages of the poorer country-folk were still there, distributed in the south still much as in the Iron Age, and much as before, too, in the Highland west and north. In Wales there was even a return to life in hill-forts, probably a Government measure entrusting local defence and security to a kind of Home Guard among their occupants. Roman-provincial manufactured goods were almost every-where in use, as we can see from pottery: but pottery, from the second century onwards, was more and more a regional product, adapting Roman-provincial models to native work-manship. And as with the material, so with the spiritual: Roman and native religion mingled greatly; and in art there was more and more barbaric sculpture, and even a little metal-work reflecting occasional La Tène designs (pp. 129-31, 139).

In short, the native personality of Britain was reasserting itself; and that not simply on the Highland margins, where prehistoric life had been least altered and there was kinship with the peoples beyond the Roman dominion, but gradually throughout the Roman dominion itself. Meanwhile, Roman power was declining throughout the Empire. Presently, it plunged headlong into crisis: foreign war, civil war and anarchy, and a general economic collapse. Intense and repeated effort rescued it. Yet the threat of disaster never disappeared again for long. The Empire after 284, under Diocletian and his successors, was prodigiously altered and reorganized. But it was a world under siege; and every unit in it had got to accept the 'New Order' or perish. Britain, however, spared by the wars of the crisis period (p. 145) and resentful of its economic shocks, was not very ready to conform. Already, during the earlier crisis years, there had been a separate Empire in Gaul: it seemed quite justifiable, when the official administration was too remote and unreliable to govern provinces properly. So now in 286, while Diocletian was still busy elsewhere, a fresh 'regional Emperor' proclaimed himself in Britain.

This was Carausius, the commander of the Channel and North Sea fleet. His command was important for an ominous reason. The Saxons, barbarians from north-west Germany, had begun to raid the British coast by sea, and coastal forts had to be built and manned against them. These defences of the 'Saxon Shore'—from the Wash to the Solent, with Richborough on the Kent coast at their centre (Pl. XVIII)—were not completed till after Carausius's time. But his sea and coastal forces gave him an easy mastery of Britain, and he and his successor Allectus maintained an effective independence until 296, when it was extinguished by the victory of Constantius, western co-ruler of the Diocletianic Empire. The 'New Order', in fact, was for the time being a success; and by now the too self-centred people of Britain were very ready to welcome it. For to fight Constantius, Allectus had brought away the northern garrisons; and the tribes of Scotland, after three generations of recovery from Severus' punishment, had a new opportunity. They swarmed in, and Constantius had to clear them out and punish them afresh before he could reorganize the north and once more restore the Wall.

His work was good. When his great son Constantine went from York to fight for and win the sole rule of the Empire, no barbarian enemy moved. The fourth century began with tranquillity in Britain: the ruined towns were in some degree restored, and the villas flourished—though the actual land-workers were now in the main 'a depressed class', bound to the soil, while peasant cultivations were partly turned to pasture, and the sea had begun to eat into the reclaimed land of the Fens. But with all this, the town magnates and villa-owners, privileged as they were, had to bear the main burden of responsibility for payment of the crushing Imperial taxes, under which every province of the Empire groaned. There was less and less margin for recouping loss, if things went wrong; and they did. As well as the Saxon danger on the east, there had for some time been an Irish danger on the west; and before 350 the northern danger had grown serious again.

At last, in 367, the three united: the Picts of the north and the Scots of Ireland and the Saxons from the east combined together in a great barbarian onslaught upon provincial Britain. It never really recovered. The peasantry, with their prehistoric simplicity of life and work, survived: but the villa system was in great part ruined. Roman dominion indeed was restored, and its grip even tightened: there was safety behind most town walls; signal-towers improved the east coast defences; a stronger hold was taken of Wales. But in 383 a usurper, Maximus, set out from Britain to win himself an Empire of the West: he may have bargained with the barbarians for peace when he led the troops away, but when he fell they swept in; and once more Roman rule had to be restored. This time, it appears, the Wall was abandoned; friendly northerners were brought down into Wales: the garrisons held little more than Yorkshire and the Saxon Shore. Then again a usurper took the troops abroad; and in 410, the year when Rome itself fell before the Goths, the emperor Honorius resigned Britain to the Britons.

Native vitality had outlasted Roman imperialism. It would be wrong to dismiss the Roman occupation as a mere lengthy episode, which passed without leaving anything behind. But what was left behind was not what Rome had meant to impose. It was what Britain took from Rome and made its own. The fighting spirit, which had grown to dominate the Celtic Iron Age (pp. 134, 135-6), was indeed quenched within the Province, while it lived on fiercely in the north. But even the northern fighting men learned from Rome, and in time combined against her in a national unity—that of the Picts—such as the old charioteering warriors could never sustain. And presently the southerners, for their part, came to do something better still.

Roman rule is usually believed to have weakened the provincial Britons. But it plainly raised their average standard of life; and security, which for long periods it gave, need not be

enervating.   Moreover, the tribal system of local self-govern-
ment was politically good.   The weight of the towns indeed
proved too heavy for the country; but by the third century
there was a better balance: Roman and native elements were
each contributing (p. 146) to something like a genuinely
Romano-British culture.   Hence came the 'separatist' feeling
against the central government, which might, certainly, re-
trieve lapses and disasters, but grew ever more oppressive and
rapacious.   Truly, there was not much flesh left on the bones
of Roman Britain by the end.   But the life was there.

Continuity with the life of Prehistoric Britain had never
broken; and though the natives had lost much, they had not
failed to gain from Rome.   The roads and the greater town
sites did not vanish.   Coinage went on, still in descent from
Roman types for all its tiny size.   There were material gains
without a doubt; and there were also spiritual.   Ultimately,
the greatest of these was Christianity: it was from Roman
Britain, where it had long since been planted, and from the civilized Continent with which Roman Britain made the link, that
the Celtic Church took root in Ireland and the West, keeping
alive the Faith and civilized literacy together, to spread them
presently back into Britain, and far into barbarian Europe.   At
the same time, there was a great reflowering of Celtic art,
which out of old La Tène and Provincial and Late-Roman
motives, raised up a superb new native style, in metalwork and
enamelling as of old, and then in Christian manuscript and
sculpture.

There must have been a feeling that Britain, which had
shared the whole growth of European culture in the prehistoric past, and had then shared in its consummation under
Rome, was still truly, and in its own right, part of the civilized
world.   And this is no mere fancy: one can see it from what
actually happened, now after Roman rule had ceased.   The
southern Britons set about fighting the Picts and Scots as the
Roman armies had.   At first they were weak; and they also
had to deal with something still more formidable: the continual menace of the Saxons from the eastern sea.   There is no
need to doubt the old story of a bargain with the Saxon to

keep off the Pict, of which the Saxon made his opportunity of settling in Britain to take it for himself. From the middle years of the fifth century, Saxons and Angles and Frisians and Jutes—all our pagan Germanic forefathers—came steadily in, and they conquered much. But gradually, and under an inspiration that was both Christian-Roman and native Celtic, the Britons rallied; and a war-leader arose whose name was Arthur. He has become legendary, but his resistance was real. By about 500 it had not only beaten the Picts, but it had weakened and obstructed the Germanic invaders for more than a generation to come. And thanks to that success, and in spite of all the Anglo-Saxon winnings later, what came at last to be England was not something wholly Germanic and new. English indeed the Anglo-Saxons made it, but it was not their work alone. For blended in it was that same native vitality which Rome had not suppressed, and which the Celtic West and the Picts and Scots too shared—the inherited vitality of Prehistoric Britain.

Chapter Seven

ARCHÆOLOGY

WE started with ape-men, and have ended with Anglo-Saxons. The human history of the half a million or so intervening years has been told, sketchily and laconically in its early parts, but with increasing detail and accuracy. After the first chapter—that is to say, after Britain assumed its island form—the reader may well have been irked by a certain repetitiveness in the story. Chapter after chapter, almost page after page, has shown a recurring theme: the invasion of that island from the Continent. The impact of these waves of invasion beats monotonously through the narrative. From Spain and the Mediterranean, from northern France, the Low Countries and Scandinavia they roll, each, when it arrives, sweeping over a lesser or a greater part of Britain and altering its character. Often before it reaches the Highland Zone the force of the wave is spent and it breaks up on the mountain scarps to filter more weakly into the regions beyond.

As writers we regret this monotony, but as prehistorians we cannot alter it. Such was the pattern of British prehistory, a pattern made inevitable by Britain's position as a fertile island accessible to a restless Continental population.

To many the number of these prehistoric incursions may be new and surprising. They may feel incredulous and suspect them to be creations of the archæologist's imagination. But see how uninterruptedly they run on into historic times, when each has a proper name attached and seems not incredible at all, but simple and familiar. We all know 1066, and before that it was the Danes and Norsemen, then the Anglo-Saxons, the rather different invasion of the Romans, and before them the earliest historically recorded incursion, that of the Belgæ. There is no break in continuity and no difference of character between these immigrations and the nameless ones that preceded them. Indeed, the archæological method has, of course, been applied to the historical invasions, and has given substance and precision to scanty and inaccurate written records.

If this account of early Britain has been monotonous, it has also, we are only too well aware, been full of gaps. These will many of them be closed during the next decade, if anything so essentially peaceable as archæological research is possible in those years. In the present century knowledge has accumulated at an astonishing speed. It was not at first merely a question of closing gaps, but of setting up the bare framework; incomplete though our information remains, it is immense when compared with the blank which confronted our immediate ancestors when they tried to look back beyond the Roman conquest. A century ago the whole of the time covered by this book was a void vaguely peopled with 'ancient Britons', while the idea that any of these shadowy characters should have been about before 4004 would have seemed dubious to all and blasphemous to many. The rapid growth of man's knowledge of his own past has been so remarkable and the change it has worked upon his whole outlook so great that it seems justifiable to write at some length of the history and methods of archæology.

The pioneers were men who travelled the countryside to further the topographical studies which were among the enthusiasms of the English Renaissance. Conspicuous among them was Leland, who in the time of Henry VIII toured England and recorded what he saw of her antiquities, generally medieval castles, abbeys and the like, but including among them such conspicuous prehistoric monuments as caught his eye and his interest. The Elizabethan age produced Camden, who in 1586 published his bulky volume, *Britannia*, in which was collected a mass of material from medieval writings, but also facts and speculations concerning prehistory. The outstanding figure of the seventeenth century was John Aubrey, an itinerant after the manner of Leland, whose careful field notes are still of the greatest value to present-day students. Even Defoe, preoccupied though he was with commerce, paused to comment on such famous sites as Stonehenge, and incidentally to rebuke the antiquaries of his day for their habit of idle speculation.

All these earlier workers can be seen as the harbingers of the outburst of antiquarian fervour which was one of the results of that great revolution in taste and cultural values, the Romantic Movement.   Many of us must have stumbled upon one of those gloomy, dripping and uncomfortable grottoes dear to the eighteenth- and early nineteenth-century landscape gardener, and read the verses in praise of caves and hermits and ivy inscribed on their walls.   To the macabre and morbid side of the Movement prehistoric antiquity was bound to appeal; it could contribute the 'sightless skulls and crumbling bones', the altar stones on which blood might have flowed and victims writhed in 'horrid', fascinating anguish.   Above all, it offered a setting for the 'white-haired Druid bard sublime'. The great champion and popularizer of the Druids was William Stukeley, a leader during the earlier phase of the Romantic Movement.   In the first decade of the eighteenth century, when he was studying medicine and developing his strong scientific bent, one would have thought him a legitimate child of the Age of Reason, yet he was to end his days as one of the most fantastical of Romantics.   Archæology was at first but one of the many scientific interests which prompted him to keep smelly anatomical specimens in his room at Cambridge and alarm the College with sudden explosions.   After 1718, however, when he became first secretary of the newly formed Society of Antiquaries, it preoccupied him more and more exclusively.   At first he used his scientific training to carry out accurate field work, and in particular to survey and plan all the complexities of Avebury and Stonehenge.   But gradually another side of his nature better suited to the Romantic taste asserted itself; he grew increasingly fascinated by the Druids, and conceived that he had a mission to reconcile and relate their supposed doctrines with Christianity, and above all with the conception of the Trinity.   This change of heart it was which led him to build extravagant theories on the sober and sound foundations of his earlier work at Avebury and Stonehenge, to see in their stone rings and avenues 'a snake proceeding from a circle . . . the eternal procession of the Son from the First Cause'.

Antiquarianism was now the fashion; young gentlemen rode about the country in search of the Gothick and any remains of the more remote past that might present themselves. Land-owners began to concern themselves with the monuments they found on their estates. The results of the fashion ranged in value from Samuel Lysons' fine publications of Roman villas, and the accurate and exhaustive account of Wiltshire antiquities left by Sir Richard Colt Hoare, to the mischievous pillaging of barrows undertaken by a number of gentlemen whose names it is kinder to forget. One among them, rather later, whose ravages can be forgiven him because they were both trivial and picturesque, deserves special place. When this antiquary wished to secure for his collection the contents of a barrow that stood on the property of another, he appeared on the site in an ample cloak and settled down as though to rest or contemplate the beauties of rugged nature. In reality, however, his hands were feverishly busy under the folds of his cloak, excavating the grave and assembling the booty.

As the nineteenth century advanced the social status of archæology gradually changed in accordance with the changing structure of English society. The power of the upper classes to act as sole arbiters of taste and fashion was slipping from them as the rising middle class assumed control. We find archæo-logical research passing into the hands of professional or retired business men, and in those hands it was inevitable and right, if a little sad, that the subject should grow more sober and scientific, more in harmony with the gospel of the Prince Consort than it had been in its extravagant youth as a standard-bearer of the Romantic Movement.

In a purely practical way, too, the Industrial Revolution affected archæology. Never before had the soil of England been so perpetually disturbed, so deeply cut about by the hand of man. Every time that a bank or a factory went up, a canal or railway line was driven, or a quarry sunk, there was good chance that some long-hidden antiquity might be uncovered. To house all these finds, and others the fruits of deliberate archæological excavation, the middle class subscribed its money to build museums in provincial towns, for it usually lacked both the arrogance and the means which had enabled the eighteenth-century antiquaries to install their collections in their own mansions.

As well as museums, local antiquarian societies were founded. All over the countryside they sprang up, with an enthusiastic membership of squires and doctors and parsons, interested ladies and a few noblemen, all eager to attend and give lectures and to make delightful excursions into the country, armed with notebooks and picnic hampers. It is easy to laugh at them, but these societies have given and continue to give invaluable service to learning. Let anyone who encounters one of their excursions and watches the party, as it turns out of its buses to stream across fields, crowd over stiles, surge into country houses and toil with limbs often no longer young to the tops of hills, pause and think with some pride of the English tradition which, with all its absurdity, it worthily represents.

Soon after the middle of the nineteenth century archæology was to be profoundly affected by that happening which did more to liberate the human mind than anything since the day when Copernicus realized that the earth went round the sun: the formulation by Darwin of the principles of evolution. Less than a century after the publication of the *Origin of Species* in 1859 it is still hard to appreciate what a tremendous striking off of chains that was. While thinking people had not, of course, always shared the general public's complete acceptance of the 'received' story of the creation and Archbishop Ussher's date for it, nevertheless it narrowly circumscribed their thought.

Into the wide vista of speculation and study finally laid open by Darwin and Huxley, no one was more bound to advance than the archæologist. Man could now be fitted into geological time, and this aspect of archæological research developed most rapidly. Immediately the Frenchman Boucher de Perthes' claim to have found humanly shaped implements in early gravels became acceptable, and the Neanderthal skull from Gibraltar, which had lain incognito since its discovery in 1848, was hailed as one of the precursors of Adam, a being who could now be recognized by respectable people.

The half-century after the appearance of the *Origin of Species* was a time of steady progress in archæological studies. Field workers such as Greenwell and Mortimer in Yorkshire and Cunnington in Wiltshire laboured to produce a mass of factual material on which classifications and generalizations could gradually be built. The great Manchester professor Boyd Dawkins did much to reconcile the geological approaches to archæology with the humanistic.

Overtopping them all was an unusual and latterly eccentric figure, a figure great enough to be an exception to the main trend of his times. General Lane-Fox Pitt-Rivers was a man who would seem more in place among eighteenth-century antiquaries. After a career as a Guards officer he inherited vast estates round Cranborne Chase; he could ride, it was said, from Rushmore to the sea without leaving his own land. Cranborne Chase is scattered with antiquities of many kinds, and the General was now able to satisfy the interest in primitive material culture and excavation which had hitherto been only an immense spare-time hobby. He had many greater eccentricities. He planted his grounds with exotic trees and shrubs and filled them with alarmingly exotic animals, and on Sundays obliged his tenants to come to listen to the brass band which played in his 'Larmer Tree Grounds'. When excavating he would drive off to the site in a high dogcart, accompanied by his carefully trained assistants, perched on penny-farthing bicycles, and displaying the General's colours round the brims of their boater hats. This man, who is personally so reminiscent of the eighteenth century, was, in fact, the immediate inspiration of the scientific archæology of the twentieth. In the objectivity and detail of his excavation and the exhaustiveness of his publication he has never been outdone. His vast *Excavations on Cranborne Chase*, which appeared between 1887 and 1898, is in most respects a model of what such a publication should be when money is unlimited. In the private museum on his estate models were not only carved from solid mahogany, but were of meticulous accuracy. As a reward, his work can still be used today, often to support ideas of which he could have no conception.

The present century has seen another great change in prehistoric studies.   Hitherto, as we have shown, it had not been the academic scholars who were interested in prehistory, nor yet the scientists, apart from its purely geological aspects, but the gentry, and then also the professional men, the parsons, lawyers and doctors, whose affairs took them out of doors.   But now more and more scholars, led by some of the Hellenists, began to concern themselves with barbarian archæology, while, on the other hand, laboratory methods were utilized to make it more scientific.   As the subject in this way grew increasingly wide and complex, it demanded to become a full-time study. While amateurs still make invaluable contributions to archæo-logy, its leaders are now professionals working at universities and museums.   Probably past Fellows of the Society of Anti-quaries would be shocked at the young men and women who sit on their red-leather benches today, people who use the study of antiquity as a means of earning their bread, and not as a cultivated pastime and opportunity for unrestrained speculation.   But they would have to recognize that their achievements in recent years have been very great.   Since it ceased to be an elegant pastime and became a serious discipline what methods have been developed in archæology?   How have the material remains of human life been made to tell a coherent story and bring news of the unrecorded passage of thousands of generations?

Self-consciousness is the most distinctive attribute of man, and throughout history its processes and discoveries have grown more and more sensitive and complex.   We have already seen how inevitable it was that in the nineteenth century the mean of this growing self-consciousness should become more scientific—a trend represented most clearly for individual consciousness by the birth of psychology, while archæology provided for the historical self-awareness of the species.   Both subjects are among various methodical attempts made by men to discover how they became what they find themselves to be. At first archæology was concerned only with the extension of the historical sequence.   It was a telescope trained on the first tracks of man in time, and in a sense its view was bound to be more 'scientific' than that of ordinary history.   It could not be concerned with the heroic ghosts of great men, or the emotions of spiritual and intellectual conflict. If its methods were turned to investigate the early 1940's it would easily detect the war and the decline in the standard of life, it would see American support through the evidence of Spam tins, but most certainly it would overlook Winston Churchill. Yet for long archæology was concerned with the purely historical process of fitting a series of events into a chronological framework. But in this country already before the war it had gone so far towards achieving this, had amassed so much knowledge of the successive prehistoric invasions of Britain, of foreign contacts and internal developments, that a change in the main aims of research was apparent. The historical sequence had become for many less interesting than the patterns of society. The ways of life of prehistoric communities were to be studied statically, just as some schools of anthropology study contemporary societies. The economic bases of existence are the first concern, then details of material culture, religion and art. If the danger of the older historical method was to pay too much attention to events in time, to migrations, invasions and cultural influences, the fear for this more recent method is that it should lose us in a morass of insignificant detail, as contemporary Mass Observation is often lost. If the former is sometimes unsound, the latter often makes one yawn. A full combination of the two is evidently what is needed, a study of society always in a state of becoming, a Tolstoyan breadth of movement.

For the pursuit of both methods archæology has devised new techniques, many of them dependent on the help of the natural sciences. These it is the main purpose of this chapter to describe, but first the writer feels bound to insist that although archæological methods are often scientific, prehistory is no more a science than is psychology. Mercifully it is a humane subject, deeply involved in all the uncertainties of human emotion, thought and action. The methods with which we are concerned are used by the archæologist to discover, study and interpret the material remains which make the prehistorian's substitute for written documents. Once these are prepared, the creative task of the prehistorian is not to be distinguished from that of the historian.

Discovery, Study and Interpretation: let the methods be considered under these simple heads.

DISCOVERY.—There is a natural inclination to divide the material documents of prehistory into two: field monuments, actual marks on the earth's surface left by prehistoric man, and museum material, artifacts that can be collected and studied indoors. Yet in many ways they are not to be distinguished intellectually as forms of evidence for the writing of prehistory, and perhaps the division is less in the remains than in those who study them. Certainly the two types of man have often been recognized; on one hand the outdoor type who may combine archæology with a strong sense for the country and its tradition; such a man is likely to have an instinctive under-standing of topography and local characteristics and perhaps some practical skills, but will hardly be able to grapple with the wider implications of his knowledge. The other type of man, it is supposed, should be found in his study contemplating stones, bronzes and pots or their images in books; he may be full of erudite theories but is liable to go astray from lack of practical sense and ordinary nous. In fact such a portrait, if it was not always a caricature, is one today. The pure strain of arm-chair theorist is extinct, and any prehistorian of the first rank must combine little eyes practised in the detailed scrutiny of excavations and big eyes familiar with the whole scene of prehistoric Britain and its Continental background.

Both forms of prehistoric remains, monuments and objects, have of course always been discovered, but not until the questioning Renaissance were they in the least understood; before that, as we have seen, such things were usually attributed to fairies, giants or to the devil. But the remains identified since Tudor times often provide material for research, while surveys and other records of sites now destroyed are guides to modern discovery. Even from medieval times place and field names and boundary marks give valuable clues.

Most archæological discoveries are still the result of chance. Before the industrial revolution it was by ploughing, peat-cutting and gravel-digging that men most frequently stumbled upon their ancestral remains, but now, as we have seen, all manner of more violent and extensive assaults are made upon the face of the earth. The sinking of deep foundations, the cutting of railways and by-pass roads, and the trenching for public utilities which goes with the interminable extension of our towns, all these and many other activities have accelerated the pace of chance discovery. The conduct of a modern war, with its great increase in industrial building and the levelling of huge tracts for aerodromes, causes a further acceleration in chance discovery; indeed in exceptional conditions, such as that of the hidden masonry of Roman London, revelations may even be made by high explosives.

What proportion of chance finds fails to be recorded can never be known, but probably with the present widespread interest in antiquity it is not very high. Indeed, that an excessive enthusiasm is not uncommon is well shown by the now classic story of an exasperated official of the British Museum, who, on being hopefully shown some flints, cried, "Madam, take them back to the gravel path where they belong." The agencies for recording discoveries are both public and private; sometimes, as this story proves, individuals may take their finds directly to a national museum, but more often they filter through the network of local societies which cover the whole country. If, for example, a farmer ploughs out a bronze-age cist, the chances are that some devoted member of the local society or an official of the local museum will either be told or will learn of it through one of the channels of rural rumour and will in turn notify the officials of the society. The cist will then be investigated, and if it proves sufficiently important a report will be sent to a central museum or to an officer of the Ancient Monuments department of the Ministry of Works. This will lead to inspection and perhaps full excavation. It will not surprise those familiar with human affairs of this sort that there may sometimes be faction; news of the farmer's discovery may travel various channels and the parties summoned encounter one another unwillingly at the graveside. However, the ultimate cause of knowledge is seldom damaged.

Plate XVII

Hadrian's Wall, looking east towards its ascent of Sewingshields Crags, from the north gate of Housesteads Fort, Northumberland

Plate XVIII

Crown Copyright reserved

The Roman works of Richborough Castle, Kent, from the air. The outer wall and ditches are of the late " Saxon Shore " fort ; within are the triple ditches of a slightly earlier fort, and the

Excavation is included in the next section, for it is essentially the study of a field monument; nevertheless it is also a means to what is virtually chance discovery. Sometimes the results of a dig are so unexpected that they may be so described, as for instance the uncovering of the unique treasure of the ship-burial at Sutton Hoo; sometimes, and indeed quite frequently, the excavation of one type of monument may strike upon another quite different. There are countless examples of such fortunate stumbling—the neolithic camp and long barrow under the Iron Age fort of Maiden Castle: the important Roman samian ware kiln on the site of the British city of Camulodunum.

One new technique is going to play an increasing part in the discovery of concealed sites. Air photography, so successfully used in modern warfare, can equally well be made to reveal the activities of prehistoric men. There are two main methods, the first depending on inequalities of level, the second on inequalities of colour. For the first method the right time of day must be chosen, when a low sun magnifies by shadows the slight surface irregularities of banks and ditches, mounds and hollows. To secure the best results by the second type of air photograph it is the time of year and not the time of day which must be considered, for it depends on differences in colour of vegetation growing on disturbed ground. Plants, whether grass or corn or sugar beet, tend to be well grown and richly pigmented when they are rooted over old hollows, such as pits and ditches, where their roots can get down into the deep soil which has silted into them. On the other hand, they are naturally poor and scanty in the shallow soil over former banks, mounds and walls. For example, imagine a cornfield where a round barrow (p. 185) has been gradually ploughed down until it is perfectly level. At a certain time in the summer the impoverished corn growing over the central mound, being prematurely ripened, would show from the air as a pale disc while the plants thriving in the silt of the surrounding ditch would stand out as a dark ring. Two of the most spectacular discoveries made by this crop mark method are the Bronze Age temple of Arminghall and the Roman town of Caistor-by-Norwich where every building was clearly planned in pale lines in the corn.

STUDY.—We come now to our second head, the study of the material discovered. If this is some form of portable object it commonly goes to a museum, local or national according to its importance, for expert examination. Archæology has now accumulated enough information for it to be rare for experts to have any difficulty in dating finds or assigning them to a recognized culture, merely by looking at them. This certainty with which an archæologist can date a scrap of bronze or even a wretched potsherd, to some people seems almost miraculous, to others dubious. But it is a matter of experience, of having handled such things for years, together with some visual and tactile sensibility: very much the same qualifications as are required to distinguish the quality of foodstuffs or materials or the work of different painters. A form of connoisseurship though often without the usually accepted implication of elegance. Almost all the things made by man can with experience be recognized in this way and be used with more or less accuracy for the identification of the culture to which they belong. This special effluvium of each age, down to its smallest items, is a fascinating thing.

Of all prehistoric artifacts the most useful to the archæologist for evidence of age and culture is pottery. This is for several reasons. To begin with, it has the essential quality of lastingness: any properly fired ware is indestructible in ordinary conditions. On the other hand, it is very easily breakable, so that on any site where people have lived there tends to be more of it than of anything else. Again, clay is very variable and slight differences in mixing, handling and firing it produce distinctive and readily identifiable wares; similarly it is a highly flexible medium which allows an infinite range of distinctive forms, styles, modes of ornament. It is valuable again for quite a different reason; many objects, bronzes for instance, may be made by a few specialists, last for a long time and be moved long distances about the map simply as articles of trade. In contrast, prehistoric pottery is usually made by the women of each local community and is not easily transportable, nor is it at all likely to have a long life before being broken; it therefore gives far more reliable evidence than bronzes for the movement or persistence of peoples. While the appearance of a few knives or brooches on a site may only mean the visit of a prehistoric Autolycus, new pottery almost certainly indicates the arrival of a new population. It is for all these reasons that pottery has come to have a very special place among the material documents of prehistory, and all archæologists have to acquire some skill in reading it.

Beyond mere identification are more detailed studies to which ideally many types of find should be subjected if they are to make their full contribution to knowledge, and this is the opportunity beyond all others for making use of a variety of scientific techniques. Some of these techniques are most pleasing in their ingenuity and a few of them can be described. The source of raw materials is of obvious interest for an understanding of trade and primitive economics: potsherds can be analysed to learn whether they have been made on the spot from local clay by the women of a community or whether they appear to have been brought from some distance and are therefore probably the work of a specialist potter selling his wares more widely. Stone axes can be 'sliced' and the source of the rock detected geologically; by this means it has been proved, for example, that a single factory in north Wales exported axes over much of Britain (p. 37). Similarly, from an analysis of copper, bronze and iron it is often possible to identify the exact source of the metal ore, perhaps far distant. It was the spectroscopic examination of the blue faience beads of the Wessex culture that made it perfectly certain that they were actual imports from Egypt (p. 70).

Among other small points it is worth mentioning that the inside of all domestic vessels should be carefully tested to see if any substance remains to give information on prehistoric food or drink. One very clever device comes from Scandinavian archæologists. When clay is fired to make pottery, any perishable scraps mixed with it are of course burnt out, leaving a cavity behind them. In the conditions under which primitive potting was done it was easy enough for grains of corn to be caught up in the clay, and if a cast is taken from the cavity, a replica of the grain is made and the exact species can be identified. In this way much has been learnt about prehistoric crops and the changes in the species of corn grown at different periods.

These methods are applicable when the material for study consists of objects; when, on the other hand, it is some form of field monument (p. 185) that form of study known as excavation must be undertaken before any more detailed analysis is possible.

We can let ourselves go a little on the subject of excavation: so many people visit digs, yet have very little idea what they are witnessing, either as a more or less scientific operation, or as a social activity involving all the curious-looking people they see at work. Individuals covering the widest possible range in age, in beauty, and in dress, are to be seen using theodolites, plane-tables, compasses, tape-measures, masons' trowels, tooth-brushes, often with exceptional seriousness and concentration. Sometimes, again, a dig may rather resemble a medieval Last Judgment: at the visitor's approach human figures suddenly raise themselves in holes in the ground. What is the meaning of these scenes so incompletely understood by most visitors?

An excavation represents archæology's nearest approach to a scientific experiment. Yet certainly it is not one: there can be no fixed 'control', no accurate repetition, and the social and individual human element must remain far more significant than in a laboratory experiment. Nor can it be so precisely directed.

It is decided that a dig shall take place, sometimes because it is believed that it will yield some badly needed information, but far more commonly because the site is in danger from the builder or some other menace. The work may be the responsibility of an individual, or of a local or a national society (the more official digs of the department of Ancient Monuments are not considered here), but the chances are that an appeal will have to be issued for funds. It is fortunate if some well-to-do person in the neighbourhood is interested, or if a local authority realizes the possibilities of prestige and an attraction for tourists and gives financial help.

A director is appointed and is left to collect a team of assistants. Friends or even relatives often volunteer, students may be sent by their university, and all are liable to bring other friends with them. The effect of propinquity on human relationships can hardly be over-estimated, and few excavations of any size or duration are without some love interest. Indeed, there is no doubt that love has saved archæology a considerable sum in wage bills.

At the appointed date the party begins to assemble; often too many come at the beginning and too few remain to the end. Some lodge in hotels or rooms or with the director; romantic characters will often camp out on the site. The more elaborate equipment is of course provided, but local shops must usually be searched for minor necessities such as labels, envelopes, paper bags, empty sweet-tins and brushes; in particular it has now become an almost universal custom to buy the elegant little wire trays of pastrycooks for use in drying potsherds.

Then, of course, in addition to his more or less skilled assistants the director has to find his labour force. 'Do you actually dig yourself?' is a very frequent question. The answer is that although at the beginning of an excavation the more energetic assistants may use a spade or pick, before long there is usually far too much non-manual work to be done and paid labour is a necessity. In days of unemployment painfully too many workmen would come forward, but at other times it might be difficult to collect a team of the excessively old and young from the Exchange. It is unlikely in the first season of a dig that any of the men will have had experience of excavation, yet quite soon they sort themselves out into those with a natural skill, who are entrusted with the more delicate work, and those others who are usually left to shift top-soil or to other occupations where clumsiness does no harm. Often men become deeply interested and well-informed and their knowledge of local soil-conditions may be of great value. Sometimes an elderly man will emerge to act as tea-maker and general batman; he may also try to rear beans or vegetable marrows on the spoil-heaps.

This human aspect of a dig is likely to have a considerable

effect upon its success as a scientific operation. Faction and discontent are a great handicap, and individual morale is equally important. It may be an impediment if a woman is utterly unwilling to risk scratching her nails, but it is far more serious if young men show signs of ceasing to shave, for slovenliness may appear also in their work. There is a legend that on a certain well-known excavation overseas dirty crockery of one meal was put through a hole into a box fixed under the table and taken out again, unwashed, for the next. This was also scientifically an unreliable dig. Absence of mind is an altogether different thing, far more endearing but hardly less dangerous. A certain scholar who wore numerous and bulky clothes and was continuously too optimistic about his own memory had always to be searched in the evening of a day's digging, for crucial finds lay in all his pockets and there was still some chance, in the evening, that he might remember where they came from.

Enough has been said to suggest that a heavy responsibility falls upon the director on the purely administrative side: he must collect money, assistants and labour, maintain harmony and direction, keep accounts involving intricate varieties in wage, insurance and bonus rates, and at the same time do what he can to train students and enlighten helpers. But this is all of secondary importance: his main task, and the one for which he is selected, is of course the scientific conduct of the excavation; work which calls for judgment, for just the right blend of courage with caution, of scepticism and common sense with imagination. If he has these qualities in wrong proportions he may nibble round his problem too long in indecision, or he may push ahead too fast and destroy evidence before the problem is fully understood; he may be too quick to build a theoretical interpretation of the history of a site, or he may fail ever to make one at all.

It is almost impossible to give any generalized account of methods: every site is unique and demands invention and improvisation; what is more possible is to state a few principles and then to describe some particular examples.

It seems that when it is reduced to fundamentals excavation

has three main concerns, two active and a third passive. It must make a vertical study of strata and a horizontal study of pattern, its passive duty being the meticulous record of all aspects of these studies. Perhaps the principles of stratification and pattern can be most clearly explained by an analogue which war will have made familiar to many people. The shattering of the walls of old houses has not infrequently exposed successive layers of wallpaper pasted one over another to satisfy the changing tastes of generations of tenants. Beginning, perhaps, with the light sprigs or elegant formalities of the eighteenth century, they will pass through various phases of Victorian pomp and *art nouveau* to finish either with modernistic brown and orange triangles or a coat of distemper. Plainly these layers can be studied vertically and made to show when the house was first occupied, when successive tenants redecorated, and, finally, approximately when it was destroyed; alternatively they can be peeled off horizontally, each paper being studied as a whole and its design appreciated. So when an excavator is concerned with a site used over some considerable period he can cut through the superimposed strata to establish the historical sequence of periods, and he can lay bare and study each stratum or period as a complete, static, entity. It is interesting to notice that these two simple principles of stratification and pattern correspond exactly to the two main schools of thought in prehistory that have been defined (p. 158). Clearly the historical approach demands concentration on the vertical method, the sociological on the horizontal one; and it is therefore only to be expected that the younger sociological school complain that excavators have in the past been content merely to cut sections to establish the sequence of events in, say, a village and have neglected to open out horizontally to discover the plan of the whole village at any one period. In the practical as in the intellectual field there is no doubt that the ideal would be the fullest possible combination of the two methods, but at this point economic considerations intrude. Life is short and archæology poorly endowed: the total excavation of a successive series of settlements demands a great expenditure of time and money. A tug-of-war between the two interests ending in a variety of compromises seems therefore to be inevitable and perhaps not altogether unhappy.

To return now to the actual conduct of a dig based on these ideas, the passive principle of recording must not be any longer neglected. For the first step on most types of excavation is to survey the site in its untouched state, planning, photographing and, if necessary, contouring all its features. Next it is usual to begin to establish the history of the site by means of stratification, and for this purpose some kind of trench will probably be cut across it in which various horizons may be revealed and, with good luck, dated by finds of pottery or other material. In all stratigraphical work the first essential is to keep all finds from each layer separate, and workmen are furnished with carefully labelled containers in which they must put each find according to the level from which it has been taken. At the end of the day these must be collected and the contents individually and indelibly marked. This cutting of trial trenches may strike upon some structural feature which will demand the opening of a wider area of excavation in order to pursue it. It must not be supposed that 'structural feature' here need mean anything so substantial as a stone foundation. It is possible by skilful digging to detect almost any disturbance made in virgin soil, for the natural formation can never be restored. Excavators can therefore trace the line of filled-up ditches and palisades, or can establish the whole plan of a house by delicately probing to find the slot sunk to take a beam or the post-holes to take uprights. Naturally the difficulty of this kind of work varies widely with the soil; in chalk it can be the easiest thing in the world; in gravel it is infernally difficult, and there is every gradation in between. Again, the stone Highland Zone country presents problems and demands skills all of its own. From this point it is impossible to continue with any general account; sometimes there may be only one historical horizon, sometimes many; there may be several different structural features to follow or there may be none: there is no normal procedure. It will therefore only be helpful to describe and show pictures of a few digs that illustrate special problems and the techniques used to solve them.

It will be appropriate to begin with an excavation covering an early period and which shows stratigraphical work at its simplest, uncomplicated by any structural features. About 8000 years ago when Europe was still adjusting fairly rapidly after the retreat of the ice sheets, the East Anglian fenland area was at a higher level and therefore far more habitable than it became in historical times. At that time a sandy ridge at a site now known

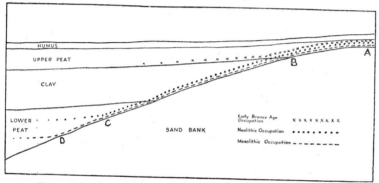

FIG. 27.—Sectional diagram of the excavation at Peacock's Farm, Cambs.

as Peacock's Farm (Fig. 27) made a suitable squatting-place for Mesolithic fishers and fowlers, and from then onward into the Early Bronze Age it was intermittently occupied. But during the same period the area round the sand-bank was silting up with natural deposits: first a slow accumulation of peat, then a rapid deposition of clay during a time of flooding, then another period of peat-formation. It will be seen how this meant a continual reduction in the area free for occupation —like a holiday beach when the tide is rising—until at last the whole sandy island was covered and became uninhabitable. The purpose of the Peacock's Farm excavation was to cut down on to the flanks of the sand ridge, establish the sequence of human occupation, and correlate it with the periods of climatic and geographical change marked by the natural deposits. A series of pits was sunk at intervals from the summit of the ridge down its side to the foot, the lowest one being as much as 16 feet deep. This was in itself a perfectly straightforward operation, but it was made difficult, and even hazardous, by the fact that as they were below sea-level, the deeper pits constantly filled with water and threatened to collapse. Indeed the last hole did subside and the director had to fly for his life, but not before his aim was completely achieved. As the diagram shows, during the Mesolithic period people occupied the bank from A to D and their rubbish scattered out into the surrounding peat at level D; by the time the Neolithic inhabitants arrived the bank was uncovered only from A to C, but peat was still forming and the Neolithic remains tail out into it about a foot from the top at C; it was therefore only after the Neolithic occupation that the great inundation of the fen area represented by clay occurred, while this episode was over and peat again forming before Early Bronze Age folk arrived to find only the top of the ridge from A to B uncovered. So the Peacock's Farm excavation established beyond all doubt that the subsidence that caused the flooding of the fenland, for which evidence exists also elsewhere, happened between the beginning of the Neolithic and the Early Bronze Ages. An analysis of the tree pollen in the two peat beds (see p. 174) made it possible also to link up this event with the changes in our forests which took place during the period.

The second example represents a very different type of work: the excavation of a round barrow by the 'quadrant' method now commonly used. By this method a quarter of the barrow is removed at a time, but between each an undisturbed baulk is left standing; it is easy to see from Plate XIX, i, how this secures that two complete cross sections of the mound remain to the last, showing the various tips and layers of which it is composed and also giving an invaluable guide for the restoration of the barrow to its original appearance when the dig is complete. This particular barrow was a simple affair covering a pit grave where a Bronze Age burial was accompanied by twelve exquisite tanged and barbed flint arrow-heads. The full advantage of the method is, however, better displayed in the diagram of a round barrow (Fig. 28) where the cross section proves that an original Early Bronze Age barrow (cross-hatched) was added in the Middle Bronze Age (stippled) when a secondary burial took place.

Fortified settlements of various kinds, the majority Iron Age hill-forts (p. 185), are among the commonest and most important field monument in this country, and recognized techniques have been developed for their excavation. Usually the main problems which have to be solved are (1) how the ramparts were built; (2) when they were built; this will probably be a complicated matter for, as in a medieval castle, they have often been altered and added to at various times; (3) the relation of these periods of rampart-construction with the remains of dwellings found inside. A famous example of work of this kind is the excavation of Maiden Castle, and

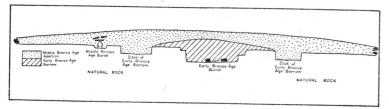

FIG. 28.—Section cut through a round barrow at Sutton, Glamorganshire.

except for the unusual size and elaboration of the place, it is sufficiently representative of its type. Plate XX, i, shows how sections are cut right through banks, and the silting of ditches, and makes it clear how such cuttings reveal the successive modifications of the defences: ramparts of no less than six periods are visible in this particular section. The stages in the silting-up of the ditch or of its re-excavation are also significant. Plate XIX, ii, is a good example of superposition in the interior of the camp; the square masonry foundations of a small Roman building are seen lying above the storage pits of Iron Age huts; finally Plate XX, ii, gives a view of one of the most stylish pieces of excavation ever achieved, that of the eastern entrance to Maiden Castle. The intricacy of the problems there were very great, for roads and gates had been remodelled at least six times and this elaborate chequer-work of cuttings and baulks was necessary to keep check of so many horizons.

The diagram, Fig. 29, introduces the fourth example, which

has been adopted as a useful comparison with Peacock's Farm.

The site of the British city of Camulodunum at Colchester, like Peacock's Farm, was completely underground with no trace visible on the surface, and at both sites the main task was to study by simple stratification successive periods of occupation. But whereas at Peacock's Farm the strata represented several thousand years of remote barbarism, at Colchester they summed up less than a century of familiar British history. There was no question at the latter site of a single compact

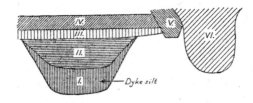

DIAGRAMMATIC SECTION
A KEY TO CHRONOLOGY

I. Cunobeline period, and partial silting of Dyke. C. 5–43/4 A.D.

II. Claudian conquest. Dyke filling. 43/4 A.D.

III. 1st Roman phase of occupation. 43/4 — 48 A.D.

IV 2nd (Main) Roman occupation. Colonia built 49–61 A.D.

V. Boudicca 61 A.D.

VI. Late pits 61–65 A.D.

FIG. 29.—Composite section showing historical sequence at Camulodunum, Colchester.

section, trenches had to be cut over an area of many acres before the historical sequence shown in the composite section (Fig. 29) could be pieced together. When, however, this had been done it was possible with some certainty to link up the various horizons, the ditches, roads, squalid huts and traces of burning and destruction with known events. These trenches cut in the fields on the outskirts of Colchester detected the ramparts of Cymbeline's capital, their destruction by the Romans, Roman industrial occupation connected with the building of the near-by Colonia, evidence of the violence of Queen Boudicca's attack, some traces of a temporary refortification of the site, and finally Roman clearance and pacification. Here the association of archæology with history is seen at its most intimate.

The last and latest example of practical excavation has been chosen to illustrate a highly specialized technique devised to cope with an individual problem. Everyone has heard of the Sutton Hoo ship burial, which is to be connected with the seventh century pagan kings of East Anglia. Under its covering mound the funeral ship had completely decayed, but the iron clamps which had held the boards together were still in position, and the soil was slightly discoloured where the wood had been. With patient and delicate work (the principal excavator weighed some 18 stone) it was found possible slowly to cut away the earth up to the discoloration and the nails until a ghost of the ship which had received the treasure lay there in the soil. This remarkable feat may also be taken as representative on a large scale of many small operations of skill which have to be performed on all types of dig when delicate objects are uncovered. These are the occasions when unskilled labour has to stand aside while the most practised hands use delicate tools—knives, hairpins, paintbrushes, and, when necessary, various preservatives are applied.

These five specimen digs give some idea of the endless variety of excavation equally with the simplicity of the underlying principles and objectives. The most arduous part of the excavator's task, whatever the type of dig, is that of recording results. His first concern may be to understand the significance of everything he sees, to fit each new detail into his wider interpretation of the site as a whole; but whether he understands a thing or not it must be recorded. He and his assistants must be constantly engaged with written notes, plans, sections and photographs of each stage of each operation so that even when some feature has been removed it is possible to interpret it in the light of later evidence. For this is the test of record-keeping: that it should perpetuate ephemeral evidence for all time. It may be that something incomprehensible when it is encountered at the beginning of an excavation is quite understandable at the end, or it may be necessary to wait for the findings of many further digs before an explanation is possible. It has already been told how the meticulous records made by General Pitt-Rivers in the 1880's and '90's keep his excavations alive as sources for modern research.

The end of a dig is usually melancholy. Everyone goes home, trenches have to be filled in and latrines cleared away. Exceptionally what has been uncovered is handed over to the Ministry of Works for preservation, but far more often it is a question of putting back, of restoring a site as nearly as possible to its virgin state. It is particularly galling also on the financial side, for while every excavator would like to use his last penny on constructive work, he must always keep a considerable sum in reserve for this 'filling in'.

But even with the last sod unrolled and stamped a little unevenly back into place, the work of an excavation is not nearly finished; indeed for many participators it has not begun. For now all special categories of finds must be sent to the experts for their reports. There are in this country a few men and women who prepare these specialist reports for almost every dig; how they remain sane, if they do, is astounding. There is one to whom all animal bones go for identification, others specialize in human anatomy, and one in particular is expert in extracting information even from cremated remains. There are experts on the pottery of each period, experts on charcoal, on plant remains and on the species of snails. In the late summer when the excavation season is over, the post brings scrubby packet after packet of relics to these people, who have been rash enough to know more about something than anyone else.

One form of specialist study there is which asks for rather fuller treatment here. This is pollen analysis. Every season trees spill their pollen and it drifts in invisible clouds on to the earth, where in favourable conditions it may be preserved for thousands of years. Each species of tree has its own distinctive pollen grain; if, then, samples of soil are taken and examined microscopically it is possible to identify all the trees growing in the area at the time the soil deposit was forming, and by counting the grains to estimate their relative numbers. There have been great changes in the tree population since the end of the Ice Age, among the simplest and most conspicuous being the displacement of pine by oak forest at the end of Boreal times (about 5000 B.C.) and the first arrival of the beech during the Bronze Age. At first the presence in the soil deposits of archæological finds did much to fix the date of these forest phases; but once the forest history is established for a region then it is clear that pollen analysis may help to date archæological horizons. At Peacock's Farm, for example, analysis of the lower peat showed the pine dwindling sharply in numbers at just about the time of the Mesolithic occupation, which is thus dated to the end of the Boreal phase.

While the experts are making their detailed reports the director has to work up his records of the dig for publication. Fair copies of plans, sections and special diagrams must be prepared (many excavators are good draughtsmen and do this work for themselves) and finds drawn and photographed. Finally his account of the actual digging, of the finds and of the interpretation of the site must be followed by some attempt to give them their proper place in European prehistory. It is not surprising that the publication of a large dig covering several seasons' work may take years to complete; it is even easy to understand if, very occasionally, an excavator allows himself to be overwhelmed by age and the burden of the task and fails to publish at all.

INTERPRETATION.—The question of fitting the results of a particular dig into its wider background leads at once to the third section, Interpretation. We have to consider how, from the very raw material of archæology, history is made. Prehistory deals with the study of man in time, and within the narrow limits of our globe, in space: the scattered scraps of material evidence found by chance or by intention have to be interpreted with these two aspects in mind. For the former a simple extension of the stratigraphical method is the strongest instrument. Before the essential chronological framework for British prehistory could be made secure it was necessary to establish the normal sequence of cultures over the country at large. If it is found that all over the country wherever in the silting of a ditch, the contents of a tomb or the horizons of a settlement, the remains of cultures have accumulated one above another, culture B overlies A and underlies C, then A–B–C obviously represents this normal sequence. It might, for instance, be the almost invariable and universal succession of Windmill Hill–Beaker–Urn (pp. 29, 52, 76). On the other hand, when B occurs only in a limited region and elsewhere C directly overlies A, then the prehistorian will probably infer that B represents some event, perhaps an invasion from the Continent, that failed to affect the country as a whole. In some circumstances it may be legitimate to explain this limitation by the fact that the rest of the land was already strongly held by the possessors of the A culture. To establish each individual culture in its entirety the evidence of association must of course be used, one particular cultural element perhaps serving to unite others: as, for instance, the occurrence of plain Windmill Hill pottery in both causewayed camps and long barrows shows this type of settlement and this type of tomb to belong to the same Neolithic culture.

There is another method which the prehistorian can use to study the time aspect of his subject. This is the typological one whose principles have already been explained. The sliding passage of the generations through time can be detected not only in the falling of layer upon layer of remains of their material culture (stratigraphy) but also in the gradual evolution of traditional forms for the design of objects, a tradition handed on from hand and eye to hand and eye in which natural conservatism is gradually modified, generally in the direction of greater efficiency or ease of manufacture, but also at last by the processes of degeneration. Conservatism is sufficiently strong, however, to make an abrupt change in the fashioning of a familiar article almost impossible, and there are many typological sequences, like that of the spearhead (p. 79), which proceed by tiny steps, trending in a certain direction much like the processes of biological evolution traced by palæontology. If a sudden break does occur then the prehistorian will suspect some external influence, probably again a migration or invasion, when an alien tradition cuts across the old. The spearhead

Plate XIX

EXCAVATION TECHNIQUE

Breach Farm, Pembrokeshire ; digging a round barrow by the quadrant method

Maiden Castle ; Roman temple overlying the storage pits of the Iron Age occupation

Plate XX

EXCAVATION TECHNIQUE
Maiden Castle (*left*)
Section cut through the
rampart and living-floors
within. (*below*) Excavation
of the east entrance by
the grid method

illustrates this point very well, for the Celtic invaders of the Late Bronze Age introduced a new form which made a complete break from the old British types which had developed during the five hundred years of the Middle Bronze Age. Sometimes typology can show the first centres of immigration, for there the earliest forms will be found while the more evolved types coming later in the sequence are spread more widely; this method of interpretation has been effectively used for the Anglo-Saxon settlements, the distribution of the cruciform brooch having proved to be particularly revealing. To find the source of new cultures appearing in this country the prehistorian naturally turns to the Continent, where he may be able to find close parallels to the early types in the British sequence and so localize the place of origin.

For all work of this kind, in which the space aspect of the subject is foremost, the prehistorian uses distribution-maps. In these the find-spots of the particular category of object which is being studied, or the group of such types known to represent one culture, are plotted on a map, of one locality, of the whole of Britain, or the whole of the Continent according to the scope of the enquiry. It is easy to understand how such maps reveal very simply the main areas of settlement of the bearers of a given culture, their lines of entry and perhaps their place of origin: contrast, for example, the mainly western distribution of megaliths with the eastern bias of beakers. It is mainly, then, from the analysis of stratification, typology and distribution that prehistorians have drawn their picture of man's development in time and movements in space. There remains of course the static, sociological, type of study which has evolved many means of interpretation for its own peculiar problems; but it has already been suggested this can only take its proper place as a part of the more dynamic treatment of prehistory. Its methods generally need less explanation than those we have been discussing. The first aim is to explain the economic basis of a society and its structure. It is not difficult to see how the tools and implements in use, the houses and their equipment, the presence or absence of visible field-systems will show whether the community depends on hunting or agriculture,

N

whether cultivation is by hoe or plough. Again, the food refuse will leave no doubt as to the presence or absence of domestic animals and, when they do occur, of the relative importance of the different kinds and the extent to which their meat was supplemented by that of wild game. As for social structure it is clear that the form of dwelling, whether in flimsy huts, isolated farmsteads, in hamlets or substantial villages, will be relevant; similarly a larger house in a village of small ones, or rich graves among the more impoverished, will probably betray the existence of a privileged ruling class. The size of settlements and cemeteries will help to give a very rough idea of population numbers. Other methods are more ingenious: for instance, if the plant remains discovered in certain types of settlement can be shown invariably to belong to one season, say perhaps autumnal seeds and nuts, then it may be supposed that their owners used these settlements only at that time of year and at other seasons lived elsewhere.

For all the many other elements in the culture of a society—religion, art, industry and craftsmanship—it is simply a matter of observation and common sense with an intelligent consideration for the inter-relationship between all the parts. How art, perhaps, is developed in the service of religion, how religion is sometimes concerned in furthering economic ends, how the material equipment is limited by environment, and so forth.

These then are some of the methods used to turn material things into history, but they are in fact no more than convenient tools in the service of the individual mind. The prehistorian's own gifts are far more important; his success will depend on his historical sense, his sensibility in relation to things and to style and, above all, to the intuition necessary for all original research—intuition being of course (equally with feminine intuition) really a delicate intelligence based on a wide semi-conscious accumulation of past perceptions and detailed facts. The prehistorian's eyes have scrutinized and his fingers felt hundreds upon hundreds of objects—potsherds, bronzes, flints—and always as a backcloth to his mind hangs a map of Britain, of Europe, of the world and the changing cultural patterns playing over it. So it is that when some new fact presents itself he can answer at once the question is this something to be expected, something in harmony with existing knowledge, or is it something odd which calls for explanation —the question that is at the root of all research.

Finally, dare we ask what it is all for? Why do prehistorians devote so much talent and industry to finding out what our species has been doing during the last half-million years? The answer is one with the question. Archæology traces from its beginning the very process which now obliges man to go smelling out his own tracks in this way. No doubt we had more peace of mind when we thought that Eden lay at the centre of an earth round which the sun revolved, and that man was set down a perfectly created being at a given and not too remote date. But our species has specialized in the development of the brain and, however this may be explained, we cannot escape the outcome. The brain that let man shape the first tool inevitably led him on to rediscover the fact that he had done so: the two processes are linked by an unbroken chain of cell-divisions. The strain and burden of the increasing complexity of our self-consciousness is severe; if in some ways conscience does make cowards of us all, it certainly calls for great courage. For information on this subject does not bring understanding; archæology does not explain the strange fate of our species any more than physics explains the existence of the universe. Perhaps in time (and at least we can now view ourselves in time with a half-million years' perspective) some harmony will emerge; and meanwhile, having started, we are bound to go on to get some more of the apparent facts right.

BIBLIOGRAPHY

(The list is for the most part limited to books published in the last fifteen years, 1932–1946. Simpler and more inexpensive books are marked ★.)

GENERAL
Prehistory and Civilization.
- ★V. Gordon Childe, *Man Makes Himself*. London: Watts, 1936. (Thinker's Library), 1939.
- ★V. Gordon Childe, *What Happened in History*. (Pelican Books, A 108.) Harmondsworth: Penguin Books, 1942.
- ★Grahame (J. G. D.) Clark, *Archaeology and Society*. London: Methuen, 2nd ed., 1947.

EUROPE
- C. S. Coon, *The Races of Europe*. New York: Macmillan, 1939.
- C. F. C. Hawkes, *The Prehistoric Foundations of Europe: to the Mycenean Age*. London: Methuen, 1940.
- ★Edith Plant, *Man's Unwritten Past*. (Realms of Natural Science Series.) Oxford University Press (London: Cumberlege), 1942.

Palæolithic:
- ★M. C. Burkitt, *The Old Stone Age*. Cambridge University Press, 1933.
- ★W. B. Wright, *Tools and the Man*. London: Bell, 1939.
- ★Dorothy Davison, *Men of the Dawn*. London: Watts (Thinker's Library), 1934.

Mesolithic:
- J. G. D. Clark, *The Mesolithic Settlement of Northern Europe*. Cambridge University Press, 1936.

Mesolithic to Bronze Age:
- V. Gordon Childe, *The Dawn of European Civilization* (2nd edn.). London: Kegan Paul, 1939.

BRITAIN (mainly Mesolithic onwards)
- ★V. Gordon Childe, *Prehistoric Communities of the British Isles*. London and Edinburgh: Chambers, 1940.
  At present the standard work: contains full earlier bibliography.
- ★Sir Cyril Fox, *The Personality of Britain: its Influence on Inhabitant and Invader in Prehistoric and Early Historic Times* (4th edn.). Cardiff: National Museum of Wales, 1943.
- ★Jacquetta Hawkes, *Early Britain* (Britain in Pictures Series). London: Collins, 1945.

England:
- ★Grahame (J. G. D.) Clark, *Prehistoric England*. London: Batsford, 1940.

181

Wales:
>   ★W. F. Grimes, *A Guide to the Collection Illustrating the Prehistory of Wales.*
>   Cardiff: National Museum of Wales, 1939.

Scotland:
>   V. Gordon Childe, *The Prehistory of Scotland.*   London: Kegan Paul, 1935.
>   ★V. Gordon Childe, *Prehistoric Scotland.* (Historical Association Pam-
>   phlets, no. 115.)   London: Bell, 1940.

Special Counties.
>   ★W. J. Varley and J. Wilfrid Jackson, *Prehistoric Cheshire.* (Handbook
>   to the History of Cheshire, no. 1.)   Chester: Cheshire Rural Com-
>   munity Council, 1940.
>   ★M. E. Cunnington, *An Introduction to the Archæology of Wiltshire* (3rd edn.).
>   Devizes: Woodward, 1934.
>   ★E. Cecil Curwen, *The Archæology of Sussex.* (County Archæologies
>   Series.)   London: Methuen, 1937.

★Other volumes in the County Archæologies Series (London: Methuen)
are:
>   H. J. E. Peake, *The Archæology of Berkshire,* 1930.
>   H. O'Neill Hencken, *The Archæology of Cornwall and Scilly,* 1932.
>   R. F. Jessup, *The Archæology of Kent,* 1930.
>   C. E. Vulliamy, *The Archæology of Middlesex and London,* 1930.
>   Dina P. Dobson, *The Archæology of Somerset,* 1931.
>   F. and H. W. Elgee, *The Archæology of Yorkshire,* 1932.

Special Sites (including some books earlier than 1932):
>   ★Frank Stevens, *Stonehenge: Today and Yesterday.* (The Official Guide
>   to Stonehenge.)   London: H.M. Stationery Office (latest edn.), 1938.
>   ★A. Bulleid, *The Lake-Villages of Somerset.* (Somerset Folk Series, no.
>   16.)   London: Folk Press, 1924.
>   A. Bulleid and H. St. George Gray, *The Glastonbury Lake-Village.* London
>   and Edinburgh: Chambers, 2 vols., 1911–17.
>   *Reports of the Research Committee of the Society of Antiquaries:*
>   R. E. M. and T. V. Wheeler, *Verulamium: a Belgic and two Roman Cities.*
>   Oxford University Press (London: Cumberlege), 1936.
>   R. E. M. Wheeler, *Maiden Castle.*   Oxford University Press (London:
>   Cumberlege), 1943.
>   C. F. C. Hawkes and M. R. Hull, *Camulodunum.*   Oxford University
>   Press (London: Cumberlege), 1947.

Later Iron Age: Roman Britain:
>   Art:
>   E. Thurlow Leeds, *Celtic Ornament (to A.D. 700).*   Oxford: Clarendon
>   Press, 1933.

General:
*R. G. Collingwood, *Roman Britain* (latest edn.). Oxford: Clarendon Press, 1934.
R. G. Collingwood and J. N. L. Myres, *Roman Britain and the English Settlements*. (The Oxford History of England, Vol. 1: 2nd edn.) Oxford: Clarendon Press, 1936.

Illustrated Regional Guides to Ancient Monuments, H.M. Office of Works:
*Vol. I, *Northern England*
*Vol. II, *Southern England* } London: H.M. Stationery Office,
*Vol. III, *E. Anglia and Midlands* } 1935–7.
*Vol. IV, *South Wales*, 1938.

Field Archæology, Maps, and Air-Photography (including some publications earlier than 1933):

Ordnance Survey publications: London, H.M. Stationery Office:
Field Archæology (notes for beginners). 2nd edn., 1936.
Maps:
Megalithic Survey (maps, ¼ mile to inch, showing distribution of long barrows, megaliths, dwelling-sites, flint-mines, with lists and explanatory text), comprising:
Map of Neolithic Wessex.
Map of the Trent Basin.
Map of South Wales.
Celtic Earthworks of Salisbury Plain (maps, 1 : 25,000, showing Celtic fields, earthworks, and barrows: one so far published):
Old Sarum (map covering the district around). Revised edn., 1937.
Period Map (with explanatory letterpress):
Roman Britain. 2nd edn., 1928.
Air-Photography (author, O. G. S. Crawford):
Air-Photography and Archæology. (Wessex district: illustrated with air-photographs and maps.) 2nd edn., 1928.
Air-Photography for Archæologists (the subject illustrated by typical examples). 1929.
O. G. S. Crawford and A. Keiller, *Wessex from the Air*. Oxford: Clarendon Press, 1928.

PERIODICALS

General quarterly review of archæology, equally for the specialist and the ordinary reader:
Antiquity, edited by O. G. S. Crawford and Roland Austin. Gloucester: 24 Parkend Road; appears regularly in March, June, September and December.

Journals published by Societies:

The Prehistoric Society:

Proceedings of the Prehistoric Society, edited by J. G. D. Clark (University Museum of Archæology and Ethnology, Downing Street, Cambridge). Contains, in addition to articles, a full summary account of each year's excavations; appears normally half-yearly.

Society for the Promotion of Roman Studies (50 Bedford Square, London, W.C.1):

The Journal of Roman Studies. Contains, in addition to articles, a full summary account of each year's excavations: may include prehistoric (usually Iron Age) as well as Roman material; appears normally half-yearly.

The following are concerned with archæology of both prehistoric and later periods:

Society of Antiquaries (Burlington House, London, W.1):

The Antiquaries Journal (normally quarterly).

Archæologia (normally a large annual volume).

Royal Archæological Institute (Lancaster House, London, S.W.1):

The Archæological Journal (normally half-yearly).

Wales: Cambrian Archæological Association (Whitford, Holywell, Flintshire):

Archæologia Cambrensis (normally half-yearly).

Scotland: Society of Antiquaries of Scotland (Edinburgh):

Proceedings of the Society (an annual volume).

Most English counties have an archæological society normally publishing a journal annually (a few more often).

The Congress of Archæological Societies (in union with the Society of Antiquaries: Burlington House, London, W.1) published a small annual *Report of the Research Committee* of the Congress, which gave a summary account of all discoveries made during the year, and a bibliography of all articles in periodicals, and principal books, published relating to Prehistoric, Roman, post-Roman and Medieval archæology, for the whole of the British Isles. This appeared to 1939 inclusive: it will now be continued by similar annual Reports to be published by the new Council for British Archæology (c/o Institute of Archæology, Inner Circle, Regent's Park, London, N.W.1), which will first issue a general *Survey and Policy of Research* reviewing the whole field of archæology in Britain.

APPENDIX

A S it may be far more enjoyable to visit prehistoric sites than to read about them, this section has been prepared to serve as a rough guide. It has been designed entirely for this purpose; thus, the regions into which the countryside is divided have been drawn for convenience in visiting and not for their cultural homogeneity, sites have been selected for their spectacular quality and not for their scientific importance, the style is necessarily uncouth but compact with information.

Unfortunately it is impossible to make such a work either complete or consistent: some regions have been far more fully explored and published than others, while the writer's personal knowledge is equally uneven. Nevertheless it is the only attempt at a comprehensive guide that has been made, and until there are resources to publish a really exhaustive survey it should be of value to those who like to salt their present enjoyment of the country with sudden reminders of its past.

A Guide to the Prehistoric and Roman Antiquities of Great Britain

As in the main text of the book, the Roman period is relatively less fully treated than the prehistoric; in particular for Roman roads, though surviving stretches may be mentioned, no attempt has been made to give a coherent picture of the system as a whole. This can be readily and pleasantly studied in the Ordnance Survey Map of Roman Britain. Before going on to the gazetteer itself, it may be helpful to provide a list of the types of monument most frequently found in Great Britain:

I. *Barrows:* (Pl. XXI)
    (A) Long Barrows. Larger, as a rule, at one end than the other and therefore generally pear- or wedge-shaped. Neolithic.
    (B) Round Barrows. These must be subdivided into—
        (i) Bowl barrows, a simple pudding-shaped mound often surrounded by a ditch. Usually Early or Middle Bronze Age; occasionally Roman (then often rather conical in form) or Saxon.

(ii) Bell barrows, with the mound separated from the ditch by a level platform. Early to Middle Bronze Age.

(iii) Disc barrows, a ditch with a bank on the outside, encircling either a level space or one or more small tumps. Early to Middle Bronze Age. Other varieties must here be passed over.

II. *Megalithic Tombs.*—Communal burial-vaults built of huge stones to a great variety of plans. The covering mound or cairn may be long or round; the relationship between the long form and the non-megalithic long barrow is complicated, and still rather obscure. Neolithic to Early Bronze Age.

III. *Circles, Henges, Stone Rows and Avenues.*—Surviving circles are of standing stones, but wood was also used, sometimes whole trunks. There may be a single ring of stones or a number, either concentric or side by side. The usually recognized mark of the 'henge' is an enclosing bank and ditch, often with the bank *outside* the ditch and with one or more entrances. Single or double lines of standing stones may be found separately or associated with circles. Throughout the Bronze Age.

IV. *Camps or Forts, Brochs.*—The Neolithic causewayed camp (p. 29) is distinctive; the great majority of the rest belong to the Iron Age (which in Scotland also covers the Roman period). The names camp or fort are interchangeable, but there is some tendency to employ the former when speaking of earth or chalk ramparts, the latter for stone-built ramparts usual in mountainous country. They are of great variety and it is impossible here to make any simple classification (Pl. XXII). They may have single, double, or multiple ramparts and cover anything from 1 to 80 acres; commonly they are on hills, and the ramparts follow the line of the contours, but there are also many plateau camps where the plan tends to be circular. Small and perfectly circular forts or 'castles', which occur in Cornwall and are very frequent in Scotland, can be grouped together as a distinct (though not wholly uniform) type. The broch is an exclusively Scottish variety of this class, originally rising into a tall circular tower. There is also the promontory camp, in which the spur of a hill or a coastal headland is cut off by ramparts running across the neck, while the other sides are protected by the natural features.

V. *Linear Earthworks* (*dykes*).—Long straight or meandering lines of one or more bank and ditch, generally designed to protect or demarcate large tracts of country. The bank may always be expected to run on the builder's side of the ditch. Usually either Belgic or post-Roman.

VI. *Roman Antiquities.*—These generally need no definition, but it should be made clear that, in contrast with terminology used for Iron Age earthworks, the word fort is used only to describe permanent military works, while camp is reserved for entrenchments of temporary use, including those of an army on the march.

Each regional section will open with some account of the most significant geographical features; a more general account of the structure of Britain and its effect on early settlement has been given above, in the first chapter.

I. *SOUTH-EASTERN ENGLAND*

The dominant natural features of this region are the two great chalk ridges of the North and the South Downs that run through Kent and Sussex to converge in Hampshire and unite ultimately with the main chalk massif of Wessex. These two ridges represent the surviving edges of what was once a great elongated vault of chalk, the whole central area having been gradually broken up and denuded. That is why the abrupt, broken edges of the North Downs face south, those of the South Downs north, while both on their opposite sides slope gradually, one to the Thames the other to the Channel. All who have stood in summer at any of the famous view-points on the steep scarps —looking northwards, say, from Chanctonbury or southwards from the Hog's Back—are familiar with the placid blue expanse of the Weald and also with the sandy ridges, often tree-covered, that lie islanded within it. The central sand ridge, best defined in the hills of the Haslemere region and in Ashdown Forest, makes as it were the central prong of a trident of which the outer pair are formed by the North and South Downs; it is the hard core of the vault still resisting denudation while the softer clays on either side (the Vale of Kent and of Sussex) have worn away. These three prongs of higher ground and the vales between them, bounded by the Thames valley and the coastal plain, make up our present region.

(North Downs)

It will be suitable to begin with the North Downs and the country to the north of them. Starting from the famous narrow spine of the Hog's Back these Downs run through Surrey and Kent to be cut short by the sea between Dover and Folkestone. Their line is broken into sections by the northward-flowing rivers Wey, Mole, Darenth, Medway and Stour. As their chalk is often overlaid with clays and other deposits which supported trees and undergrowth, the North Downs were not very attractive to prehistoric settlement and are therefore relatively poor in monuments. Beginning at the western extremity, the first site to mention is off the chalk, on an eminence formed of Bagshot Sand. This is 'Cæsar's Camp', west of the main road from Farnham to Aldershot, an Iron Age entrenchment of no great importance; two other camps lying between the Downs and the Thames are at Weybridge and Wimbledon Common. The first of these is the St. George's Hill camp not far from Brooklands, which has been engulfed in a housing estate but is still very largely intact. It has a good dominating position between the Wey and the Mole at the point where the two rivers approach most nearly to one another and where both are fordable. Perhaps the most accessible monument of all for the Londoner is the Iron Age enclosure towards the west end of Wimbledon Common; it covers about 12 acres, is roughly circular and allows part of its ramparts to add to the hazards of the golf course. After naming another 'Cæsar's Camp', near Holwood, 3 miles south-east of Bromley, we can cross the North Downs to note three camps on the edge of the Greensand escarpment which runs along the southern side of the Downs. All three have fine prospects over the Weald and are well worth visiting. The most westerly is on Hascombe Hill, about 5 miles south-east of Godalming, and is approached by a gradual climb from Hascombe village; the central example is Holmbury, to the west of Leith Hill and probably the most attractive site in Surrey. It can be reached on foot from Holmbury St. Mary, and some of the ramparts, especially where they are double on the west and north, are well enough preserved to be quite imposing. Only a few miles to the east, and east of Leith Hill, is the third camp, Anstiebury, a circular earthwork crowning a steep-sided hill. On the North Downs themselves there is little of note before the Medway gap, where on both sides of the valley there are well-known megalithic tombs of the New Stone Age as well as a few quite interesting round barrows. This group of megaliths is in extraordinary isolation, for there are no others east of Rollright on the Oxford–Warwickshire borders (p. 226). They are attractively set among woods and lie near the Pilgrims' Way just off the edge of the Downs; the most important are Addington, 'the Chestnuts' and Coldrum on the west side of the valley, Countless Stones and Kit's Coty on the east. Taking the western area first, a large round barrow east of the road between Trottescliffe and Wrotham Heath is sufficiently uncommon in this part of the country to be worth mentioning before going further east along the road from Wrotham Heath to Addington, where there are two megalithic sites. The first is a rather tumbled group of sarsens known as 'the Chestnuts' while some 50 yards to the south-east of them the road cuts right through the remains of a megalithic long barrow, which can be seen to have had the oblong enclosure of standing stones and a small rectangular chamber characteristic of this Medway group. The form is, however, even better shown at the Coldrum barrow, which lies a mile and a half north of Addington and can be reached by taking the road from Trottescliffe past the church to Coldrum farm. Here the chamber built of massive stones is well preserved, and when excavated (in 1910) was found to contain the bones of at least 22 individuals, apparently typical Mediterraneans, slight in build, long-headed and with delicate features. The other members of the Medway megalithic group are about 5 miles to the east on the other side of the river —which may best be crossed at Aylesford. Of these the most famous, indeed perhaps the best known megalithic tomb in Britain, is Kit's Coty, above the Maidstone–Rochester road about $1\frac{1}{2}$ miles north-east of Aylesford. Three large upright stones support a wide covering slab to form a chamber which originally stood at one end of a long barrow. About 500 yards to the south a confused group of recumbent stones are the relics of another tomb, probably similar to Coldrum in plan. These are named the Countless Stones, for attached to them is that widespread legend of a magic which makes it impossible to number them correctly. There are remains of other megalithic structures in the immediate neighbourhood, among them the White Horse and Coffin Stones. In the same area an important site of a very different age must be noticed: the Iron Age camp on Oldbury Hill near Ightham, whose fine ramparts are single for most of its circumference but are double on the west side. This camp has been excavated and dated to the later part of the Iron Age. Another most interesting and unusual feature of Oldbury Hill are the two 'rock shelters'—places naturally protected by overhanging rocks that have been occupied by Old Stone Age hunters. Such sites are rare in this country, and especially unexpected in the generally mild landscape of Kent; they yielded excellent tools of the late Acheulio–Levallois phase.

(Canterbury District)

Continuing on our western line there are two sites to be mentioned that lie well off the northern side of the Downs. The first is the Neolithic long barrow called Jullieberrie's or Julaber's Grave (Julaber was a giant), in Chilham parish 6 miles south-west of Canterbury. The second site is an Iron Age one, Bigbury camp at Harbledown, 3 miles west of Canterbury, where the Pilgrims' Way cuts right through the earthwork. It is a small roughly rectangular enclosure with a defensive annex on the north side; excavation has dated it to the Belgic period.

This is probably the best point at which to digress from the itinerary which follows the uplands and their prehistoric sites in order to mention the Roman sites with which east Kent is unusually well endowed. Among the wonderful medieval possessions of Canterbury itself there are a few relics of the Roman town of Durovernum (the south side of the castle wall, the Dane John barrow and a good deal of Roman material re-used in St. Mildred's church and the city walls), but the most important sites, other than Rochester, are the four 'Forts of the Saxon Shore' (p. 147) of Reculver (Regulbium), Richborough (Rutupiae), Dover (Dubris) and Stutfall Castle, Lympne (Lemanis). All are worth seeing. Reculver is at a point west of Herne Bay which in Roman times commanded the northern entry of the Wantsum Channel which separated the Isle of Thanet from the mainland. In Tudor times the outline of the fort was complete, but in subsequent centuries it was rapidly eaten away by the sea, and now, although the encroachment has been checked, the walls that survive are ruinous and much eroded. The twin towers, which are all that survive of a medieval church, contain much Roman building material; standing on the cliff they are a famous landmark for sailors. Richborough, now well inland to the north of Sandwich, when in commission was on an island at the southern end of the Wantsum. It has been fairly thoroughly excavated and is an important and interesting site. As well as the ditches of earlier Roman earthworks, and the foundations of a great stone monument and other Roman structures, the rectangular walls of the Saxon Shore fort are exceptionally impressive, standing in some places as much as 25 feet high, with external ditches and remains of gates; many of the objects found during the excavation are to be seen in the museum on the site (Pl. XVIII).

(Dover—Hythe)

At Dover the fort has disappeared under the modern town, but there is one most remarkable Roman building, the lighthouse (pharos) which still stands to a height of 40 feet within the Castle precincts. It is an octagonal tower showing the characteristic masonry in which courses of stone blocks are bound with courses of red tiles; the windows are Roman work, but the large west door is a Norman addition. The last of the four Kentish forts, known as Stutfall Castle, stands south of Lympne (near Hythe) on a slight hill-slope overlooking Romney Marsh; in the Roman period it was approached by an arm of the sea. It has been much damaged by land-slips, but the walls are still impressive and the greater part of a turret survives at the north-west angle; it has five sides instead of the rectangular plan usual with these forts.

Before leaving these Roman sites note should be made of the foundations of a Roman villa which can be seen on the cliff of East Wear Bay, at Folkestone.

(South Downs)

We have now picked out most of the monuments worth visiting in Surrey and Kent, those which belong to the northern and eastern part of the denuded vault (p. 187). There remains its southern edge, roughly coincident with the county of Sussex. The South Downs have little of the overlying deposits which discouraged early settlement on the North Downs; their relatively bare chalk was always more open and therefore more attractive to prehistoric man, and as they have since been little cultivated they form what is almost a natural museum of ancient sites. But before mounting on to them we must turn for a moment to Pevensey where, on a spur of sand projecting into the Pevensey marshes, is the only Fort of the Saxon Shore in Sussex, and among the most impressive Roman ruins in the country. The walls of this fort of Anderida, built late in the third century, still stand to a height of 20 feet and enclose an oval area of some 8 acres; they are strengthened by ten large bastions. The castle which occupies the eastern end of the enclosure is a Norman work.

To order the abundance of the antiquities of the South Downs, it will be best to study them in the blocks into which they are divided by the rivers Cuckmere, Ouse, Adur and Arun. We can begin with the most easterly of these blocks, that which lies between the great chalk cliffs of Beachy Head and the Cuckmere gap. Eastbourne offers an obvious starting-point. The way over the Downs from Eastbourne to Jevington passes many round barrows, including some of the bell variety, and on Coombe Hill close by Jevington is a small Neolithic causewayed camp, of characteristic plan (p. 29) but difficult to distinguish on the ground. Some $2\frac{1}{2}$ miles due east from here is a Neolithic long barrow; there is another, of small size, at Litlington and a third to the north of Alfriston. From Coombe an attractive path leads to the main eminence of this block of downland, the area centred on Windover Hill. Windover is famous for the chalk-cut figure of the 'Long Man' which from its northern slope looks out over Wilmington village to the Weald. The Long Man is a plain naturalistic figure with a pole (apparently) in either hand; it has, however, the distinctions of being one of the largest representations of the human body in the world and of remaining stubbornly undatable. It is perhaps not prehistoric in its present form. On the slopes of Windover Hill round about the Long Man there are several other antiquities: a fine round barrow just above his head and a long one a little to the west, while away beyond his right hand are pits and bumps that may mark the site of flint mines. A little farther east again is the finest of the long barrows on this section of Down, that known as Hunter's Burgh. Turning south down the Cuckmere Valley we come to Alfriston, whose long barrow has been mentioned, and to Litlington where on the sides of Fore Down the lynchets of a Celtic field system (p. 91) show up very clearly.

We have now reached the second natural section of downland, that lying between the Cuckmere and the Ouse, a compact block which reaches its highest point at Firle Beacon. Crossing the Cuckmere at Alfriston and mounting towards the ridgeway that leads up to Firle, a long barrow 164 feet long and flanked by deep ditches lies on the left of the track while about 300 yards farther on there is another on the right, just above Winton chalk pit. All the way to the summit of the Beacon there are numbers of round barrows, and the hill itself is topped with a large bowl barrow and a long barrow. The branch 'ridgeway' leading due south from Firle Beacon towards Seaford passes more imposing bowl barrows, the best known being Five Lords Burgh which stands where five parishes (now reduced to four) had their junction point. Mention can also be made of an Iron Age camp on Seaford Head, on the coast between Seaford and the mouth of the Cuckmere. The Downs towards Lewes are divided from the Firle range but are still contained between Cuckmere and Ouse. The most important monument there is the camp on Mount Caburn, a roughly circular hill-fort, with a single rampart and ditch on all sides save the north where there are two banks. It is small, but has been exceptionally fully excavated; it was possible to show that it was inhabited throughout the Iron Age down to the time of the Roman Conquest. At its maximum it seems to have had a population of about 300 living in daub and wattle huts with the characteristic deep storage pits sunk in the chalk. There is some evidence to suggest that during the last part of the Iron Age the lord of the Caburn may have had some sort of hegemony over all the downlands east of the Adur. There is also here above Lewes the last of the four long barrows known on this Cuckmere–Ouse section of Down.

The third block of the South Downs, that between Ouse and Adur, is far more substantial than the two already described and consists of three portions—a southern range in the triangle between Lewes, Newhaven and Brighton, the magnificent unbroken ridge that terminates at Ditchling Beacon, and the more diverse hills west of the main Brighton road. The southern portion is notable chiefly for Neolithic sites. It has two long barrows, one at Rottingdean and another at Piddinghoe; it should be noted that after this there are no long barrows known for a distance of nearly 30 miles, when they begin again in the extreme west of Sussex. But the most important Neolithic site on this part of the Downs is the causewayed camp of Whitehawk which is on the north-east outskirts of Brighton, just south of the grandstand on the racecourse. It is partly obliterated by the pulling-up ground of the course, by allotments and roads, but it is still just possible to see the curious characteristic plan of rings of interrupted banks and ditches (p. 29) here, as many as four in number.

Just outside Brighton to the north is another camp, Hollingbury, at the end of a spur running south from the main Ditchling ridge. This camp was occupied during the earlier part of the Iron Age and is the only place where visitors can see a partial reconstruction of the timberwork which was a feature of the ramparts of so many camps of the period.

The Ditchling ridge offers perfect conditions for walking and is well sown with round barrows and minor earthworks, but has nothing individually noteworthy. Indeed, the only other site which need be named in the whole of this Ouse–Adur block is the Devil's Dyke camp on the hill just north of the Dyke station, where a little pleasure-railway runs up on to the Downs from Brighton. This camp was occupied in the Belgic period of the Iron Age; it is oval in plan and has quite well-preserved ramparts.

The fourth block is formed by the continuous ridge and southward-pointing spurs between the rivers Adur and Arun; here for the first time the coastal plain attains a considerable width, so that the principal watering-place, Worthing, is some distance from the Downs. This section of Down is noteworthy for two things, first that it includes more than half of the known South Down flint-mining centres, and second, that in Cissbury it has the camp with the largest area of any in Sussex. If the broad valley of the Adur is crossed at Beeding and Bramber, the first site of note along the main northern ridge is Chanctonbury Ring, a very minor camp made conspicuous and lovely by the beech clump which covers it. Under this clump are the foundations of a Roman Temple. A delightful ridgeway leads southward from Chanctonbury to Cissbury, which lies on a southern spur about 3 miles north of Worthing. The single rampart and ditch of Cissbury, enclosing an oval area of no less than 60 acres, was originally (as in so many camps of this type) faced with wood, and it has been calculated that some 10,000 uprights at least 15 feet long must have been used. The pitting which shows inside the western end of Cissbury and outside on the south marks the filled-in shafts of flint mines, probably over 200 of them. Several have been opened at different times, some of them by no less a person than General Pitt-Rivers, and have been proved to be Neolithic.

Other flint-mining centres in this part of the Downs are on Harrow Hill (4 miles north-west of Cissbury), Church Hill, Findon (1½ miles west of Cissbury) and Blackpatch (3 miles west). Excavations have been made among them all and while the mining at Harrow Hill seems to have been mainly in Neolithic times, the other two centres certainly continued in use well into the Bronze Age. All these mining areas show on the surface as broken and irregular patches of mounds and hollows.

The fifth section of the South Downs now to be described lies to the west of the Arun, but has no well-defined western limit as it becomes one with the main chalk massif of Wessex.

West of the Arun the chalk widens out and is much more wooded; this is the country of magnificent beech hangers. Crossing the delicious water meadows of the Arun at Amberley, it is worth keeping to the northern foot of the Downs to visit the Roman villa at Bignor and so to climb up once more by

Stane Street, the Roman road from Chichester which cuts boldly across the Downs at this point. The Roman road leads one immediately to remains some 2000 years earlier, for on the spur of Bignor Hill known as Barkhale Down is a small, unexplored example of a Neolithic causewayed camp. Between this point and the Midhurst–Chichester road there is a fine uninterrupted ridgeway passing through the usual scatter of round barrows, especially fine groups, mainly of the bowl type, standing on Waltham, Graffham and Heyshott Downs. But it is well to the south of this northern scarp that the most interesting site is to be found. Many people know Goodwood as one of the loveliest racecourses in the country; on the hill overlooking it from the west is a fine earthwork known as the Trundle, the circular rampart being like a hoop or 'trundle'. This is an Iron Age camp; inside is a much smaller and fainter ring, clearly visible only from the air, which represents part of the defences of a Neolithic causewayed camp. This is perhaps the moment to call attention to Chichester, as its position on the coastal plain is almost due south from the Trundle. There is not very much to be seen of Roman Chichester (Regnum or Noviomagus), but one of the most important inscriptions in Britain is to be seen built into the wall of the portico of the Council House in North Street. This is the Cogidubnus stone which records the dedication of a temple by the authority of this Celtic king, a vassal of the Roman Empire; it must have been set up as early as A.D. 60–70. There are interesting stretches of linear earthworks (dykes) to the north of the town, possibly (like those at Colchester and St. Albans, pp. 247, 250) built by the Belgæ who had a settlement somewhere near what was later to be the site of Regnum. About 15 miles west of Chichester, Porchester on the north side of Portsmouth harbour is perhaps the finest of all the forts of the Saxon shore; practically the whole of the rectangular walls and their bastions are standing right at the water's edge. As at Pevensey (p. 192), there is a Norman castle in one corner of the Roman fort.

The Downs west of the Midhurst–Chichester road are beautifully varied between woods and open grass, while there are occasional groves of yew trees, with their strange atmosphere, like that of Kingley Vale. Bow Hill against Kingley Vale is particularly rich in antiquities; on the crest are four large round barrows, two bowl and two bell, known as the Devil's Humps; they have been dated to the Early Bronze Age. About a mile west of them, on the western spur of Bow Hill, is a fine example of a type of barrow extremely rare except on Salisbury Plain, a double bell barrow with two mounds standing on a platform with an oval ditch. On the nearby Stoughton Down there are two small long barrows, while another, called Baverse's Thumb, is a little farther north on Telegraph Hill. These three long barrows (the last in Sussex) represent the recommencement of this type of monument after the gap in their distribution which occurs in central Sussex (p. 194). On the ridgeway between this point and the Cocking Gap on the Midhurst road there are many round barrows including a notable group named the Devil's Jumps just north-west of Monkton Down.

Moving now westward to the junction of the South Downs with the wider chalklands of Hampshire, we find a number of varied and not precisely datable minor earthworks (notably on Butser Hill), and, on Old Winchester Hill, a single-ramparted Iron Age camp with a number of barrows standing within it. Here, overlooking the Meon Valley, we are on the threshold of Wessex. We will advance just far enough over it, another ten miles, to reach Winchester itself, where above the Itchen to the south of the city is the well-known camp of St. Catharine's Hill, which represents the native stronghold that was in use through the Iron Age until it was sacked by the Belgæ. Of Roman Winchester (Venta Belgarum) remains can only be seen in the City Museum; there are also relics indicating a previous Belgic occupation on its site.

II. WESSEX

This section will give the widest possible interpretation to the term Wessex, for it will not only cover the main chalk uplands of Hampshire, Wiltshire and Dorset, but will also be stretched to include the 'White Horse Hills', cut off though these are by the Vales of Pewsey and Kennet. South of these vales Wessex is a basin of chalk, filled in the middle with clays and sands; in effect, a ring of chalk hills with their steep scarps facing outward and their inner sides sloping gradually down to the central basin that is largely occupied by the sandy territories of the New Forest. We have already followed those out-thrust fingers of chalk the North and South Downs to their junction with the Hampshire Downs; these in their turn form a more or less continuous plateau with Salisbury Plain, while to the south-west the Plain runs into the Western Downs which include Cranborne Chase. From here the chalk not only runs on westward, but also swings sharply east, into the spine of the Purbeck Hills: then, having been broken by the sea, it re-emerges at the Needles of the Isle of Wight and terminates in a narrow ridge running west and east across that island. This southern rim of the chalk basin is of course infinitely slender when compared with the great northern arc of the Hampshire Downs and Salisbury Plain. The basin is drained by a fan of rivers rising in or beyond the chalk uplands and flowing into the sea between Selsey and Purbeck; from east to west these are the Itchen, Test, Avon, Stour and Frome.

Archæologically Wessex is in many respects the richest and most significant region in the whole country; it possesses so many monuments that it will be possible to mention only the most outstanding.

(North Hampshire Downs)

Setting out from our previous starting-point of Cæsar's Camp, Aldershot (p. 188; and incidentally another Cæsar's Camp, that at Easthampstead 10 miles northward, ought perhaps to be mentioned), we enter the new region from the North Downs and are immediately on the ancient track called the Harroway. There are no major prehistoric sites east of Basingstoke, but northward, between the chalk and the Roman town of Silchester, there is the multi-ramparted Iron Age camp of Bullsdown. Silchester itself is a most fascinating site; the complete circuit of the walls of the small provincial town of Calleva Atrebatum stand there among fields and heaths, with nothing more inside them than a small medieval parish church and an old farmhouse. These walls are probably Severan in age, but outside are banks and ditches belonging to the earlier Roman defences of Flavian times. Returning to the chalk, just west of Basingstoke and east of the Roman road from Silchester to Winchester, is the much damaged Iron Age camp of Winklebury, and from it an old ridgeway westward along the northern scarp of the Downs passes close to the south of two other camps, Ladle Hill and Beacon Hill. Ladle Hill, a camp of circular plan, is of interest mainly because it was never finished and so still shows the method by which the rampart was dug in sections; a good example of disc barrow can be seen 40 yards down the hill on its western side. Ladle Hill is a conspicuous, dominating site and so also is Beacon Hill (the Berkshire Beacon) just to the west. The camp there has an hour-glass plan and there are a number of 'hut-circles' within the ramparts; from its walls a dozen other hill-forts are visible. A mile or so to the south of Beacon Hill is the Seven Barrows group of large round barrows, while a long barrow lies on the southern slope of the ridge at Woodcote, about 3 miles south-west of Beacon Hill. Again following the commanding ridgeway of the northern scarp of the Downs we reach Walbury, a site which occupies one of the highest points of chalk in the whole country (959 feet). It is also the largest camp in Hampshire (82 acres); the single rampart is roughly quadrangular. There is a long barrow at Combe Gibbet a quarter of a mile westward, and five good round barrows three-quarters of a mile farther on again; and, where this ridge of the Hampshire North Downs merges into Salisbury Plain, there is a noteworthy megalithic-chambered long barrow at Tidcombe. From this site a track leads back eastward to Fosbury, a large, irregularly shaped camp with double ramparts. Special mention should also here be made to the Kenwardstone, a recumbent slab carved with patterns recalling those of north Wales and Ireland (p. 45) but most unexpected here between Fosbury and Tidcombe.

(Central Hampshire)

We have now followed the Northern Hampshire Downs to the limit of the county and the verge of Salisbury Plain, and we must turn southward to survey the antiquities lying on the lower country to the south and on the uplands of the South Hampshire Downs beyond. Andover is the main town which lies towards the centre of this area, while the Test valley provides a dominant geographical feature, and one which was of great significance in prehistoric times. Returning to start again on the eastern side of the area, the camp of Tidbury 6 miles east of Andover is just worth naming, together with the Andyke, a linear earthwork (bank and ditch) which cuts off a headland down against the Test some 2 miles west of the camp. But of considerably greater interest is Bury Hill camp, just outside Andover to the south-west. Here there is an inner ring of multiple ramparts dating from the later phase of the Iron Age, while the single outer rampart belongs to the earlier Iron Age; between this and Andover town is the larger but simpler camp of Balksbury. Mounting now on to the principal ridge of the South Hampshire Downs, two long barrows on Moody's Down just south of the village of Barton Stacey should be noted, together with a third example on Chilbolton Down a little to the west. This leads us on to where the Iron Age camps of Woolbury and Danebury lie east and west respectively of the narrow valley of the Test where it cuts through the Downs. Woolbury, with its single rampart of irregular plan, is undistinguished though beautifully sited, but Danebury is an exceptionally imposing and highly complex fort with three approximately circular ramparts, the innermost of very great size, although masked by a plantation of beech and pine. Only 600 yards north of this magnificent Iron Age camp is a characteristic pair of Neolithic long barrows. Moving again westward, at the end of the South Hampshire Downs where they join the Plain, we encounter Quarley Hill camp, where a single line of ramparts follows the contour of an isolated pear-shaped hill, conspicuous from the Southern Railway just on the Salisbury side of Grately station; it has been dated to the earlier part of the Iron Age and overlies earlier boundary-ditches.

(*South Hampshire*)

Before embarking upon the survey of the immense archæological riches of Salisbury Plain and Cranborne Chase, we must name the scattered sites of southern Hampshire, few and far between on the sands and clays at the centre of the Hampshire basin (p. 198). We penetrated as far as Winchester while dealing with the south-eastern region (p. 197); 4 miles to the west of the city Merdon Castle suggests an interesting mixture of periods, for an outer rampart which is almost certainly prehistoric encloses the massive earthen keep and bailey works of a Norman castle. Leaping southward, the remains of Roman Clausentum are to be found within the grounds of Bitterne Manor on the outskirts of Southampton: a strange place, with an atmosphere quite its own.

It is impossible to name all the minor embanked enclosures that exist in the New Forest and round its north-eastern edge, but right on the southern fringe of the Forest, Buckland Rings, near Lymington, is a fine triple-ramparted camp, of an irregular plan, dating from the later part of the Iron Age. Finally in this area there remains Hengistbury Head, where a double line of bank and ditch isolates the promontory which juts between Christchurch Harbour (certainly a leading port in prehistoric times) and the sea; excavation has identified Bronze Age barrows, and a succession of Iron Age and Roman occupations.

(Berkshire Downs)

We will now leave Hampshire and return to the north, not far from the point where we left the North Hampshire Downs at Fosbury and Tidcombe (p. 199). The Berkshire Downs, which together with the Marlborough Downs are often known as the White Horse Hills, form only an outlier of the main chalk plateau of Wessex, from which they are separated by the Kennet and the Vale of Pewsey. This outlying position is emphasized by the fact that they drain northward into the Thames. We can start, then, at the east end of the Berkshire Downs, along the length of which runs the ancient green track known as the Ridgeway, while below, along their northern foot, follows the Icknield Way. These Downs are quite prolific in monuments, and no individual mention can be made of the round barrows which are scattered along them, most plentifully on the slopes to the south of the Ridgeway. North of their eastern extremity, and overlooking the Thames, note should be made of Sinodun (a bogus antiquary's name this), a modest but beautifully sited camp which encircles one of the two hills known as Wittenham Clumps. Dorchester, too, can be named here, though it lies just across the Thames; its Roman defences are largely invisible, but the Dyke Hills earthworks seem to defend an Iron Age promontory-site on the head between Thames and Thame. Returning to the Ridgeway, at Churn Knob in Blewbury parish it passes a long barrow, and some miles farther on a camp known either as Letcombe Castle or Segsbury. Here the scarp of the Downs, so familiar to those who follow the G.W.R. to Swindon, is extremely steep, and the stretch of the Ridgeway past Uffington makes one of the loveliest and most moving of walks. The Way here passes just above the famous White Horse, whose fantastic form (p. 125) we now know to have been cut into the chalk at the end of the Iron Age about 2000 years ago. It is said that any wish made while standing in the horse's eye will surely come true. Close above and to the west of the White Horse is Uffington Castle, a notable Iron Age camp whose single rampart and ditch enclose the highest point of the Berkshire Downs; an interesting entrance should be noticed on the west side. Only just over a mile farther on, the Ridgeway passes Wayland's Smithy, hardly less well known than the White Horse itself. Wayland's Smithy, despite its legendary association with the iron-smith, is actually a Neolithic long barrow with a cruciform megalithic chamber, an eastern outlier of the chambered long barrows of the Cotswold region (pp. 227-32).

On the milder southern slopes of the Downs in this area is yet another well-known site, Lambourn Seven Barrows, lying in a hollow 2 miles north of Lambourn village. This is a group of round barrows numbering nearer 20 than 7, and including some of the disc type; several have been dug and have yielded relics of the Early, Middle and Late Bronze Age. It is just worth mentioning also Alfred's Castle, a small but striking Iron Age camp about 3 miles west of the Severn Barrows and 2 south of Wayland's Smithy; there are fine bowl barrows on Idstone Down close by to the south of Alfred's Castle. Membury is another large camp in this area, right on the county boundary.

There are a number of camps in southern Berkshire on the spurs leading towards the Kennet valley: Perborough, Oareborough, Borough Hill, Bussocks and Grimbury are all in a small area north of Newbury.

(*Wansdyke*)

We have now to cross into Wiltshire, and this affords a convenient moment to mention that remarkable earthwork, the Wansdyke. This is a 60-mile line of bank and ditch facing northward; it is known to be post-Roman (or very late Roman) and may have been built in the fifth century by the Britons against the Saxon invaders. The extreme eastern end of it is encountered here at Inkpen on the Wiltshire-Hampshire-Berkshire borders, and from this point it runs by Chisbury camp (to the south of the Hungerford–Marlborough road) and is then lost within the confines of Savernake Forest. But west of the Forest, near the railway embankment, it begins again and in imposing form goes almost due west past West Woods, then more northerly to Kennet and Silbury Hill, then to Morgan's Hill where its line coincides with that of the Roman road to Bath; it passes from Wiltshire into Somerset (where we shall meet it again, p. 214) between Corsham and Atworth.

(*Marlborough Downs*)

Following the course of the Wansdyke has led us right across the county and we must return to the Marlborough Downs, but before going on it is well to make it clear once more that as from this point south across Salisbury Plain and Cranborne Chase we are dealing with what is archæologically the richest part of England (p. 4); it is quite impossible to give individual mention to the majority of monuments. There are, for instance, about one hundred long barrows in Wiltshire alone, and round barrows innumerable. It is only possible to call attention to the areas of greatest concentration and to name a very few barrows of exceptional interest.

The first site to be noticed is Liddington Castle, a camp lying beside the continuation of the Berkshire Ridgeway to the south-east of Swindon; it is, however, less fine than the magnificent

Barbury Castle, whose double ramparts adjoin Hackpen Hill about half-way between Swindon and Marlborough. Just outside Marlborough to the west there is a long barrow with a megalithic chamber on Manton Down, near Manton House. Now we are approaching that wonderful group of ancient monuments that centre upon Avebury, 5 miles west from Marlborough. First there is the great temple itself (p. 57), and the Avenue of standing stones, leading to Overton Hill, where the second circle known as the Sanctuary is now marked out with accurately-placed but unsightly concrete blocks. Conspicuous by the roadside near the Sanctuary is a well-known group of round barrows, part of a concentration of barrows in this sacred area. At Beckhampton are the two large standing stones called Adam and Eve, while north-west of Avebury is the causewayed camp of Windmill Hill, which has given its name to the leading Neolithic culture of Britain (p. 29); on this hill also there are some large round barrows. There still remain in this really astonishing neighbourhood, Silbury Hill, apparently a huge round barrow but almost too big to be believed, and the chambered long barrow of West Kennet; Silbury is close to the north, and West Kennet to the south, of the Marlborough–Chippenham road. The Downs on the southern side of the road in this region can show another half-dozen long barrows, and at Knap Hill above Alton Priors there is an unexplored Neolithic causewayed camp, and also a Belgic Iron Age enclosure. On the western edge of the Marlborough Downs are Oldbury, a formidable double-ramparted camp in Cherhill parish, and Oliver's Castle farther south on a spur of Roundway Down. Wansdyke (p. 203) runs between these two camps.

(Salisbury Plain)

We have now dealt with the principal sites of the Marlborough Downs and can cross the Vale of Pewsey to reach the northern edge of Salisbury Plain. The Plain is, of course, thickly studded with round and long barrows, especially round Stonehenge where, as at Avebury, there was evidently an eagerness to bury the dead near a sacred place. Starting as we are from the north, there is nothing worth special mention before Bratton Castle, a spectacular camp near Westbury; south of Bratton, beautifully placed in open country above the Wylye, on the north side of the valley 2½ miles east-south-east of Warminster, are two more Iron Age camps, mysterious for their closeness to one another, Battlesbury and Scratchbury. The latter has a single rampart, irregular in outline, and an apparently earlier inner ring; the former is round and has double ramparts. Why so much labour should have been expended in duplicate, and whether they were ever both in use at the same time is at present unknown.

About half-way between Bratton and Stonehenge there are exceptionally fine long barrows round Tilshead, one of them, at 400 feet, is probably the longest in the county. Stonehenge itself, three miles west of Amesbury on the Warminster road, is perhaps too well known to need further description (p. 59), but some of the associated features should be noted. There is the faintly marked line of the 'Avenue' (two parallel banks with flanking ditches clearly visible from the air), which runs from the temple north-east, then forks to send one arm south to the Avon, while another goes north to the so-called Cursus. This is a long narrow rectangular area enclosed between banks which runs east and west on the northern side of Stonehenge; its purpose is uncertain—Stukeley ingeniously suggested that it must have been a chariot-racing course.

No less than 300 barrows cluster round Stonehenge, and among them there is a notable group forming a line south of the Cursus; it includes huge examples of the bell and bowl types and one of the 'twin' variety in which two barrows are enclosed by one ditch. A second even better group (Pl. XXI), and one which includes a long barrow, is west of the temple at the Winterbourne cross-roads, while a third, perhaps the finest group of barrows in the county, is on Normanton Down, due south from Stonehenge. These are not only varied in type (disc, bowl, bell, twin bell), extremely well preserved and imposing, but are also of special interest for the wealth of the Bronze Age burials which they covered; the grave goods included ornaments of gold and of amber.

The immediate Amesbury district is also of considerable interest. The road from Stonehenge to Amesbury cuts through a large earthwork, known absurdly as Vespasian's Camp, on

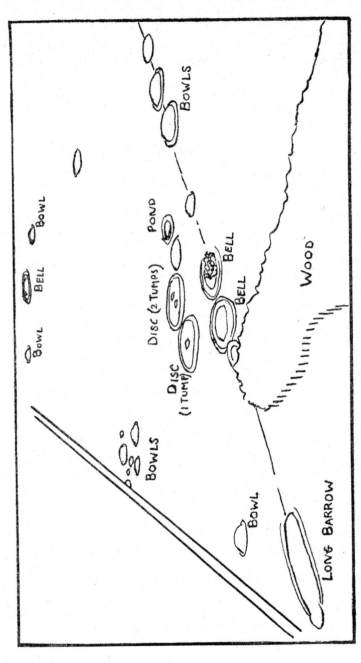

Fig. 30.—Key to Pl. XXI. The group of barrows at Winterbourne Cross-roads, near Stonehenge.

Plate XXI

Types of burial mound.   The group of barrows at Winterbourne Cross-roads, near Stonehenge
(*see key sketch opposite*)

Plate XXII

Crown Copyright reserved

Types of fortification. Two Iron Age hill-forts in Dorset ; Hod
Hill (*top*), multiple-ramparted, with a Roman fort constructed
in the lower corner ; Hambledon Hill (*bottom*), another multiple-
ramparted type

a promontory overlooking the Avon. Just outside Amesbury to the north-east, near Durrington, is the remarkable Bronze Age monument which, since its excavation in the 1920's, has been known as Woodhenge. This name indicates the fact that it is apparently a smaller structure more or less of the Stonehenge type, but with wooden instead of stone architecture. The numerous concentric circles of holes which once held wooden posts are now marked with concrete blocks looking even more hideous than those at the Sanctuary (p. 204). Immediately to the north of Woodhenge, Durrington Walls is a penannular earthwork with the ditch inside the bank; this plan suggests that it, too, is a sacred site.

Leaving now a region which is perhaps archæologically the most important in Britain, we find beside the Winterbourne Stoke–Wylye road, 7 miles from Stonehenge, an exceptionally fine camp, Yarnbury, built on almost level ground. The main earthwork has three well-preserved banks, but inside them are faint traces of another ring, which has been proved to belong to a camp of the earlier Iron Age. A few miles eastward, on the Downs near Codford, is a circular earthwork and a good group of barrows. Drawing close to Salisbury itself, it should be said that the huge earthworks of Old Sarum that mark the site of the early medieval town probably incorporate the remains of an Iron Age camp. About 4 miles north-east of the city is a well-known circular camp, Figsbury Rings; it is a mournful yet most striking place, with the curious feature of an inner ring of ditch with no corresponding bank.

(Cranborne Chase)

To the west and south of Salisbury we enter Cranborne Chase, another region of immense archæological importance, and of archæological sentiment too, for the Chase contains the house of General Pitt-Rivers, and was the centre of his greatest activities. The finds from many of his digs are housed in the museum which he established on his estate at Farnham, reached by a right-hand turn from the Salisbury–Blandford road. Beginning in the north we can note on the left of the Salisbury to Shaftesbury road an almost perfectly circular earthwork, the camp of Chiselbury, while 3 or 4 miles westward, still just within the bounds of the Chase, is Castle Ditches. This second camp is on a wooded greensand hill dominating a stretch of the Nadder a mile and a half from Tisbury; it has multiple ramparts of heart-shaped outline, very strong indeed on the south-east side. The walk from Chiselbury along Swallowcliffe Down (leaving Castle Ditches to the north) is a lovely one, and so is its continuation (past a long barrow) to Whitesheet Hill. A crossing of the little Don valley brings us to the much overgrown camp of Castle Rings, which occupies the east end of the greensand ridge of Shaftesbury.

We have now covered the northern part of the Chase between Ebble and Nadder; considerably richer is the great stretch of wild chalk upland south and west of the Nadder with spurs running away towards the south-east, a region drained by minor tributaries of the Avon and Stour. Few highways pass so many antiquities as the bold stretch of the Salisbury–Blandford road where it crosses this area. This road follows the line of the Roman one from Old Sarum to Dorchester (Dorset) until a point about half-way to Blandford where, by the turning to Pentridge, the Roman road dramatically leaves it and can be seen going straight on while the modern road bears to the right. A little before this point the road has passed the Romano-British village of Woodyates excavated by Pitt-Rivers; this settlement lies just in front of the three-mile-long linear earthwork of Bokerly Dyke, which can be seen climbing up the hill on the left-hand side of the road towards Pentridge and Tidpit Down. Behind this dyke (which faces north-east) there are three long barrows in a straight line among a number of round ones. In the triangle between the modern Blandford road, the Roman road and the side road to Cranborne village, there is one of the largest barrow groups in the county; it includes two diminutive long barrows as well as bowl, bell and notable disc types. A little farther along the Blandford road, just past the turn to Gussage and opposite the Farnham road, are the two Thickthorn long barrows; there are three more on the other side of the Gussage road, and two others again north of the main road between Chettle and Tarrant Gunville.

Thickthorn offers a suitable point from which to make two sudden excursions off our road, one northwards, the other to the south. The first takes us to the higher downs north of the Blandford road, past the famous but now inconspicuous Romano-British village sites of Woodcuts (set between clusters of round barrows) and Rotherley, to Winkelbury camp, a fine site on a spur overlooking the source of the Ebble and close to Berwick St. John. Returning to the neighbourhood of Thickthorn, the second excursion takes us across the Blandford road south-westerly along the by-road which follows the Gussage Brook, then across the Allen Brook to the Knowlton Circles. This is a most remarkable group of banked enclosures, that appear from their plan with the ditch inside the bank to be sacred sites or 'henges'. Of the four probable examples only one is well preserved; here a certain natural strangeness (the place is, in some quite peculiar way, remote) is enhanced by the presence inside the prehistoric ring of a ruined church and derelict church-yard. Near by to the east of this circle is a very large round barrow under a clump of trees; air photography has shown it to have encircling ditch at some distance from the mound. If we return yet again to the Blandford road and follow it to within 4 miles of that most enchanting country town, we pass on the right-hand side one of the finest and least damaged of Wessex long barrows, that of Pimperne. The line of Iron Age camps which stand along the south-west limit of the Chase overlooking the Stour valley can now be described. The most southerly, half-way between Blandford and Wimborne, is the imposing Badbury Rings, made so conspicuous by the round clump of pine trees that fills its centre. This strong, oval camp has a double line of ramparts surrounded by a third, much weaker. The Roman road to Dorchester (which we left on the Blandford road) grazes past the north-west side of this camp, with its central causeway flanked by well-marked banks and ditches. A little beyond Badbury on the south-west a line of Roman barrows have, in the frequent practice of their time, been raised by the roadside. Buzbury Rings, between Badbury and Blandford above the river Tarrant, is an insignificant-looking earthwork, but 6 miles to the north-west of Blandford, over-looking the Stour in the westernmost extremity of Cranborne Chase, we reach two camps which together are more impressive than any others in Wessex save Maiden Castle; their setting, too, is very lovely (Pl. XXII). These camps are on isolated hills,

P

south-western outliers of the main Cranborne Chase massif. At Hambledon Hill, the more northerly of the two, three huge ramparts enclose the top of a long narrow spur; there is a long barrow at the centre (where the earthwork is at its narrowest and bends slightly), and there appear to be signs of a Neolithic causewayed camp near the southern end. The second site, Hod Hill, is a big squarish hill separated from Hambledon by the pretty road that runs from Steepleton Iwerne to Okeford and Shillingstone; the camp, as it follows the contours, is squarish also; on three sides there are triple banks, but on the steep side overlooking the Stour these are reduced to two. By the south-west corner is a fine entrance where the ramparts stand 40 feet above the ditch. Most curious and unexpected of all is the small Roman camp which has been made by cutting off the north-west angle of the older camp. Excavations at Hod Hill discovered material of the later Iron Age, as well as important Roman military and other remains. Hod and Hambledon Hills are exceptional in their closeness to one another (the best comparison, on a smaller scale, is offered by Scratchbury and Battlebury, p. 205) and in their noble situation; few sites are better worth a visit.

This account of Cranborne Chase has hitherto ignored the eastern area which lies due south of Salisbury along the west side of the Avon. In the north of this territory (Woodbury (p. 101) is invisible except from the air) there is Clearbury Ring, in a strong position on an isolated hill in the angle between Ebble and Avon, a single-ramparted rectangular camp entirely filled with beech trees and Scots pine. Four miles south of Clearbury is the much larger Whitsbury Castle Ditches, an oval camp with triple ramparts. One portion of a meandering dyke known as Grims Ditch runs from Clearbury to Whitsbury, but the longer arm follows a zigzag course due westward until it crosses the Salisbury–Blandford road a little to the north of Bokerly Dyke. Within these arms of dyke and north-west of Whitsbury there is an extensive Romano-British enclosure, an Iron Age farm site and numbers of round barrows on the barren and inhospitable Rockbourne Down; there is also a long barrow at the place called the Duck's Nest. Just to the south there is a tree-grown and undistinguished camp on Damerham Knoll and another beyond it on the top of Pentridge or Pembury

Knoll; south-west again is a very neatly dug kite-shaped earth-work, almost certainly a Roman pastoral enclosure, known as Soldier's Ring.

(*West Hampshire—Dorset*)

Having described the major monuments of Cranborne Chase we can turn to the parts of Hampshire and Dorset west of the Stour, a region which cannot compare with Salisbury Plain and the Chase but is nevertheless quite rich in antiquities. The promontory fort of Hengistbury Head on the Avon–Stour estuary has already been mentioned (p. 201). Behind Bourne-mouth on the Corfe Hills there are quantities of round barrows but nothing of special note until we come to the heart-shaped camp of Spettisbury, between Wimborne and Blandford. Standing on the edge of Spettisbury village, it has been cut through by the railway; quite by chance this cutting revealed a Celtic war cemetery that contained interesting late Iron Age grave-goods, including swords and sword sheaths, currency bars, brooches and a cauldron. The camp stands on this west side of the Stour looking over towards Badbury Rings.

A more prolific area is the great chalk ridge (the southern rim of the basin defined on p. 198) stretching from Purbeck past Dorchester on to its western edge at Eggardun and Chil-combe. There are plenty of barrows on the Purbeck pro-montory, but it is from Poxwell, Osmington and White Horse Hill that the more interesting country begins. Along White Horse Hill (the name refers to a chalk-cut equestrian figure of George III) goes a fine ridgeway which passes a cluster of round barrows north of Sutton Poyntz. West of that village, on a spur running south from the main ridge, is Chalbury camp; it has stone-built ramparts and a fine position overlooking Weymouth Bay. Returning to the ridgeway, there are excep-tional clusters of round barrows on either side of it east of Came Wood and between it and the Dorchester–Weymouth road. One long barrow can be recognized to the north of a tree-set round barrow which is known as Culliford Tree. From this point, where the ridgeway joins the Dorchester road, it is only a mile and a half northward to Maiden Castle, the most spectacular

Iron Age camp in Britain and one which needs no further description here (pp. 114, 128, 171). There are several fine round barrows near it, including the well-known Clandon barrow (close by on the north-west), which yielded an amber cup and gold ornaments that now form part of the admirable prehistoric collections in the Dorchester Museum. Before, however, we can push farther west along the chalk ridge we should continue northward along the road towards Dorchester; on the right-hand side on the outskirts of the town is the oval embankment of Maumbury Rings, a site with a most varied history. Originally it seems to have been a Bronze Age sacred site of the 'henge' type; some 1500 years later it was remodelled as a Roman amphitheatre for the citizens of Durnovaria (Dorchester); in the seventeenth century it was cut about to serve as a gun emplacement for the Parliamentary forces; in 1940 it formed part of an anti-invasion road block. Just west of Dorchester on a low hill above the railway tunnel, overlooking the Frome, is the extensive but not very strong single-ramparted camp of Poundbury; a stretch of the aqueduct which served Durnovaria is to be seen here—but only with very great difficulty.

In all the attractive downland country north of Dorchester there are scattered round barrows, and on Smacam Down east of Sydling St. Nicholas there is a long barrow and several minor earthworks, but the one site really worthy of comment is Cerne Abbas. It is an agreeable relief to interrupt the monotonous catalogue of camps, barrows and the rest with a unique monument. Most people have heard of the Cerne Abbas giant, a huge fertility-figure cut in the hillside just north of the village. It is probably of Roman date and may illustrate the combination of a Celtic fertility personification with Hercules, for the giant holds a club in his right hand, while there is a possible suggestion of a 'lion skin' (now overgrown) on his other arm. Near him is a small square earthwork, perhaps a sacred enclosure.

We will now retreat south again to the ridge of chalk to pick up the ridgeway which we left south of Maiden Castle on the Weymouth road at Bincombe. This Way continues west of the road, passing many round barrows; notably good examples of the bell-and-bowl type are to be seen on Brankham Hill, which leads up towards the Hardy Monument on Blackdown. Blackdown itself is not chalk but sandy heath; it is dotted with round barrows including two bells. Near here, north-east of Portisham, are interesting remains of a megalithic chamber known as the Hell Stone; a large roof slab is supported on 9 uprights. This chamber in its present form is much restored, it may once have been contained in a long barrow. West of Portisham on Hampton Down stands what is left of a stone circle, while just north of Abbotsbury (with its incomparable swannery) is the Grey Mare and Her Colts, which, like the Hell Stone, is the burial-chamber of a long barrow. Farther west again, and this is a lovely walk above the sea, there is another stone circle south-west of Little Bredy. A third of this group of Dorset stone circles is the Nine Stones at Winterborne Abbas on the left of the Dorchester–Bridport road. Quite a short distance farther along, and on the same side of the road, there is a long barrow at Longlands. The road continues to pass round barrows, and just beyond Kingston Russell a long barrow should be noticed, again on the left; also an odd 200-foot strip of dyke with a ditch along both sides. There are many large round barrows, one with a monolith on it, between this point and Watcombe Down to the south-east. From Kingston Russell to the southern end of the chalk ridge at Chilcombe Down this road still passes several dykes, barrows and an earth circle opposite the turning to Litton Cheyney. We need not, however, end this section at Chilcombe, but far more nobly at the northern side of this last westward extension of the chalk. A track leaving the road a mile before Chilcombe, and passing Stancombe Barn, crosses an expanse of wild bare down to Eggardun. Eggardun marks the end of the chalk which we have been travelling for so long; it is the setting of a well-known Hardy scene, and it is in its own right a striking and dramatic place. The strong, multiple-banked camp looks out over Powerstock and all the more wooded country to the north; here Wessex is at an end, and our south-western region begins.

III. THE SOUTH-WEST

The ending of the chalk in the west makes a profound break in the character of the country, and we shall therefore include in the south-western region that part of Dorset which lies beyond it, together with Somerset, Devon and Cornwall. This includes the southern tip of the great strip of limestone (the 'Jurassic Belt') that runs from Portland Bill to Northumberland. Once we have pushed on south and west beyond the limestone we are in true Highland Zone country (p. 3) with the Old Red Sandstone of the Quantocks and Exmoor, the great granite masses of Dartmoor and Bodmin Moor, and then the lesser ones of St. Austell, Redruth and Land's End. Away to the north the region is bounded by the Mendips. These are intermediate in age, for their limestone is more ancient than that of the Jurassic belt, being comparable rather with the Pennine rocks.

(Bath—Bristol)

We will approach this region by way of this northern extension, our point of departure being the southern extremity of the Cotswolds (p. 232). There are several places worth visiting near Bath (whose baths and other Roman remains should, of course, be seen), though none is of outstanding interest. On Landsdown to the north are many round barrows and a camp (Littledown), to the south-east Bathampton has more barrows and a larger camp, covered in Roman times by fields and now by a golf course. Both this and Stantonbury camp near Stanton Prior to the west of Bath have the added interest of adjoining the line of Wansdyke, the most impressive earthwork in Somerset, whose more easterly portion we have already traced in Wessex (p. 203). From Stantonbury the Wansdyke has been traced over Dundry Hill, and more doubtfully right across the country to the sea at Portishead. Another monument in the Bath district which is worthy of mention is Stony Littleton long barrow, near the village of Wellow about 4 miles south of the city. This is a fine and intact example of chambered long barrow, an outlier of the Cotswold group. The megalithic chamber is of the typologically early form with a central passage and pairs of side chambers. Another noteworthy though much damaged example of this kind of monument, with the enchanting name of Fairy Toot, is some 12 miles to the west, on the north slopes of the Mendips at Nempnett Thrubwell. In between these two is another megalithic monument of a very different

type. At Stanton Drew, a village 4 miles north-east of Nempnett Thrubwell and 6½ south and a little east of Bristol, in a
meadow near the river Clew, is a complex of standing stones
including three circles, avenues and several other megalithic
groups. Finally about 4 miles north-west of Nempnett Thrubwell there is a megalithic chamber, without covering mound,
behind Cornerpool farm at Redhill, Wrington. We are now
near Bristol and note should be made of Cadbury Camp about
8 miles west of the city. It is a fine camp with 2 and sometimes
3 ramparts and with a splendid view over the Bristol Channel
and Severn Mouth. There are many lesser camps in the neighbourhood—Wain's Hill (Clevedon Pill), Failand and Rhodyate
Hill (Yatton).

(Mendips and Quantocks)

Turning southwards again we come to the Mendips, one of
the archæologically richest and best explored areas in the south-
west, and remarkable above all for the Palæolithic cave dwellings
found in its limestone ravines. If we begin at the western end
of the Mendips there are two coastal camps, a southern one
represented by a series of banks and ditches cutting off the
promontory of Brean Down, and a northern one, Worlebury,
on the hill just north of Weston Super Mare. Worlebury is
protected to the north by natural escarpments and on the west
by the sea, but the other two sides have colossal ramparts of
rough limestone blocks. Moving eastward along the Mendips
away from the sea we pass many round barrows, and another
Iron Age camp with massive limestone walls at Dolbury; yet
another camp lies on the north-east side of Burrington Combe
just above the village of that name. But Burrington Combe
brings us to one of the great Palæolithic centres. This Combe
is a cleft in the north face of the Mendips, less spectacular than
Cheddar but still very impressive. It has several caves, a number
of which contained Pleistocene animal remains, while one,
Aveline's Hole, was frequented by Palæolithic hunters and has
yielded some good finds, including a Magdalenian type of
harpoon (p. 18), shell necklaces and important human skeletal
remains. Cheddar Gorge itself lies due south straight across

the Mendip ridge; although too much a show place, it remains magnificent. The prime show cavern of the Gorge, called Gough's Cave, contained quantities of Palæolithic implements in flint and bone, as well as 'Cheddar Man', a skeleton which is on view near the cave mouth. Several other caves in the Gorge have produced Palæolithic finds, the most interesting being the fine Solutrean flint (so rare in this country) from Soldier's Hole, a small cave reached by a steep scramble some 200 yards above Gough's. Pushing on eastward now from these famous cave areas of Burrington and Cheddar, high on the crest of Mendip, we come to Charterhouse, near which, in addition to the well-known Roman lead-mining centre, there is an Iron Age earthwork and the important site of Gorsey Bigbury situated about 300 yards from Longwood Farm. Gorsey Bigbury is a notable example of the Bronze Age 'henge' whose circular bank, about 160 feet across, has its ditch on the inner side.

We now approach the richest area of all Mendip. Priddy is the centre of an area where barrows abound; the heaths round about are sown with more than a hundred round barrows; on North Hill west of the Miners' Arms are the finest examples of all, in two main groups, Priddy Nine Barrows and (to the north of them) the Ashen Hill group which consist of eight bowl barrows in a row. There is also a long barrow at Priddy, while the Priddy Rings close by the Castle of Comfort inn, are an interesting though undated series of earthen circles, each about 550 feet in diameter. Northward from Priddy there is a long barrow at Chewton Mendip and yet another, together with an Iron Age camp, on Pen Hill; southward, the third centre for Palæolithic cave sites. In Ebbor Gorge are several caves that have been occupied by Palæolithic hunters, but most spectacular, best known and most easily visited of all, is Wookey Hole, where the river Axe flows through the caverns which its waters have worn in the limestone. At one period during the Pleistocene this cave was an hyæna den, when masses of animal bones accumulated on the floor; later it was occupied first by Aurignacian and then by Solutrean hunters (p. 17). We can end this westward route along the Mendips by mentioning the strong multiple-ramparted Iron Age camp of Maesbury, 3 miles west of Wells, and then (on the northern side of the ridge) a fine specimen of promontory camp which can be seen on Blacker's Hill near Chilcompton. Beyond the Mendips to the south, Brent Knoll, an isolated hill 2 miles north-west of Burnham, has a camp on it, while Meare, 3 miles west of Glastonbury, and Glastonbury itself, are famous for their lake dwellings (p. 114); there is little enough to be seen of them in the field, but a fascinating collection of finds is housed in the museum, and more, from both villages, is well shown in the Castle Museum at Taunton. Away to the east of Glastonbury, South Cadbury is the most powerful camp in Somerset and, as 'Camelot', a centre of Arthurian legend. This camp has four distinct lines of huge ramparts with ditches cut in the rock; in some places dry-stone walling survives along the inside of the banks. A dozen miles to the south-west, in the parish of Stoke-sub-Hamdon, is another imposing camp, Hamdon or Ham Hill, of enormous size (though partly damaged by the famous stone-quarries), which has yielded some excellent Iron Age material now exhibited in Taunton Museum.

The liassic Polden Hills have slight archæological interest, but the Quantocks, where ancient Devonian rocks support a dense growth of heather, and whose tree-filled valleys are stocked with red deer, there are many antiquities though at present little explored. On the main ridge between Quantoxhead and Mendip are many round barrows; the best camp, a double-ramparted example, is Dowsborough or Danesborough on the north side of the hill above the village of Dodington. A circular earthwork known as Trendle Ring (cf. the Sussex Trundle, p. 196) lies on the slopes above Bicknoller, and Daws Castle on the coast at Watchet is worth visiting, though very much eroded.

(Exmoor)

We can now leave the Quantocks for that far greater mass of Devonian rocks, the Brendon Hills and Exmoor. Approaching first by the Brendons, we find the usual crop of round barrows on the moors and two camps that are worth naming: the triangular Clatworth Castle, and Elworthy Barrows camp, finely situated on an open common 2 miles north-east from Clatworthy. The

Brendons lead up to the noble bare summit of Dunkery Beacon over 1700 feet above sea-level and the highest point on Exmoor. From the Beacon (where there are several badly damaged stone-built round barrows) stretches a wonderful prospect of moorland which includes a bird's-eye view of Staddon Hill camp, Ash-combe.   A path leading down the north side of Dunkery passes a stone circle to the south of Porlock church; it is about 80 feet across and has 10 standing and 6 fallen stones.   A better circle can also be mentioned here although it stands on Exmoor 6 miles to the south, 7 furlongs south-west of the Barle Bridge at Withy-pool.   This example has 37 upright stones and a diameter of 120 feet.   The adjoining portion of Exmoor between the Exe and the Barle has many round barrows.   To the north-east of Dunkery, across the valley in which Porlock lies, is Selworthy Beacon, where there are more barrows to be seen and a sub-stantial square earthwork called Bury Castle.   On the same stretch of upland there is another camp, East Mylne, on Mine-head North Hill; Bat's Castle is a camp east of Minehead, and there is yet another in Dunster deer-park.   Other sites on this northern, seaward, edge of Exmoor are the late Roman coastal signal-station of Old Burrow Walls, at Glenthorne just across the Devon border, and Countisbury Camp, by Lynmouth. In this same corner of Devon is the Mattocks Down Menhir (or Standing Stone), while the famous tourists' attraction, the Valley of the Rocks west of Lynton, has a hut-circle and en-closure of the 'pound' type (p. 77); near here also is Cewydd's Stone, and a camp at Martinhoe.   Turning south, there are the well-known Chapman Barrows west of Blackmoor Gate (by Challacombe Common), and near by are barrows and a triangle of standing stones on Homer Down.   West of Blackmoor Gate is Kentisbury Barrow, and south of Challacombe, Shoulsbury Common has a good camp.   Other camps (now again within the Somerset portion of Exmoor) are Cow Castle at Simonsbath, Whitestanton above the river Yarty, Old Bury Castle near Dulverton, and Brewer's and Mounsey Castles, both overlook-ing the Barle.   The striking earthwork which dominates the junction of Exe and Haddon may be medieval.

Before we advance right into the south-western peninsula we must retreat a little to cover a region hitherto neglected, that part of Dorset west of the chalk which we reached in our last section at Eggardun Hill. It is not notably well supplied with antiquities, but there are a few sites of interest. Leaving Eggardun the first is Pilsdon Pen, a bold dark hill towering above the road from Beaminster to Axminster; crowning the summit is a strong Iron Age camp with elaborate entrance works. On the southern slopes of the Blackdown Hills north of the road from Axminster to Honiton are the camps of Stockland Great Castle and Membury. Hembury, 4 miles beyond Honiton on the Cullompton road, is a camp rather similar to Pilsdon which excavation has shown to have been occupied during the greater part of the Iron Age, and, what is more important, to cover the site of a Neolithic causewayed camp, the most westerly of its kind known in Britain. In this imposition of an Iron Age upon a Neolithic earthwork it recalls Maiden Castle (p. 40) and the Trundle in Sussex (p. 196). Immediately to the south of Hembury in the region east of the Exe estuary are a number of monuments, including camps at Woodbury Castle, and Blackbury, and good examples of round barrow on Venn Otley Common, Farway and Gittisham Hills; Farway also has a camp.

West of the Exe, the Haldon Hills are lovely but not archæologically well endowed, despite the Neolithic house site mentioned on p. 30; note need only be made of Penhill Camp and Ugbrooke Castle Dyke. On Milber Down, near Newton Abbot, is an interesting camp dated by excavation to the later Iron Age, adjoined by a smaller earthwork. Also near Newton Abbot is Torbryan, whose limestone caves have yielded remains of cavebear, hyæna and other animals of the later Pleistocene; traces of contemporary Palæolithic man are dubious here, and at the better known cave on Windmill Hill at Brixham, where extinct animal remains have been found in quantity, he is represented only by a few scattered implements. But in the most famous of these Devon caves, Kent's Cavern, a mile due east from the harbour at Torquay, Mousterian, Aurignacian and later Palæolithic inplements have been excavated in different parts of the cave, together with similar animal remains; this cave was the scene of the pioneer researches of M'Enery and Pengelly respectively in the early and middle nineteenth century.

(Dartmoor)

We are now on the eastern fringe of Dartmoor, that great granite mass which even more than Exmoor is a land where the prehistoric past still asserts itself. The whole area, which is about 20 miles from north to south and 15 from east to west, is so thickly scattered with the 'hut circles' (which are the stone foundations of round huts, often of Bronze Age date), with rows and rings of standing stones, pounds (enclosed groups of huts) and other monuments that it is only possible to single out a few exceptionally interesting areas. If we come from Exeter the first important site is just west of Drewsteignton, where the so-called Spinster's rock is a megalithic burial chamber akin to the Cornish dolmens (p. 221 ff.). In the north part of the Moor the Nine Stones, Belstone, 3 miles south-east of Oke-hampton, is a stone circle, and a large group of hut circles beside the Tavy 3 miles east of Lydford should also be mentioned. South-east of Chagford and north of the Two Bridges–Moreton-hampstead road there is a stone row at Metherall, a circle just west of it at Fernworthy, and south-west from there again the better known circle of the Grey Wethers—these stand about 3 miles north of Postbridge, where the 'megalithic' bridge should be examined. Further east and south of Chagford there is an interesting area between Shapley Common and Wide-combe-in-the-Moor where there are great numbers of round barrows and the interesting Bronze Age enclosure of Grims-pound (p. 77). In this same neighbourhood, between Grims-pound and Warren House there are some easily accessible stone rows, while at Foales Arrishes on the main road between Hayor and Widecombe the hut circles and Celtic field boundaries are exceptionally fine. Going westward along the Tavistock road, before reaching Two Bridges there are some remarkable stone cists; one of them, with a surrounding stone setting and associated stone row, is the finest in the Moor. There are more cists on Royal Hill south-east of Two Bridges. Continuing along the Tavistock road from Two Bridges there is a varied group of monuments at Merivale; these include quadruple stone rows, standing stones, cists and hut circles. Among all the abundance of Dartmoor perhaps the richest area is that to the south-east drained by the Plym, Yealm, Erme and Avon, above all the Erme valley and the area round the Upper Plym; hut circles are abundant throughout this region. The Erme valley antiquities may be approached from Harford. There is a stone row with circle on Burford Down, and farther north, west of Hillson's House, is a particularly impressive stone row associated with circles and cairns. A row of small but closely set stones starts from a circle on Staldon Moor, and, after crossing the Erme, ends with a small cairn on Green Hill some $2\frac{1}{4}$ miles away. East of the Erme, on Butterdon Hill, is another exceptionally long stone row measuring over a mile to its end north of Spurrell's Cross. The Upper Plym area is approached from the Cornwood–Sheepstor road. This area is thickly covered with remains of many kinds of which the following are particularly worth seeing: Trowlesworthy Down (stone rows and circles), Yellowmead (quadruple circle), Ditsworthy Warren (cist, hut circles and stone rows that include the tallest standing stone on the Moor, nearly 18 feet in height). Farther north near Down Tor is another interesting stone row and circle. Away to the south from here Blackdown Camp, Loddiswell, is sufficiently striking to be named.

(Cornwall)

We can now penetrate into Cornwall, where the four granite moorlands of Bodmin, St. Austell, Redruth and Land's End, particularly the first and last of the four, are the areas of greatest archæological importance; only for the Iron Age can other areas show anything comparable. There is some very peculiar quality in the bare landscape of western Cornwall and the Cornish moorlands, something which includes a profound sense of its antiquity. Standing in such a landscape, the power of prehistoric monuments to move the imagination is greatly increased.

Bodmin Moor is as full of interest as Dartmoor, and in general its antiquities are similar. If we are coming from Dartmoor we reach this Moor in the south-west and immediately encounter some of the most remarkable monuments in the county. In the parish of St. Clear is the well-known and striking megalithic chamber of Trethevy; it has an ante-chamber and a chamber divided by a slab with a small gap at the lower edge large enough to allow a man to crawl through from ante- into main chamber. The whole is covered with a colossal capstone and is of an exceptional height; all traces of the covering mound have disappeared. Less than 3 miles to the north-east, in Linkinhorne parish, are the finest stone circles in Cornwall; these are the Hurlers, three circles standing in line. Immediately above them, Stowe Hill is crowned with a single stone rampart, probably a Bronze Age fort, and on the same hill is the natural but freakish rock-formation known as the Cheesewring. A large stone cist is still visible in the round barrow between Stowe Hill and the Hurlers whence came the unique ribbed gold beaker (p. 72) so long in the possession of the Royal Family as treasure trove and now in the British Museum. The neighbouring hill of Caradon has a number of fine round barrows on its summit. About 3 miles north of Stowe Hill is a small stone circle, the Nine Maidens; another 5 miles to the west on the slopes of Hawks Tor in Blisland parish is the Stripple Stones, a large circle which from its possession of a surrounding bank with internal ditch, qualifies as a 'henge' (p. 186). The entrance to the Stripple Stones faces westward in the direction of a smaller circle, the Trippet Stones, while about 2 miles northward is yet another stone ring, the smallest of the group, near the farm of Leaze. We are now on the southern edge of another of Bodmin's most prolific areas, that which is centred on the great granite outcrop of Rough Tor. Just south and south-west of the Tor are two large stone circles, those of St. Breward and Stannon, both in Fernacre parish, which differ from all the rest in that the stones are quite irregularly spaced and variable in size. These circles are both associated with clusters of Bronze Age hut-villages, which are indeed very numerous along the banks of the upper De Lank river and north of Rough Tor. Those are of particular interest where the huts adjoin clearly marked outlines of little cultivation plots. Rough Tor itself, like Stowe Hill, carries a stone walled enclosure, possibly contemporary with the Bronze Age huts near by. The two weirdly-weathered rock outcrops of the tor form the narrow ends of this stronghold; a double rampart runs between them on the west side, but to the east, where it is precipitous, there are no defences to be seen. Inside the area are a few huts and three springs of water.

Leaving Bodmin Moor behind, there is a good Iron Age ring fort (p. 186) at Tregear, about 8 miles west from Rough Tor. Still larger and more impressive is Castle-an-Dinas in the parish of St. Columb Major north-east of St. Austell Moor; it has three huge circular earthen ramparts, the outer one measuring 850 feet across. It is possible that this great fort may have been connected with the control of the tin trade (p. 112). Between these two forts is the megalithic chamber on the slopes of the ridge above Pawton (St. Breoke) which has an enormous capstone, and some 2 miles to the west in St. Columb Major is the Nine Maidens, the only noteworthy row of standing stones in Cornwall. On Trevelgue Head a mile or so outside Newquay on the east is a fine specimen of Cornish promontory fort, proved by excavation to be of Iron Age date, and containing huts and a contemporary iron-mine.

The next region of any note is Redruth Moor where the three-peaked granite hill of Carn Brea between Camborne and Redruth is of great interest. The summit has been defended by a number of dry-stone walls embracing an area as much as 1100 feet long and including the two summits now occupied by the medieval castle and monument. These ambitious ramparts probably date from the Iron Age, but inside them some of the huts contained Neolithic material; two hoards of British coins were also found here. A megalithic tomb which is worth visiting is Giant's Quoit, Caerwynen (Camborne parish), 4 miles south-west from Carn Brea. It has three uprights supporting a large capstone and, like so many Cornish megaliths, has been largely denuded of its mound. Before going farther westward to the richest of all Cornish regions, the moorlands of Land's End, we should note the Iron Age ring-fort of Castle Dore, on the road leading south to the coast at Fowey, which was occupied both in the Iron Age and in post-Roman times, and is associated with the legend of King Mark, Tristan and Iseult; and farther west, we should also turn southward to the promontory which ends in the Lizard. There are several forts along the southern side of the Holford Estuary, and at Halligye near Trelowarren there is a quite outstanding example of the earth-house or 'fogou' (the Cornish name), a series of subterranean passages 54 feet long and 6 feet high in an excellent state of preservation. Farther south down the peninsula in the parish of St. Keverne is a large stone cist, probably of the Early Bronze Age, known as the Three Brothers of Grogith.

We can now complete our survey of this whole south-western region by extending it through the Penwith peninsula to Land's End, a piece of country as full of antiquities as any in Britain.

Entering it from the east the first site to note is the second Castle-an-Dinas (see p. 223), where three concentric ramparts crown a hill-top in Gulval parish. It is itself a fine example of the circular Cornish fort, but its special interest lies in its protective association with the neighbouring Iron Age village of Chysauster, a relation similar to that which we shall meet again farther west at Chun. Chysauster, an important site which has been very fully excavated, now lies open to visitors who can see the 8 large sub-rectangular houses arranged in pairs along a street. Individual houses are of the courtyard plan which seems akin to that of the Scottish brochs; rooms built in the thickness of the wall open on to a central court which seems generally to have been unroofed. There are several other such village sites in Penwith, notably one at Porthmeor in Zennor parish, which has been fully excavated, and shown to have been occupied mainly in the Roman period. About 3 miles due north on a high ridge is the famous megalithic chamber ('dolmen') of Zennor. This is the nearest counterpart to Trethevy (p. 221), but here there is no hole to give access from the ante-chamber into the chamber; the 18-foot-long capstone has been pushed off sideways. Zennor is the easternmost of a close-set group of megaliths. Another with its circular covering mound and retaining wall still well preserved is at Pennance near the track between Kerrowe and Boskednan, still in the parish of Zennor; a very similar one is near by at Treen close to the turf track from Gurnard's Head to Bospor-thennis. Next comes Lanyon Quoit, the best known and most visited of all Cornish megaliths, standing by the roadside between Penzance and Morvah. In its present form it is a gigantic three-legged table standing 5 feet high; before its collapse and restoration during the first half of the nineteenth century it was possible to ride a horse under the capstone. A mile to the north is the interesting stone of Men-an-Tol, a large slab with a round hole through the centre; this is evidently the only surviving relic of some megalithic chamber in which it must have served as a 'porthole' (p. 231) stone at the entrance between ante-chamber and chamber or elsewhere. There is one of the familiar Nine Maidens circles close at hand at Boskednan. On Gurnard's Head is another of the very numerous Cornish coastal promontory-forts, or 'cliff castles', of the Iron Age. Within 2 miles westward we come to another centre of interest, inland at Chun in Morvah parish. The Iron Age fort of Chun stands on a high hill commanding the Land's End district; it is a most characteristic example of Cornish circular fort, and one which has been extensively excavated. It has two concentric rings of massive granite ramparts, each with a ditch outside; to the west there is a carefully screened entrance and inside huts were built round against the wall. It may date from early in the third century B.C. On the same hill is the megalithic 'dolmen' of Chun Quoit, a rectangular cist with the characteristic large coverstone; there is another very like it in the adjoining parish of Madron which has the name of Mulfra Quoit (Frontispiece). About 2 miles farther west in dreary heathland in the parish of St. Just is the small megalithic gallery of Tregaseal; near it are two circles, one of them largely destroyed, known as the Dancing Stones and also by that name which is applied indiscriminately to most Penwith circles, the Nine Maidens. Not far to the south on the hill of Chapel Carn Brea, the round hill above Land's End, there is a fine round cairn which has been proved to cover a megalithic chamber resembling that of Tregaseal. Just to the east is Chapel Euny, a well-preserved little chamber in a round barrow on the way from Brane and Tredinney in Sancred parish. Just south of these tombs is a good stone circle, the Nine Maidens, Boscawen-un. In the southern bulge of the peninsula there is another circle, Rosemodres, near Boleigh. There are two very tall stones standing within a quarter of a mile to the north-east, in Buryon parish. If we are to end at Land's End itself, the adjoining promontory-fort of Maen's Castle should be named, together with a closed megalithic cist on the farm of Tregiffian Vean.

IV. *THE COTSWOLDS*

We have already dealt with that part of the Thames basin rimmed by the White Horse Hills and later we shall come to the Chilterns; the present section is concerned with all that region of the upper Thames and its affluents which is formed by the oolitic limestone of Oxfordshire and Gloucestershire. It should be remembered that this upland area forms the base of the Jurassic Belt (p. 119) which stretches up from here through Northamptonshire and Lincolnshire and on to the Yorkshire Moors, and which in prehistoric times formed a more or less open route linking areas of primary settlement in Wessex with north-eastern England.

The Cotswolds are from our present viewpoint a most interesting area, but a description of its antiquities will be more than ever monotonous, so greatly do chambered long barrows and Iron Age camps preponderate among them.

(North Oxfordshire)

We left region II (Wessex) in its nearest point at Dorchester; the best line of approach to the Cotswolds necessitates a leap across to the north of Oxfordshire, perhaps while leaping taking note of the Roman site of Alchester just south of Bicester and linked with Dorchester by Roman road. Our leap, however, is to take us to a point 3 miles north of Chipping Norton on the Oxfordshire–Warwickshire borders, where we shall find the Rollright Stones. They can be reached from Chipping Norton by a pleasant road through Over Norton; the key for entry into the circle (enclosed in unsightly railings) can be had from the White House at the cross-roads immediately to the west of the Stones. The whole group of stones comprise the King Stone, the King's Men and the Whispering Knights, and all are united in the legend which recounts how a witch turned a king and his men into stone and how they may come to life again at night. The King Stone is reached first, on the north, Warwickshire, side of the road; it is a single stone, much hollowed out on one side, which stands in the south edge of a just visible long barrow running east and west (called by Stukeley 'the Arch-Druid's barrow'); it may have formed one half of a port-hole entrance into a megalithic side chamber (a device found in Cotswold long barrows). Only a few steps farther west, but on the opposite, Oxfordshire, side of the road is the principal monument, the King's Men, a stone circle of some 70 rather strangely weathered uprights to which is attached the common folk-tale that they cannot be correctly counted. The Whispering Knights, across a field to the east, are a group of four upright stones and one fallen capstone, the whole probably the ruined chamber of a long barrow now itself vanished. Before pushing ahead towards the Cotswolds, an excursion should be made south-eastward along the Chipping Norton–Oxford road to see the Hoar Stone, which stands in a holly thicket by the cross roads on the south side of Enstone village. There are in fact three stones, the largest still 9 feet high; like the Whispering Knights they may represent the chamber of a denuded long barrow. If the road from here to the west through Taston and Chadlington is taken, an interesting long barrow will be found on the opposite side of the Chipping Norton–Burford road a mile south of Sarsden. This is the Lyneham barrow, distinguished by a large monolith standing at its north-east end. Digging revealed two megalithic chambers and within them many burials. There are also a number of round barrows in this Sarsden area.

(Northern Cotswolds)

To return from this detour to the Rollright circle: if we take the road westward just past the crossing of the Chipping Norton–Moreton-in-the-Marsh road there is a fine stone-ramparted camp on the right known as Chastleton Burrow. We are now nearing Stow-on-the-Wold and one of the greatest concentrations of Cotswold long barrows, in the neighbourhood of the attractive villages of Upper and Lower Swell. Within a thousand square yards in this region there are 5 long barrows, and 3 others at no great distance. Three lie near the Poles Wood Plantation; in one the characteristic 'horned' plan (p. 47) is visible, in the second the barrow is much decayed but a megalithic chamber towards what was the smaller, western, end is well preserved; the third and westernmost barrow has only a low mound to show but may be relatively undisturbed. There is another long barrow with no external architectural features just west of Lower Swell church; the Hoar Stone, a monolith in a field south of the village

may be the relic of yet another.   Westward along the Guiting
Power road are two more, one dilapidated and under grass,
one perfect but ploughed over—this latter example is against
Eyford Hill farm; near by are 3 round barrows.   Just north of
the road there is a much-mutilated long barrow and a number
of round ones on Cow Common.   As a group the Swell
barrows, although amazingly numerous, have been too severely
damaged by farming and by casual excavation to be very
rewarding to the visitor.   The archæologically important Iron
Age camp of Salmonsbury just east of the exquisite little town
of Bourton-on-the-Water is large but low-lying and so hardly
impressive; the most spectacular sites on this side of the Cotswolds
are rather Notgrove and Belas Knap long barrows.   Leaving
Bourton-on-the-Water the first of these is on the Salperton
road just north of Notgrove village; this long barrow, which
is of the typologically early type in which there is a central
megalithic structure approached through a forecourt between
'horns' (p. 47), has recently been re-excavated and preserved;
in plan the chamber consists of a central passage with two pairs
of side cells.   An interesting comparison to this plan is offered
by Belas Knap, which stands 2 miles south of Winchcomb and
Sudeley Castle, just above the woods of Corndean Hall.   This
site has been completely excavated and restored in such a way
as to give what must be a reasonably reliable impression of the
original appearance of Cotswold long barrows.   There is the
pear-shaped mound (in the Cotswolds generally made of stones)
with its outer retaining wall neatly built in the dry-stone technique,
and the horned forecourt at the larger end.   Belas Knap is, however, an example of a plan typologically later than Notgrove, for
the impressive portal which is approached through the forecourt
is not a real entrance at all, but a dummy which probably had
ritual uses; the actual burial-chambers are in the length of the
mound and have their entrances opening on to the long sides.
There are several other sites in this neighbourhood which repay
a visit.   Just below Belas Knap there is the Roman villa of
Wadfield, while a pleasant walk over Postlip Warren leads to
Cleeve Cloud and Cleeve Hill, where there is a variety of earthworks, including a strong camp on the brow of Cleeve Hill
overlooking Cheltenham.   This is a semicircular earthwork
with double ramparts, the ends resting on a natural cliff, now

cut back further by quarrying. Behind the camp a linear earthwork runs across Cleeve Common and passes a small circular banked enclosure of unknown date. The scarp which runs north-west from Cleeve has several minor earthworks and a quite considerable promontory-fort in Beckbury, on a spur above Hales Abbey; an outlier beyond the northern end of the escarpment is the isolated Meon Hill, crowned with a strong Iron Age camp. This is the point also at which an excursion must be made to another isolated outlier of the Cotswolds, Bredon Hill, now always to be associated with Housman's coloured counties and church bells. Rising to a thousand feet straight from the plains of the Avon Valley and the Vale of Evesham half-way between Evesham and Tewkesbury, it is indeed a striking site and one which commands tremendous views; westwards the Malverns show very clearly, sometimes even the Wrekin may be visible, while eastward the scarp of the Cotswolds (which we have just left) bounds the outlook across the plain. The north-west angle of this hill-top has been cut off by two lines of rampart, rather after the fashion of a promontory camp, and there are entrances through the centre of each. Excavation showed that this camp had been used during the later part of the Iron Age and that there had been a ferocious massacre at the inner entrance, where mutilated bodies were found in confusion and there were signs that a row of heads had been set along the gate. It is possible that this may have been the work of Belgic tribes in their extension to the south-west (p. 135).

If now we return to the Cotswold escarpment at Cleeve and follow it southward and cross the Cheltenham–Andoversford road there are the remains of a long barrow by Lineover Wood, Dowdeswell, close by the Gloucester–Stow road; and round about this village are three camps, two of them quite considerable. A well-known site not far from here is the Chedworth Roman villa, which can be reached by way of Withington (where there is a long barrow west of Swilly Bottom). It stands on heavily wooded slopes and is perhaps the most interesting villa to be seen in the whole country. If we continue southwards there is a fine though featureless long barrow known as Colnpen just south of Coln Rogers, and a promontory-fort at Ablington near the delectable but over-visited village of Bibury. This is a legitimate point from which to retreat northwards for a short distance through Aldsworth village and on to Lodge Park, the lovely dower-house of Sherborne, where, just behind this perfect example of mid-seventeenth-century architecture, there is a well-preserved long barrow with a large slab, probably part of a portal, exposed at the larger end. If we go on to turn right along the Northleach–Burford road there is a neat little circular camp on perfectly level ground just opposite the village of Windrush.

(Western Cotswolds)

We must now return to the Avon–Severn escarpment which we left at Dowdeswell near Cheltenham, in order to pursue the series of camps and long barrows which stand along this magnificent edge. Two miles south of Cheltenham there is an important camp on the summit of Leckhampton Hill, while on Crickley Hill, a fine headland above the Cheltenham–Birdlip road, is a strong promontory-fort with two lines of ramparts running across the neck. There is a number of round barrows outside this camp on Crickley Hill and long barrows on either side: one (Crippet's) at Shurdington, the other west of Coberley. Birdlip Hill to the south has a small promontory-fort, but it is known chiefly as the site of the Late Iron Age grave which yielded one of the finest of our Celtic La Tène mirrors (p. 130). Continuing west along the scarp we can first name West Tump, a long barrow, with a false entry like that of Belas Knap, in Buckholt Wood, Brimpsfield. Then there are insignificant earthworks on Cooper's Hill (which is, however, distinguished for its cheese-rolling ceremonies), but more interesting is Haresfield Beacon just above Haresfield station; this headland has a promontory camp, while the tip is cut off again by a very large bank; the situation is itself a fine one. South of Haresfield above the Stroud valley, which at this point cuts through the escarpment, there is a long barrow on Ranwick Hill. Before crossing to the wonderfully rich area south of the Stroud valley we must touch upon the group of long barrows held in the curve of that valley between Painswick, Stroud and Duntisbourne Abbots. In this region there are the remains, none of them very remarkable, of 9 long barrows: 2 close together in Miserden parish, the northern example having the stones of a chamber showing; at Througham in Bisley parish where a cottage has been built in the heart of the mound; a very long specimen (210 feet) narrow in form and sufficiently well preserved to be attractive for excavation, Juniper Hill just west of Edgeworth; and Hoar Stone (the third of this name) south of Duntisbourne Abbots, with two large stones visible. From this last site there is an easy run down to Cirencester, where there is little of the Roman town to be seen but a good collection of finds from it in the museum.

(*Southern Cotswolds*)

We are now ready to enter that region immediately south of the Stroud valley which has more spectacular sites than any other in the Cotswolds. Since we are approaching from Cirencester the first site of note is the Windmill Tump, $\frac{3}{4}$ mile south-west of the village of Rodmarton. This important barrow is planted with trees and enclosed within a modern wall which roughly outlines its oval shape; there is a fine horned forecourt and dummy portal at its larger, eastern, end with two side chambers opening on to the long north and south sides of the mound. These chambers are excellent examples of the skilful combination of megalithic with dry-stone walling and are remarkable for the small flight of steps and the porthole entrance (p. 226) through which they must be reached. The southern porthole still retains the neatly fitted dry-stone blocking which must have been made by the last users of the grave; such a survival appears to be unique. This interesting barrow is an eastern outlier of a group belonging to what is generally called the 'Avening District'. Continuing past Rodmarton, $\frac{3}{4}$ mile past the village of Cheriton, we come to Norn's Tump, a long barrow lying just behind the Nag's Head. Somewhere near this barrow there seems once to have been another which was completely destroyed, but three chambers from it are re-erected in a field beside the Avening rectory garden. If we turn north by the rectory along Step's Lane we pass on the left the tree-planted Tinglestone barrow, with a single standing stone on its larger end. This barrow is already within the property of Gatcombe Park, and it is only a little farther along the road to the park entrance where a very notable barrow is to be found on a small wooded ridge just above the entrance lodge. The best feature of this fine long barrow is a chamber opening on to the north side; the megalithic and dry-stone masonry are in excellent condition and the whole is bone dry under its huge coverstone. After Gatcombe Lodge the road bends westward and, passing on the right a monolith known as the Long Stone, enters Minchinhampton. On Minchinhampton Common are a number of earthworks, the principal one an extensive linear work of bank and ditch called the Bulwarks and dated by excavation to the Iron Age; there are also some round barrows on this Common. At Amberley just west of Minchinhampton there is a poor long barrow, Whitefields Tump, while to the south of it Amberley camp on the edge of the hill above the village seems to be linked with the Bulwarks. Two miles farther on through Woodchester, the Toots, a big long barrow, is on Selsey Hill south of King's Stanley, overlooking Stroud and the whole Vale of Gloucester and the Severn Estuary. Following the road, still with splendid views, to the south-west we come within three miles to the Nympsfield long barrow which stands on the right-hand side close to the escarpment edge. The mound has largely disappeared, but the chamber, a central passage with side cells, has recently been carefully re-excavated and restored. Only another mile along the edge and we are at Hetty Pegler's Tump, unquestionably the most impressive and best preserved of all Cotswold chambered barrows. In plan the chamber is of the same class as those of Notgrove and Nympsfield, a central passage with two pairs of side cells; but here the chamber is complete under its covering mound and we are able to feel the full power of these strange burial vaults of the New Stone Age. The camp of Uley, boldly situated on a spur just beyond the village, is well worth visiting.

We have now surveyed the greatest archæological glories of the Cotswolds, but there are a few more sites to mention in two areas. First, here in the south, there are more camps on the Severn escarpment south of Uley all the way to Bath, the finest being Sodbury, a rectangular camp above Chipping Sodbury right on the limit of the uplands. To the west of these, between the main escarpment and the Severn Estuary, is another line of camps including Damery, Bloody Acre (a good example ¾ mile north of Cromhall on the Gloucester–Bristol road), King's Weston and others. Standing forward from this line and doubtless originally right on the Severn bank is the Toots, Oldbury, another interesting camp.

(*Lydney to the Malverns*)

The second area which remains to be briefly covered here is that part of Gloucestershire and closely bordering territories lying beyond the Severn and Avon.   The first site worth noting is 7 miles up Severn side near Lydney.   In the Bathurst estate of Lydney Park, a mile south from the town, there are Iron Age defences on Camp Hill, and within the defended area the remains of a late Roman temple, with a house or hospice and baths; closer to the mansion are the remains of a small Norman castle. Continuing northward we enter the Forest of Dean, where we can note a strongly banked enclosure at Little Dean near Cinder-ford; the space enclosed is so small that it seems possible this embankment may be a Bronze Age 'henge' rather than an Iron Age camp.   Just to the north there is a much larger earthwork on Welshbury Hill.

It seems justifiable in this section to extend our survey just as far as the Malvern Hills as they may reasonably be taken as an outlying region of the Cotswold country. There are only two sites of note, both Iron Age hill-forts; the more southerly is on Midsummer Hill above Eastnor Park; the second is the much better known Herefordshire Beacon, a strong camp in a commanding position; the raised mount on the summit here may be a Norman motte and without further excavation it is difficult to distinguish the Iron Age from possible other Norman defences.   If we stand on the Malvern Hills and turn eastward we are of course looking across the Severn and Avon to the isolated crown of Bredon and beyond it to the main scarp of the Cotswolds.

V. *WALES*

(Monmouth and South Wales)

From the south-west and from the Cotswolds we come to the second western peninsula of Britain: Wales. The Welsh peninsula is a plateau of ancient rocks cut up by river valleys and surrounded on three sides by coastal plains which reach their greatest extent in Gwent and Pembrokeshire in the south, Anglesey and the Lleyn peninsula in the north. Archæologically Gwent has connexions with south-western England, for at various prehistoric periods cultural influences spread round both sides of the Bristol Channel; in our survey of field monuments this relationship will be most obviously shown by the existence in South Wales of chambered long barrows similar to those of the Cotswolds. The north naturally had connexions with northern England, notably with Yorkshire.

Approaching through Monmouthshire, the main interest in that county will be found in its Roman sites, but first something must be said of a few monuments nearer to the English border. Just by the western end of the Severn Tunnel is the Iron Age camp of Sudbrook, a triangular earthwork abutting on to the river-bank; there are three lines of defences, the innermost exceptionally powerful. Not far away at Heston Brake near Portskewett there is a megalithic grave of the parallel-sided 'gallery' type (p. 44). Before we reach Caerwent mention must be made of the neigh-bouring Iron Age camp of Llanmelin, with its imposing stone-built ramparts. At Caerwent itself are the ruins of the Roman town of Isca Silurum where the southern wall with its supporting bastions is a remarkable example of Roman town-wall architecture. The Roman legionary fortress at Caerleon (by Newport) has much of interest to show, particularly in its museum collections and the carefully restored amphitheatre; together with Chester for the north, Caerleon here in the south was the main centre for the conquest and pacification of Wales. Crossing into Wales proper, we shall find in the National Museum, Cardiff, the best displayed prehistoric and folk-culture collections in Britain; in addition the town can show a restoration of the walls of the fourth-century Roman fort raised on their original foundations. If we go westward from Cardiff across the coastal plain the first site worth visiting is the important chambered long barrow which lies under the trees of Tinkinswood near St. Nicholas on the Bridgend road. There the neat rectangular mound with its containing dry-stone walls is unusually well preserved, while the huge capstone is the most conspicuous feature of the megalithic chamber; note should also be made of the contemporary blocking of the entrance, a feature which must have been rebuilt after each interment. A little to the south of Tinkinswood at St. Lythan's on the same side of the Bridgend road there is an imposing megalithic chamber with 3 uprights supporting a capstone; this 'dolmen' is probably the chamber of a largely vanished long barrow. Coastal sites which should be visited here are the semicircular camp known as the Bulwarks still standing above the sea at Rhoose just west of Barry, and the large round barrows, one at least of them dated to the Beaker period, among the sand-dunes between Merthyr Mawr and Porthcawl.

The Gower peninsula is of greater interest. Most important is the chambered long barrow of Parc Cwm at Parc-le-Breos, closely related to the Cotswold type, the chamber having a central passage with two pairs of side cells; the remains of over twenty skeletons were found here. A second megalith is not far away in Penmaen Burrows where it stands among sand-dunes. This tomb has a passage with one side chamber preserved; the uprights are all large and there is a massive capstone. Just beyond at Reynoldston there is the more severely ruined megalithic grave of Arthur's Stone, while on the Rhossili hills oval cairns with small stone chambers are known as Swine's Houses; there is also a strongly defended camp here. But perhaps the most famous site in Gower, and indeed one of the best known in all Wales, is the Goat's Hole cave, Paviland. This cave dwelling of Old Stone Age hunters is situated in a 70-foot-deep cleft in the cliffs; it yielded quantities of animal bones, flint, bone and ivory implements and, most notoriously (p. 18), the skeleton of the 'Red Lady'. There are also other caves on the peninsula: Long Hole, Cat's Hole and Bacon Hole have all yielded Palæolithic remains. And the islet of Burry Holms, off the northwest angle of Gower, is a mesolithic settlement-site of importance.

(Black Mountains)

Before going any farther westward an excursion must be made northward to the Black Mountains (Old Red Sandstone) of Brecknockshire, for there is to be found the only large and important inland group of megaliths. These megalithic long barrows (or long cairns) lie in an arc round the western side of the Black Mountains following roughly the lines of the upper Usk and Wye valleys; as a whole they are ill explored and little known. Starting with the Usk valley in the south there is one near Crickhowell on the south side of the Brecon road opposite the entrance to Gwernvale House and another very interesting example much higher up the valley is Ty Illtyd in the parish of Llanhamlach; the incised carvings on the chamber walls here are not contemporary but appear to date from the Christian era. To the west-north-west in the valley of a tributary of the Usk are two not very noticeable long barrows, at Mynydd Troed and Ty-Isaf Farm, parish of Talgarth; a third in the same parish is that of Cwm Fforest, a little north of Ty Isaf. Across the watershed among the upper streams of the Wye are the 2 barrows of Ffostyll in Llanelieu parish; in both remains of megalithic chambers are visible within a long mound. Northward of them in Talgarth parish is the Pipton long barrow, much ruined and hidden under trees, and north-west again that of Pen-y-Wyrlod, Llanigon parish. The only other monument belonging properly to this group is Arthur's Stone, a chambered long barrow on the parish boundaries of Dorstone and Bredwardine across the Herefordshire border.

(Pembrokeshire)

We can now return to the coast and continue our westward journey into Pembrokeshire, archæologically one of the richest counties in Wales. As we go from Gower there are megaliths, though none of outstanding interest, round the lower Towy (at Llanstephan, Llangain and Llangynog) and again at Marros on the Carmarthen coast about 8 miles east of Tenby. Pembrokeshire itself was an important area of settlement by megalith-building seafarers. In the south the Hanging Stone (Burton), the Long Stone (Hubberston) and the Devil's Quoit (Angle) are three examples of megalithic tomb all of them round Milford Haven; but by far the most numerous group is in the north of the county, particularly round the Nevern valley and Newport Bay. Many of these tombs are well worth seeing. On the St. David's peninsula are Longhouse near Mathry, with an oval chamber of 6 uprights and a capstone, and a group round St. David's—Carn Llidi, Coetan Arthur, Garn Twlc and Nine Wells. Near Fishguard there is an alignment of standing stones, Parc y Meirw, Llanybyther: near Newport the noteworthy tombs of Pentre Ifan, Carreg Coitan Arthur and Cerrig y Gof. This last is a unique monument with five megalithic chambers ranged in a circle round a mound. Inland from the Nevern valley on the Pembroke-Carmarthen border there are more megaliths, including two circles, one Gors Fawr, Mynachclog Ddu (Pembrokeshire), the other Meini Gwŷr, Llandyssilio East (Carmarthen). The northern part of this region marks the starting-point of the renowned Stonehenge 'bluestones', which are thought once to have formed part of some monument here on the Presely Hills. Indeed, among the round barrows which are also found on the Presely range is at least one which covered the burial of a Beaker man, and it may have been his kinsmen who were responsible for moving the stones to Wiltshire.

(Central Wales)

Going northward we find an almost total absence of noteworthy monuments in the coastal region of Central Wales. There are no megaliths of importance for the whole stretch between Cardigan and Barmouth; there are, however, a few camps among which Pen Dinas near Aberystwyth has been excavated and shown to belong to the later Iron Age. There are practically no megalithic tombs, either, in the central mountain massif, an exception being Pen-y-Garn-Goch, Treflis, in Brecknockshire. The type of monument which does exist in these central uplands is the stone circle and alignment. First, towards the south, there are a number of circles round about the source of the Usk and Tawe, near Trecastle and Llanfihangel-nant-Bran. Other groups with a higher proportion of associated alignments are about the sources and upper stretches of the Wye and Severn; among them may be named Saeth Maen Ystradgynlais in Montgomeryshire and Llanbrynmair, Merioneth. Then on the coast of the latter county is the double circle of Carneddau Hengwm, Llanaber parish.

(North Wales and Anglesey)

But here immediately north of Barmouth and the Afon Mawddach estuary megalithic monuments suddenly become common again, including a number with long mounds, and, equally, there is an increase in hill-forts. Still in Llanaber parish is a long mound with a megalithic chamber at the east end and a dry-stone one at the centre, and there is another long mound with two chambers, both megalithic, Dyffryn, in Llanenddwyn. Another interesting example in this area is Gwern-Einion, Llanfair, where a megalithic chamber with capstone in position is built into a modern wall. After this concentration between Barmouth and Harlech there are a number of megaliths with a more scattered distribution if we move on into the Carnarvon peninsula, many of them with the simple box 'dolmen' type of chamber. The first to be reached are Penarth and Bach-wen in Clynnog parish. Not far from these two megaliths is a famous hill-fort, that of Tre'r Ceiri. This long, narrow and high-standing fort has well-preserved stone ramparts, in places with rampart-walks intact, while inside are traces of round huts. Like many other Welsh hill-forts, Tre'r Ceiri seems to have been occupied during the Roman period, but architecturally it is wholly Iron Age.

Further south at the base of the peninsula are the further megalithic chambers of Llanystumdwy and Cist Gerrig in Treflis, while towards its extremity there is a well-preserved dolmen at Mynydd-cefn-amwlch in Penllech, as well as a single example of a long mound similar to those of Merioneth with both end and central chambers—this is Tan-y-muriau, near Rhiw by the coast at Porth Nigel.

But it is in Anglesey that we again find territory where signs of the prehistoric past are constantly noticeable. Immediately along the south-east side of the island nearest the mainland are at least half a dozen megaliths, one of which, Bryn Celli Ddu at Llanddaniel-fab, is a well-known and important monument. It is a more modest version of the great passage graves in round cairns so magnificently represented in Ireland (p. 44), a similarity which is strengthened by the presence in this Welsh site of a peristalith round the mound and of a carved stone within. The two other megaliths on this side of the island which deserve mention are both in Llanedwen parish— Plas Newydd, which appears to have two chambers separated by an upright, and Bryn yr Hen Bobl, a chamber in an oval mound from which there projects a long horn. In the south-east at Aberffraw we come to the first considerable group of hut circles, of which there are many in Anglesey; there are also round cairns in this area. In the north-east angle of the island there is a camp, Din Sylwy or Bwrdd Arthur, while moving farther north in the Lligwy Bay region there is an excavated megalith called Pant-y-Saer and another at Penrhos-Lligwy; this whole quarter is also scattered with hut circles, many of them in enclosed groups, largely of the Roman period. Crossing to Holyhead island, Holyhead Mountain has much of interest to visit; there is the hill-fort of Caer y Twr with rampart walks like Tre'r Ceiri, and exceptionally fine hut circles on its slopes at Ty Mawr, where there are the foundations of at least ten round houses with well-preserved entrances. Holyhead also possesses two megaliths—Trefignath and Trearddur; the former seems to be a long cist divided into segments (p. 46).

Returning now to the mainland of Carnarvon, there used to exist a most interesting site at Penmaenmawr where on the summit of this conspicuous mountain was Braich-y-Ddinas, a large complex hill-fort with dry-stone ramparts and again, as at Tre'r Ceiri, the relics of native houses all apparently dating from the Roman period. On Penmaenmawr also late Neolithic man manufactured stone axes; and there is a good example of an embanked stone circle, known as the Druid Stones. There are several other camps here in northern Carnarvon, and others across the Conway river in Denbighshire; there are also Roman forts at Caerhun and at Caernarvon itself; but we must next notice some Denbighshire megalithic monuments. The most southerly is a remarkable example of a passage grave in a long mound, Capel Garmon, Llanrwst; there is a related type of megalith at Maen Pebyll in the same parish; both these sites may be likened to the distant Brecknockshire long cairns of the Black Mountains (p. 236). On the other hand, Tyddyn Bleiddyn just to the north in Cefn parish resembles the Merioneth group (p. 238).

Not far from Tyddyn Bleidden there is an exceptionally fine hill-fort, Dinorben, Abergele, west of Rhyl, which on the southern side has colossal ramparts reaching 60 feet in height. Other minor forts on both sides of the Vale of Clwyd as far as the Dee are too numerous to name.

With the Dee we reach the region of the west Midlands and the Welsh Marches, which are described in the next section; but we must not leave North Wales without a mention of the pair of Palæolithic cave-dwellings of CaeGwyn and Ffynnon Beuno, in the north side of the Ffynnon Beuno gorge near Tremeirchon, about 3 miles south of St. Asaph. Both have been excavated, and CaeGwyn is especially important for its evidence of a return of glacial conditions after its occupation by Palæolithic man.

VI. *WEST MIDLANDS AND THE WELSH BORDER*

Having reached as far as the Malvern Hills in our survey of western England we turned aside to cover the Welsh peninsula, to emerge at the end of the last section in Cheshire. It will now be fitting to fill in the gap between the Malverns and Cheshire by a very brief survey of the Welsh marches and the western Midlands.

The great central plain of England, the Midlands, is a triangle bounded by the limestone escarpment of the Jurassic Belt, the eastern edge of the Welsh mountains and the southern edge of the Pennines; following roughly the line of these upland boundaries flow the three great rivers of Avon, Severn and Trent. Within this triangle the plain is of New Red Sandstone and clays and is a part of the so-called Great Red Plain which borders the Pennines on the west, south and east, and runs southwestward right down to the Severn Estuary. It is mostly low, level, heavy land broken only by the minor uplands of the

Clent and Lickey hills in Worcestershire, the Wrekin district in Shropshire, Cannock Chase in Staffordshire and Charnwood Forest (the most spectacular) in Leicestershire.

This midland country is archæologically the poorest in Britain, for its heavy soils supported dense forest growths most unattractive to prehistoric man. Shropshire and Cheshire which adjoin it through the Staffordshire gap have rather more sites, especially in the southern part of Shropshire that is one with the Welsh Marches, in the Central Ridge of Cheshire (the hills between the Dee and Wear valleys) and the Cheshire fringes of the Pennines. But nowhere in the present region is the memory of prehistoric man assertive, nor his works an important feature of the landscape; nowhere is it possible to pass from one interesting site to another through a day's walk. This survey therefore will only skim over the country, picking out the relatively few scattered sites that are worth visiting. The most noteworthy are in general the Iron Age hill-forts, which like the castles of the Middle Ages, followed the line of the Marches between Wales and England.

(*Herefordshire*)

We must begin from our stopping point on the Malverns, and after mentioning King Arthur's Cave near Ross-on-Wye, occupied by Palæolithic and Mesolithic man, name some of the more important of these Iron Age camps in the rest of Herefordshire. First there is Wall Hills, a fairly strong irregularly shaped camp 1½ miles west of the charming town of Ledbury, then a line of three along the course of the Wye south-west from Hereford; these are from south to north: Caplers camp, a long narrow enclosure on the bank above the river in the parish of Woolhope; Cherry Hill less than a mile north from Fownhope, and Ethelbert's camp to the south of Dormington. There is quite a strong and interesting example here away on the west of the Wye at Aconbury about 5 miles due south of Hereford. Along the valley west of Hereford there is Credenhill camp, and then the outline of the Roman town of Magna can be seen close by the river at Kenchester. Among a few camps about the centre of the county, Risbury, ¾ mile south

R

of the village of Humber, is an outstanding example; it is roughly
oval or sub-rectangular in plan and has several lines of rampart.
Another is Ivington, 3 miles south of Leominster, a large triangular
camp with several unusual features in its plan and construction.
Perhaps the best area for camps is up in the northern angle of
the county; there is Croft Ambrey, a roughly triangular multiple-
ramparted earthwork on the highest point of a ridge $1\frac{1}{2}$ miles
north-east of Aymestry; west of it in the same parish is the
much smaller example of Pyon Wood; farther west, nearing
the Welsh border, there is a strong camp on Wapley Hill,
Staunton on Arrow, with as many as five ramparts on the north-
east side.   Right in the north there is a not very distinguished
camp of triangular plan, Brandon, $\frac{3}{4}$ mile north of Adforden (not
far away to the north the village of Leintwardine stands within
the walls of the Roman station of Bravonium).   Finally,
straddling the Shropshire border on the west side of Buckton
and Coxhall parish, there is the interesting Coxhall Knoll camp,
a narrow oval with two additional enclosures at the east end.

(Offa's Dyke)

Something must now be said of that great and ambitious
monument, Offa's Dyke, even although it falls outside our
period.   This Anglo-Saxon earthwork, a large bank with a
ditch on the west side, which cuts off the Welsh mountains from
Mercia, seems in fact to have been built by the eighth-century
Mercian king after whom it is named.   Its over-all length from
the Severn near Chepstow to Dee estuary is as much as 149 miles;
here in Herefordshire it is broken into short lengths, for the land
was so heavily forested that it was only necessary to bar the
few natural openings through it.   But from the river Arrow
a few miles west of Wapley camp there is a fine stretch running
up through Knighton and Clun Forest past Montgomery to
join the Severn just east of Welshpool; it then leaves the Severn
5 miles to the north at New Cut, and soon after this point is
doubled by Wat's Dyke which runs parallel on its east side;
together they cross the Dee near Ruabon and die out near
Prestatyn as the sea is approached along the west side of the
Dee Estuary.

(Shropshire)

This hasty excursion along the course of Offa's Dyke has taken us far to the north; if we return to our starting-point round the Hereford border the first site in south Shropshire which should be named is the large camp of Titterstone on Clee Hill about 6 miles east of Ludlow on the north side of the Kidderminster road. Or if we leave Ludlow by the Shrewsbury road at Church Stretton we find the picturesque hill of Caer Caradoc which has some rather confusing defences and many legendary associations with Caratacus (p. 137); on the west side of Church Stretton the much visited Long Mynd has some groups of round barrows. There are too many camps on the hills of the Welsh marches here to name, but an outstanding example is Ffridd Faldwyn, ½ mile west of Montgomery; this camp has complex defences dating from various periods probably beginning fairly early in the Iron Age. Excavation in the interior discovered the remains of dwellings. Pushing north again to Shrewsbury, there are noteworthy sites on both sides of the town. On the east the Wellington road soon passes to the north of Wroxeter, the site of the Roman town of Uriconium; the ruins here are remarkable, including a massive fragment of the wall of a public building and the foundations of the town's large forum. A little farther to the west the magnificently isolated spine of the Wrekin is encircled by two distinct lines of rampart, one inside the other, both with interesting entrance works at their north-east ends; it is possible that this Iron Age fort represents the chief stronghold of the Celtic tribe of the Cornovii which in Roman times was shifted down to Viroconium (cf. p. 142). About a dozen miles west of Shrewsbury on the southern side of the Severn there is a striking camp in a dominating position on Breiddin Hill, while just across, on the northern side of the river, there is a lesser camp, Oliver's Point, at Great Ness and near by at Baschurch is another, the Berth, formerly surrounded by the now shrunken waters of a mere. Continuing northward along the Welsh border districts, the next important camp is Old Oswestry, an exceptionally fine work with multiple ramparts; circular hut foundations have been found inside. It seems that this camp, like the Breiddin, Ffridd Faldwyn and others, started early in the Iron Age with very simple defences, the multiplication of earthworks being undertaken later. The next camp to be specially named is of rather a different type—this is the promontory-fort of Maiden Castle on Bickerton Hill, in the southern part of the Central Cheshire Ridge between Wrexham and Crewe. Here double ramparts (with a fine entrance way through the inner one) are continued by a circuit of natural cliffs made steeper by an artificial cutting-back of the rock face.

(Cheshire)

This southern part of the Cheshire ridge has a number of minor camps and also some round barrows. On the east bank of the little Oakmere 5 or 6 miles south-west of Northwich there is a promontory-fort, and another 4 miles due west at Kellsboro' Castle; but the most remarkable example in this area is Castle Ditches, Eddisbury, lying just north between the two last-mentioned sites. This is a long oval camp following the contours of the hill; the complex ramparts are largely stone-built, while the entrance to the south-east has a wide passage-way cut in the solid rock and a pair of flanking guard chambers. Finally, in the northern extremity of the Ridge overlooking the Weaver valley and the Mersey, it is worth mentioning the camps of Bradley, Woodhouse Hill and Helsby Hill; south of them round barrows of some note are at Houndslow and Castle Hill (Norley parish).

Moving eastward across the Weaver valley to the Pennine foothills, we find many round barrows (particularly in the region between two concentrations of barrows at Old Withington and Over Alderley), while in the extreme west of Cheshire near Macclesfield there is the rectangular camp of Cloud. At Macclesfield we are near another centre where there are many antiquities set in lovely country: this is the district east of Buxton which includes also two most famous houses, Haddon Hall and Chatsworth.

(Derbyshire)

We can take as a convenient starting-point the most important monument in the neighbourhood, the sacred site of Arbor Low.

This embanked stone circle or 'henge' is by the Buxton–Ashbourne road 3 miles west of Middleton by Youlgreave; it can be approached by the road known as Long Rake and Little Oldham's Farm. An entrenchment leads from Arbor Low towards Gib Hill, an exceptionally large Bronze Age barrow. Also in the vicinity of Arbor Low (west of Bunty Grange Farm) is a small round barrow surrounded by a bank and ditch which is of interest because excavation proved it not to belong to the Bronze Age but to cover a rich Anglo-Saxon burial. Like Stonehenge and Avebury, though to a much humbler extent, Arbor Low provided a sacred centre for burials, and the moors round are dotted with round barrows, in this countryside known by the Scandinavian name of 'low' or some variant upon it. Not many are sufficiently distinguished for particular mention, although Endlow, 2 miles south of Gib Hill, and Liff's Low 2 miles south again, contained rich and interesting Bronze Age burials. Some of these round barrows have stone chambers, though not of large size, and usually of simple box-like construction. There are two such on Minninglow Hill, 5 miles south of Arbor Low, under its conspicuous clump of trees; the larger contains as many as five slab cists or chambers. A mile to the east of them is another chambered round barrow on Greenlow Hill. There is pleasant walking to Winster and Birchover to reach an inn curiously named the Druid's Arms, and a mile westward on Harthill Moor are four large stones, probably part of a circle; near them is a small earthwork known simply as Castle Ring. Going northward to Stanton, the road passes on its left a plantation which screens a big block called the Andlestone, said once to have stood within a stone circle; a very small circle (belonging to a barrow?) still stands 300 yards to the south-west. On the right-hand side of the same road is Stanton Moor, which can show many barrows, standing stones and other remains. Here the Cork Stone is a large boulder rigged for climbing, and within a fence 400 yards to the east is a round barrow with an exposed central structure of concentric stone rings and a cist. On the northern ridge of Stanton Moor is the Nine Ladies circle, with an outlying monolith known as the King Stone. It is north of Stanton that the magnificent scenery of Haddon Hall and Chatsworth begins. East of Chatsworth in wild moorland surroundings by Bunker's Hill

Wood is the well-known barrow called Hob Hurst's House, while to the west of Chatsworth near Taddington on the moors north of Five Wells Farm there is another good example of the round barrow with stone cist, this one with two separate compartments, in the tradition of megalithic construction.

Another famous and scientifically most important archæological centre in Derbyshire is the limestone gorge of Creswell Crags on the Nottinghamshire border near Worksop. Now at a step we are back in the middle of the Palæolithic Age, for the Creswell caves, particularly those known as Mother Grundy's Parlour and the Pin Hole, are among the most significant Palæolithic cave dwellings known in Britain. The succeeding layers of occupation-rubbish in these caves together cover the immense span of time from the mid-Palæolithic to the Mesolithic, the latter being represented by the indigenous Creswellian culture (p. 18) which takes its name from this gorge. The cave deposits here also give valuable evidence for the climate-changes at the outgoing of the Ice Age. There are also other caves in the neighbourhood of Taddington and Bakewell, some occupied in later prehistoric and Roman times.

VII. *FROM THE CHILTERNS TO EAST ANGLIA*

Before extending any farther into the north we must return to cover eastern England north of the Thames, starting from the middle Thames valley, where the Chilterns continue the chalk ridge of the Berkshire Downs and themselves in turn lead on to the East Anglian Heights and the Norfolk Edge. We shall also of course have to include in this section all the lowlands south and east of the chalk escarpment, particularly Essex, Suffolk and Norfolk. In the whole of the area so defined antiquities worth visiting are fairly sparse, and a continuous itinerary is therefore rarely possible.

(*Chilterns*)

If we begin from the southern extremity of the Chilterns we must recall that the Wittenham camp (Sinodun) and Dorchester have been described in Section II though they might equally well find a place here. Farther down river Wallingford has a conspicuous rectangular earthwork which is probably an Anglo-Saxon fortification. Crossing the bend of the Thames to Henley, attention must be called to the alien monument in the grounds of Templecombe, a house on the river terrace just south of Henley. This is a megalithic tomb of most unusual plan (a ring of separate rectangular chambers approached by a covered stone passage-way) which was presented on his retirement to a Governor of Jersey. It was transported in about 1785, and is a good example of the fashion for antiquities during the Romantic Age (incidentally a most Romantic inscription has been placed on the monument describing the bloody scenes of Druid sacrifice supposedly performed on these 'altars').

There are two main ancient trackways along the southern part of the Chilterns: the Chiltern Ridgeway along the crest from the Pangbourne crossing, and the Icknield Way, just to the north of it, from Goring; they meet 2 or 3 miles south-west of Princes Risborough. There is a sprinkling of round barrows and minor earthworks on the Chilterns; a kidney-shaped 'long barrow' at Whiteleaf near Princes Risborough deserves mention, though there is little to see. There is a noteworthy camp dated to the Belgic period of the Iron Age at Cholesbury some 8 miles north-east of Princes Risborough and south of Tring. Tring perhaps gives the signal to make a diversion eastward off the main line of the Chilterns to St. Albans, where there is so very much to see—parts of the walls, gate-foundations and buildings of Roman Verulamium; the excellent museum of finds from the site; and the Roman theatre, excavated and as far as possible restored (it is a true theatre and not an amphitheatre, and the only one discovered in Britain). Above the main Roman site the earthworks in Prae Wood represent the Belgic settlement which preceded the Roman city, just as we shall find the Belgic Camulodunum which was the precursor of the Colonia at Colchester.

North-east of St. Albans there is the further Belgic earthwork of Beech Bottom Dyke, best seen on the right-hand side of the road to Harpenden. This leads on to Wheathampstead, where two now distinct sections of bank and ditch above the Lea (known as the Devil's Dyke and the Slad) form part of what was once a great Belgic stronghold (p. 124), probably that of Cassivellaunus.

Returning now to the Chiltern ridge we come to its richest area, in the neighbourhood of Dunstable. Here is a fine group of round barrows, the Five Knolls, on Dunstable Downs, 3 miles west of the town. In the northernmost of these mounds an original Early Bronze Age crouched burial was uncovered and also, quite by chance, a whole group of extended skeletons representing a massacre of Anglo-Saxons, possibly a marauding party of the fifth or sixth century which for once was worsted by the local Britons. The other notable site over here is the camp of Maiden Bower just to the west, where in addition to the Iron Age occupations of the camp itself, the site has yielded Neolithic remains. As we advance farther along the chalk it is worth noting two other Iron Age camps, Willbury, just west of Letchworth, and Arbury Banks near Ashwell. There are also the well-known Six Hills at Stevenage. This line of neat round barrows, so conspicuous by the side of the Great North Road, are not prehistoric, but examples of Roman barrow-burial.

(Royston—Newmarket)

We do not reach another area of many monuments before Royston, where there are several sites of interest mingled with the bunkers of the Therfield Heath golf course. The most important is a long barrow, a great rarity in this part of the country and indicating an eastern spread of Wessex influences. To the north-west of the Heath there is a group of round barrows (another Five Knolls) and there are a number of others on the hills round Royston. The line of the Icknield Way runs to the north of Therfield Heath to be joined by the Roman Ermine Street (the Old North Road) at Royston itself. Continuing north-east along the chalk and bearing a little southwards there are some traces to be seen of the small Roman town at Great Chesterford; also an oval earthwork, Ring Hill, at Littlebury near Audley End. Farther north at Bartlow by the source of the Granta there is another series of Roman barrows, of most uncommon size. These, together with the Six Hills, Stevenage, are perhaps the most spectacular Roman barrows in the country; they covered richly furnished burials.

On the Gog Magog hills south-east of Cambridge is a fine stretch of Roman road, the best surviving section of the road from Huntingdon and Cambridge to Colchester; there are also a few round barrows up here, and lying to the south of the track in Stapleford parish is the circular Iron Age camp of Wandlebury, with two ramparts and a ditch still surviving. The most dramatic earthwork hereabouts, however, is the Fleam Dyke, a great linear earthwork which runs from Fulbourn towards Balsham, facing south-west. It is a post-Roman construction and was probably raised by the men of East Anglia against the neighbouring Middle Angles. It was designed to block the open line made by the chalk—for the Fulbourn end rested on marshland and the other on heavy forest. The Icknield Way (Newmarket Road), which of course follows this open line, cuts through the Dyke almost at the centre. There are a number of round barrows south of Fleam Dyke, and another considerable, though much damaged, group can be found some 5 miles farther along the Icknield Way round Upper Hare Park where the ground rises for Newmarket Heath; many barrows on the Heath have been levelled in the making of the racecourse. Another very widely known East Anglian monument is the Devil's Dyke which cuts across the racecourse at its Newmarket end; this is another linear earthwork consisting of a bank and ditch even larger than that of Fleam Dyke, with which it runs parallel. Like Fleam Dyke it barred the open upland, reaching from the fens at Reach to the old forest line at Wood Ditton.

(*The Breckland*)

We are now on the verge of that wild sandy heathland known as the Brecks which occupies central Norfolk and Suffolk. It makes attractive walking country, with a very special flora and fauna of its own; the broken heaths often make good hunting-ground for flint implements, and there is a scattering of round barrows throughout the area. It is country, indeed, where a sense of the prehistoric past is strong, although sites of out-standing individual interest are few. The show archæological

site of the Brecks is, of course, Grime's Graves, the most famous
of British flint-mining centres, lying 4 miles north of Brandon
near the village of Weeting.

A wide area of heath here is covered with the bumps and hollows
of filled mineshafts, such as we have seen in southern England
on the smoother turf of the chalk downs. Some have been
excavated and one roofed and kept open so that it is possible
to go down and follow the galleries that extend along the seams
of flint. Certain of the opened shafts have been dated to the
Neolithic period, others may be of Bronze Age date; the fertility-
shrine is described on p. 39.

We have now referred to the principal antiquities of the great
upland ridge which leads up from Berkshire, and ultimately
from the Wessex centres of prehistoric culture, right into East
Anglia. It was always a relatively open strip which could form
a corridor from one side of the country to another; it is in fact
the line of the Icknield Way.

(Essex)

Most of the country to the south and east of it was far more
thickly wooded in prehistoric times, and for this reason there
are only a few isolated sites which merit description. Starting
from London, there are two Iron Age camps in Epping Forest
—Ambresbury and Loughton, and there is a fine multiple-
ramparted camp known as Wallbury near Bishop's Stortford
(an unusual type of camp for eastern England). We can note
an Anglo-Saxon earthwork by the gas-works at Witham, but
the main centre of interest here is at Colchester. Here, first of
all, are the huge Belgic dykes which defended Cunobelin's
capital of Camulodunum (p. 132), best seen in Lexden Park
to the west of the town. The Belgic city itself (in reality a loose
scatter of habitations) had its densest concentration just west of
Colchester on the slopes rising from the by-pass road; there were
doubtless wharves here on the side of the Colne. Today there
is little more to be seen than a notice-board which the Corpora-
tion has set up on the by-pass, but the abundant Belgic finds
from the area are in the Castle Museum in Colchester, as are
also the quite exceptional Roman collections drawn from the

Colonia underlying the modern town. It is difficult to dig a
drain in Colchester without turning up some sign of the Roman
occupation. The principal ruins of the Colonia still to be seen
are long stretches of the town wall, with a small gateway on
the north and a large one, the Balkerne Gate, on the west, and
the foundations of the great temple of Claudius, which are
preserved intact beneath the Norman Castle (which also, with
the adjoining Holly Trees Mansion, houses the Museum).
There are also various excavated remains of structures in the
surrounding grounds. The other East Anglian sites most worth
visiting (though there are a few Iron Age camps, *e.g.* at Warham
in north Norfolk) are also Roman. In the late third and fourth
centuries the south-east coasts of the Province of Britain were
fortified against the attacks of marauding Saxons and other barbarians—the more southerly of these forts of the Saxon Shore
have already been encountered in Kent and Sussex (p. 191 ff.).
Others in the present region are at Bradwell (Essex), Burgh
Castle just east of Great Yarmouth and Brancaster on the north
Norfolk coast. The site of the Roman town at Caistor-next-
Norwich (Venta Icenorum), like that of the near-by Early
Bronze Age timber 'henge' at Arminghall, is better visible from
the air than from the ground; the same applies to the several
groups of round barrows in this area just south of Norwich.
Because of the now world-famous treasures found there, mention
should perhaps be made of the Sutton Hoo barrows south of
Woodbridge in Suffolk. The really astonishing ship-burial found
in one of them dates from the seventh century A.D., and its
treasures are now in the British Museum. Minor remains from
other barrows in the group are in Ipswich Museum which,
however, is more worth visiting for its great collections of
Palæolithic flint implements.

VIII. *LINCOLNSHIRE AND YORKSHIRE*

The main geological features of Lincolnshire and Yorkshire
are continuations of formations which begin in the south. The
chalk which we have followed as the Norfolk Edge almost
to the shores of the Wash reappears, though now curving back
a little to the west, as the Lincolnshire and the Yorkshire Wolds

(separated from one another by the Humber). Similarly the limestone hills of the Jurassic Belt, after the Witham gap, stand up again in the narrow 60-mile-long ridge of the Lincolnshire Edge, then, after a considerable gap in the East Riding, spread out as the north Yorkshire Moors. Beyond the wide Vale of York, western Yorkshire is of course occupied by the carboniferous limestone and millstone grit of the Pennine Chain, and in Bowland Forest the North Riding pushes right across to the west side of the Chain, and indeed reaches not so far from the west coast.

(*Lincolnshire Wolds*)

We will start from southern Lincolnshire, where the chalk, last seen in west Norfolk, appears once more on the north side of the Wash. Lincolnshire is an exceptionally thoroughly ploughed country and even the chalk Wolds have now lost a high proportion of the prehistoric sites that formerly existed there. Before mounting on to the Wolds there are a few sites off their southern edge that cannot be altogether ignored. One is Honington Castle, a small quadrangular camp, presumably of Iron Age date, which lies in the high ground south-west of the Roman fort of Ancaster; it is strongly defended with triple ramparts and represents the nearest approach in the county to a south English type. Two other monuments which can conveniently be mentioned here are a pair of interesting dykes that probably represent Roman canals. By far the larger is Car Dyke, a ditch between banks that run for 56 miles from the Nene at Peterborough to the Witham below Lincoln. The second is the Foss Dyke which goes at right angles to Car and joins the Trent at Torksey with the Witham at Lincoln. A number of Roman finds of one kind or another have been made along their course. We can now climb the southern slopes of the Lincolnshire Wolds. One of the most characteristic types of monument here is the long barrow, now largely destroyed or reduced by agriculture; most of them (as with the Yorkshire examples) seem to be relatively late in date and to represent a gradual spread northward from the great centres of Neolithic culture in southern England. Among long barrows here at the southern end of the Wolds perhaps the best preserved are a tree-covered pair which lie on separate spurs of the same hill north of the road between Skendleby station and Claxby, and are known as the Dead Men's Graves. It is not much farther west to Horncastle, near the western edge of the Wolds, where between the little rivers Bain and Waring there once stood a small Roman fortified town, still showing some remains of walls and one corner turret. There are similar fragments in the north of the Wolds at Caistor. The largest long barrow of the Wolds is not in the southern group but just north-east of the Louth road between the villages of Swaby and Walmsgate; farther north along this road, on Balby Hill by Haugham, a group of 7 round barrows have survived to be the finest of their kind in the county. Perhaps the most distinguished survival from the past in all Lincolnshire is Lincoln itself: the Newport Arch is the only original Roman arch in Britain under which traffic still passes— it was the north gate of the Roman town and through it ran the Ermine Street. Some stretches of the Roman walls and their outer entrenchments also remain, their line enclosing the Castle and the greater part of the cathedral.

(Yorkshire Wolds)

Crossing the Humber into the largest of English counties we find the chalk continuing as the Yorkshire Wolds that form a crescent curving from the Humber at Hessle right round to the cliffs of Flamborough Head, and cut off on their south-east side the low-lying nose of Holderness between the Humber and the North Sea. They are separated from the limestone moorlands of the North Riding by the Vale of Pickering. On the Yorkshire as on the Lincolnshire Wolds agriculture has destroyed a very large number of antiquities, above all a multitude of Bronze Age barrows. Entering as we do from Lincolnshire there is little to visit in Holderness although some interesting Mesolithic finds have been made there, and there was a remarkable Neolithic and late Bronze Age lake-dwelling in the north at West Furze near Ulrome. Coming up on to the Wolds and following their crescent from its tip on the Humber, we should notice that here in the south were the clusters of small round barrows which yielded the renowned La Tène burials of the Iron Age, including several chariot burials (p. 110). The best known clusters were the Danes' Graves at Kilham just north of Great Driffield (some of which still exist), and at Arras, 3 miles east of Market Weighton. Continuing in the south there is a round barrow, formerly covering five stone cists, between Menethorpe and North Grimston: it is known as Hedon Howe. Parallel entrenchments running on either side of Weaverthorpe can be noticed. Howe Hill south of Duggleby is one of the few well-preserved round barrows on these Wolds; we can visit it to get some impression of what very many others must once have been. It is 42 yards in diameter and still over 20 feet high; it proved to cover the relics of most astonishing burial rites. There were ten inhumations, one a huge old man 6 foot 3 inches tall, and about them, buried at the same time, were no less than 53 cremations, surely evidence for funerary sacrifice on a lordly scale. Both culturally and in the physical types of the individuals buried, Howe Hill shows signs of the superposition of Beaker upon surviving Neolithic peoples. If we go 12 miles farther to the north-east we encounter another, even larger, example of these gigantic round barrows, 60 yards across and 24 feet high; this is Willy Howe near Wold Newton, which has a legend of mysterious feasting within the mound. Here towards the north-eastern termination of the Wolds at Flamborough Head and Scarborough there are many and varied antiquities. Rudston, 5 miles west of Bridlington, has a colossal monolith 25 feet high in its churchyard, one of the tallest standing stones in the whole country. A linear earthwork of three banks and two ditches runs north from Rudston to Reighton. Cutting off 5 square miles of the tip of Flamborough Head is the massive Danes' Dyke, with a bank sometimes still 18 feet high and a very wide ditch on the landward side; its age is uncertain. North-west of Hunmanby between that village and Folkton is another linear earthwork. Near here on Flotmanby Wold, right on the northern brink of the chalk, is one of the finest surviving Wold long barrows, while in a round barrow near Folkton were found the famous chalk idols (p. 69). In one of a group of three other round barrows just inland from the Gristhorpe cliffs, north of Filey, was found a Bronze Age burial in an oak coffin. At Scarborough the Roman signal station on the Castle Hill (also an Early Iron Age settlement-site) is open to the public.

(North Yorkshire Moors)

We are now approaching the limestone uplands of the North Yorkshire Moors, framed between the Vales of Pickering and York, the Tees valley and the North Sea; it is made up roughly as follows: there are the two main components of the Limestone Hills running from Scarborough to the Vale of York, and the Eastern Moorlands to the north of them. These can be further divided; the west end of the Limestone Hills is formed by the Hambletons while on their northern boundary are the Tabular Hills; in the north the Eastern Moorlands terminate in the high and lovely Cleveland Hills. This whole upland plateau, being far less cultivated than the Wolds, is rich in antiquities; in particular it is rich in round barrows—it has been calculated that there are still 10,000 of them, some large and standing singly, others tiny mounds in clusters of up to 1300. First as we approach from Scarborough we must notice the extensive complex of linear earthworks known as the Scamridge Dykes which run partly on Dalby Warren to the south of the Limestone Hills north-east of Pickering. Then 4 miles north of Pickering at Cawthorn on the edge of the Tabular Hills is a most remarkable series of Roman camps belonging to the Trajanic period; troops from the Cawthorn camps may have built the Roman road known as Wade's Causeway which runs up to them from near Malton and goes on northward to end a little inland from Whitby; when exposed winding across the moors complete with its central paved causeway it was a magnificent example of its kind. Not very far away there are two long barrows to be seen at Cropton; there are also groups of round ones in many areas of the Limestone Hills, notably on Maw and Thompsons Riggs, near the curious hill of Blakey Topping; on the south-west side, too, of this isolated hill are three standing stones thought to be the remains of a circle. There is an even richer region if, instead of turning westward from Scarborough, we go north. First, just west of Cloughton there is a good stone circle on Standing Stones Rigg; passing Ravenscar (the site of

a Roman signal station) we come to John Cross Rigg between
Robin Hood's Bay and Iburndale Head, where there is a vast
necropolis of 1300 small round barrows. This necropolis
is cut by a linear earthwork running due east and west for a
total length of $\frac{1}{2}$ a mile; it consists of 4 ramparts with 3 ditches.
The Goathland–Sleights Moor area westward from John Cross
Rigg is thick with ancient monuments. North of the Blakey
Topping area already described is Loose Howe, a barrow which
covered a remarkable Bronze Age boat burial. Along the Whin-
stone Ridge and beyond is a line of this larger type of round
barrow: by name these Howes are the Lilla, Lowen, Ann,
Fosters, Robbed, Sill, Breckon and Flat; of this list one of the
two Foster Howes and the Robbed and Flat Howes have an
encircling ring of stones (peristaliths). The line of these round
barrows brings us to Sleights Moor proper, with its Stone Circle,
High Bridestones, to the west of Flat Howe. (The Low Bridestones, it must be explained, are only the remains of field walls.)
Sleights Moor can also show some clusters of the small type
of round barrow. Immediately to the north from here across
the Esk the country is comparatively poor in antiquities, but
there is a well-preserved Roman signal station at Goldsborough
on the southern point of Runswick Bay. Moving west there
are barrows and traces of prehistoric settlement on Danby Low
Moor and Commondale, and on the spur north of Sleddale
there is a stone circle as well as small-barrow clusters; these last
are particularly plentiful also on the spur between Sleddale and
Kildale. One of the most impressive of the large type of round
barrow is Robin Hood's Butts in this region, 2 miles north of
Danby. Guisborough Moor has both large and small barrows
(some of the former with peristalith). North of Guisborough,
on the northernmost limit of this moorland country, the Eston
Hills between Middlesbrough and Saltburn have a good specimen
of a semicircular camp with the rampart ends abutting on to
a sandstone cliff. But the best hunting-ground here in the
Cleveland Hills is south of Danby, round Danby High Moor and
Castleton Ridge. The northern extremity of Danby Rigg is
sown with round barrows in the midst of which is a stone circle;
this seems also to have been a settlement-area, for the spur is
cut off first by a single rampart and then by a fine double one
(between the two lies an earth circle and three standing stones

with it). Three miles farther west there is a comparable con-
glomeration of antiquities on the spur known as Crown End,
Castleton, while south of Danby Rigg there are some larger,
named, round barrows—Pind Howes, Wolf Pit and the three
Western Howes. Passing on to the south-west of the Cleveland
Hills, there is another particularly prolific area between Bilsdale
and Ryedale: the ridge between the upper reaches of the two
has a line of the large round barrows—Flat Howe (another of
this name), Cock Howe, Green Howe and Benky Hill—while
all round the slopes are small-barrow clusters. Just across the
Bilsdale Beck is a stone circle again known as the Bridestones.
Turning south again now to complete the circuit of this North
Riding Moorlands, we come to the Hambleton Hills, a region
again scattered with round barrows, and with a long barrow
at their northern limit at Kepwick Moor, Over Silton. Towards
the south-west bounds of the Hambletons there is a semicircular
earthwork on Boltby Scar very similar to the Eston camp
(p. 256); inside are two round barrows and an unexplained oval
mound.

Still in the North Riding but off the main upland area which
has now been surveyed a few more isolated sites should be
named; a number of them are Roman, including camps and forts
on the line of the Roman road that leads north-west from
Aldborough through Catterick on the line of the present Great
North Road. Catterick itself is the site of the Roman fort of
Cataractonium, portions of whose east wall are still visible.
Just north of Catterick at the famous Scots Corner, where, while
the main north road goes ahead through the late Roman fort
of Piercebridge, the Carlisle road forks westward for the Stain-
more Pass, following its Roman predecessor. It passes through
the Roman sites of Greta Bridge, where the fort is to be seen
behind the Morritt Arms, and Bowes (another unexplored fort),
then just on the country boundary and the Pass, cuts through
the Roman legionary camp of Rey Cross where the defences
are 300 feet square; this temporary camp must have been a
forerunner of the forts at Bowes and Brough-under-Stainmore
in Westmoreland, to which the road now drops.

Others include Castle Steads, a good example of camp at
Gayles between Richmond and Barnard Castle, and the big linear
earthwork known as the Scot's Dyke which runs from Barforth-

S

on-Tees to Hindwath-on-Swale, past the great complex of
earthworks at Stanwick, where a hoard of La Tène metalwork
of the Iron Age was found. A continuation is said to have run
along the south bank of the Swale to Grinton where (but nothing
to do with the Dyke?) there is a circular earthwork called Maiden
Castle, which is approached from the east by a stone avenue.

(West Riding—Yorkshire Dales)

The West Riding of Yorkshire has a number of important and
interesting sites, particularly Roman ones, but it largely lacks
the concentration of antiquities found in the moorland of the
North Riding; there are few areas where prehistoric man still
commands the landscape. If we enter from the extreme south
there is a group of sites worth visiting north-east of Sheffield.
First there is the camp of Wincobank on a spur above the Don
valley about 3 miles from the city; it is oval in plan and its double
ramparts enclose 2½ acres; it certainly belongs to a late phase of
the Iron Age. Only 2½ miles farther to the north-east is another
even smaller camp of similar plan in Scoles Wood. A linear
earthwork of considerable scale, 11 miles in length, runs just
below the hill crests on the west side of the Don and passes close
below Wincobank camp on its route from Sheffield to Swinton;
it is generally comparable to the Scot's Dyke (p. 257), and for
the present is equally undatable.

Another industrial town with antiquities of interest in its
neighbourhood is Huddersfield. To the south-west at Almond-
bury is the exceptionally fine and impressively sited camp of
Castle Hill whose oval rampart and ditch enclose an area of about
8 acres on a lofty spur; on the west side the Iron Age works are
cut about by the motte and bailey of a Norman castle. This
camp overlooks the line of the Roman road from Slack to
Manchester, and it should be noted that the remains of an
originally Agricolan fort are to be seen at Slack on the west side
of Huddersfield while on an opposite spur is another Iron Age
oval earthwork; another fort-site comparable to Slack is farther
along this road at Castleshaw. Near here on the Lancashire
border, where it heads for Manchester across Blackstone Edge,
there is a famous strip of the Roman road in almost its original

condition, bounded by kerbstones 16 feet apart, with a central paved strip worn in places by the skid-pans of carts descending the steep hill.

To reach the next area of archæological interest we must cross the main industrial area of the West Riding and land to the north of Leeds and Bradford. Here, although strictly outside our period, attention must be called to the Anglian and Viking carvings in the church at Otley and the famous group of Anglian cross shafts in the churchyard at Ilkley—Ilkley is also a Roman fort-site. The best-known prehistoric remains here in mid-Wharfedale are the cup-and-ring marked stone (natural boulders and outcrops in which circular pits sometimes surrounded by rings have been carved; they date from the Bronze Age) which are seen at their finest among the heather on Rombald's Moor above Ilkley and Burley; just above the latter, too, is a stone circle. Another much smaller group of cup-and-ring carved rocks is on the other (north) side of the road on Snowdon Moor, while another circle, the Twelve Apostles, stands a few miles farther south towards Bingley. Near the village of Nesfield a short way beyond Ilkley on the Skipton road is a semicircular camp on a cliff edge recalling those of Eston and Boltby (pp. 256-7); a few miles across moorland to the north-east there is a fine stretch of Roman road (Watling Street) to be seen on Blubberhouses Moor. A branch from this road ran north-west, and at Long Preston on the Settle road there are two Roman camps beside its course. Farther on, in the region of Settle itself, is the well-known Victoria Cave which was occupied in the Mesolithic period and has yielded a characteristic Azilian bone harpoon (p. 22). It was inhabited again during Roman times, in the third and fourth centuries A.D. North-west of Settle we must mention the remarkable Iron Age fortified settlement which occupies the summit of the great isolated hill of Ingleborough; the elaborate stone-built walls are unhappily much damaged by modern cairns; inside traces of many huts can be seen. Fourteen miles to the south-east another cave, Dowkerbottom, between Arncliffe and Kilnsey, was also occupied in the Roman period and still contains occupation-rubbish. Arncliffe can also show an exceptionally interesting Iron Age enclosure system situated on the plateau formed by the Great Scar limestone just south of the village. Here there are two enclosures, the more southerly lined with dwellings that have immensely thick walls and in one instance at least 'beehive' corbelling. This is only one site of a number in this part of the dales, and particularly the Upper Wharfe and Skirfare valleys, where rectangular enclosures, hut circles and rectangular field systems, often also small barrows, are found in association; on the other hand these valleys are often conspicuously marked with the long 'strip lynchets' which are the remains of Anglian or later cultivation. Among these numerous 'Celtic' sites there is one near Grassington which merits special notice, for here in High Close Pasture is a very fine set of Celtic lynchets, with hut circles, probably marking the homes of their cultivators, near by in Grass Wood. South of them is the 'Druid's Circle', an oval enclosure whose bank is topped with stone blocks; this work also probably has some connexion with the settlement. Not far away at Netherside Hall, Threshfield, is a group of Bronze Age barrows.

We can now move eastward away from this lovely dale country to take note of a monument which is certainly one of the most spectacular in Yorkshire: the Devil's Arrows at Borough-bridge (Roecliffe). These are three huge blocks of millstone grit, curiously grooved by natural weathering, which stand at some little distance from one another in a line running roughly north and south; one is 18 feet high, the others 22½ feet—which is slightly more than the height of the Stonehenge uprights (though not so high as the Rudston monolith, p. 254). Little is known directly of these great stones, but they are likely to date from the Bronze Age and may not be unconnected with the fairly numerous Bronze Age remains in the neighbourhood. For instance, on Hutton Moor just north of Ripon is a settlement and a large banked circle, probably a sacred enclosure, while, more impressive, 5 miles to the north, Thornborough Moor (near West Tanfield) has more settlement-remains and three huge banked circles of a similar type.

Before leaving Yorkshire something must be said of York itself, for in addition to its wonderful medieval possessions, the city has some outstanding Roman antiquities, and the Roman collections of its Museum are exceptionally fine. Founded as a legionary fortress in about A.D. 71 York had an important history as the main military centre for the north of the Province.

The fortress was rebuilt in the fourth century, and the most prominent piece of surviving Roman architecture is one of its bastions—now known as the Multangular Tower.

IX. NORTH LANCASHIRE: CUMBERLAND AND WESTMORELAND

Beyond the gap of the Cheshire Plain where the Midlands, extending in effect to the Irish Sea, split the Highland Zone (p. 3) we enter upon another mountainous area in North Lancashire, Westmoreland and Cumberland. This was not an area of intensive prehistoric settlement, the main mountain masses were too forbidding, yet there is still quite a lot which is worth seeing: the best areas being round the south-western coast and along the valleys of the Eden and its tributaries.

(Westmoreland)

Approaching from North Lancashire there is little of note (some small undated camps on the east side of the Kent Estuary and of the river Winster near its mouth) until we cross the south tip of Windermere into the Barrow peninsula. Here there are a few Bronze Age round barrows on either side of Urswick, while Urswick Stone Walls is a small fortified site which excavation has shown to be of Roman (and perhaps Iron Age) date. Beyond the base of the peninsula there are stone circles at Ash House near Duddon Bridge and Sunken Kirk at Swinside, at Hall Foss by Bootle and at Annaside right on the coast; a more doubtful example is on the end of the peninsula at Kirkstanton. A small undated fort can be seen just north of Hall Foss. Pushing on up the coast we find yet another stone circle in Eskdale on the north side of the Boot Inn; it encloses 5 round barrows with peristaliths. There are some small long cairns together with hut circles between Raven Crag and Latterbarrow in Eskdale; near here also is the (? Iron Age) Barnscar settlement-site. Before we stop this coastal journey at St. Bees Head, there is a stone circle to be seen in the Ringlen Stones a mile west of

Egremont and some standing stones at Kinniside between here and Ennerdale.

(*Lake District*)

We have now passed up the west side of the Lake District. That District itself was hardly suitable for prehistoric settlement, and there is little to record save a few small forts—notably four in a line along the south-east side of Derwentwater, and in the same area, the famous Castle Rigg circle just west of Keswick. This circle, which is also known as the Keswick Carles, has 39 sizable stones and a diameter of about 100 feet. On the northern fringe of the Lake District is another circle at Elva Plain on the south side of the Derwent a few miles after it leaves Bassenthwaite. Isolated mention must be made of the well-excavated Roman fort just south of Ambleside, and of that of Hardknot, on the famous pass south of Scafell into Eskdale.

(*Eden Valley*)

We can now cross this main massif and survey the remains along its east side and beyond—roughly along the course of the Eden. Near the head of the Eden system there are round barrows in the Ravenstonedale area and from there west and north to Shap; in this piece of country also is a large stone circle at Gamelands near Orton. Between Orton and Shap there is an important Iron Age settlement-area (and also a long cairn) near Crosby Ravensworth, while at Shap itself there was a standing stone avenue with a circle at one end now largely destroyed by the railway. There is another round-barrow concentration between the Lowther river and Ullswater and small forts just north of that lake. In the narrow angle of land between the Lowther and Eamont rivers, close to the Castle and Roman fort of Brougham, is the monument of Mayburgh. This last is a rather anomalous form of the stone circle in which a large ring work of rubble is closely associated with standing stones.

More round barrows are north of the Eamont at this point, between it and the river Petterill. If we go down the Eamont to the Eden we find a number of forts on the hills on the east side of the valley, and here also, just north of Salkeld, is the largest stone circle of all that we have encountered in this region: Long Meg and her Daughters has a diameter of approximately 350 feet and 59 standing stones. The catalogue of circles is completed when about 7 miles due north we notice the Grey Yauds in Cumrew parish.

X. DURHAM, THE ROMAN WALL AND NORTHUMBERLAND

(Durham)

On the north side of Carlisle ran Hadrian's Wall, perhaps the most widely renowned of all our national monuments. But before saying more of it some attention must be given to the county of Durham and the portion of Northumberland which, lying between our stopping point in the North Riding (p. 256) and the Wall, would otherwise be omitted. Not that there is very much of archæological importance in this country; its covering of boulder clay allowed the growth of heavy forest, almost always unattractive to prehistoric man. Its most remarkable site is not in fact a prehistoric one, but the Roman town of Corstopitum at the modern Corbridge just east of Hexham. Some of the most interesting finds from the whole Province have been made there and are now to be seen in the museum. Also near Hexham is the conspicuous camp on Old Warden Hill. There are Roman forts also at Ebchester, Binchester, Lanchester, Chester le Street and South Shields.

(The Roman Wall)

But the great glory of this part of northern England is of course Hadrian's Wall, the great Roman frontier work which cuts across the country from the north side of the Tyne at Wallsend to Bowness on the Solway Firth (p. 143). The outline of the history of this frontier (architecturally one of the best preserved and most striking in the whole western Empire) has been given in the body of the book; nor will it be described in detail here, for Bruce's famous guide-book has been devoted to it. Its exploration does in fact provide the perfect theme for a holiday for those so minded. Thoroughly obliterated by the industrial region of Tyneside, it begins to be possible to trace and to enjoy it west of Wallbottle and Heddon on the Wall. The first site of monumental interest is, however, considerably farther west still, at Chollerford where the Wall crossed the North Tyne. Here is the fortress of Chesters (Cilurnum) with its bathhouse and the abutments of the bridge which crossed the small river below the fort. It is less than 10 miles west of Cilurnum that we reach the most famous and magnificent stretch of Hadrian's Wall where it rides the wild craggy scarp above Crag Lough. The fortress of Housesteads or Borcovicium here is one of the most important and certainly the most impressively sited, with its northern wall built immediately on the precipitous edge. The next fort, again of distinction, is Great Chesters or Æsica; at Gilsland there is an elaborate bridge-abutment for the crossing of the river Irthing and, on the cliff edge to the west, the fort of Camboglanna or Birdoswald. From this point to the Solway, the Wall still stands in intermittent stretches, but it never again has either the completeness or the grandeur of the famous length between Chollerford and Gilsland. Anyone staying at Gilsland should not fail to go into the remote country to the north to see one of the two finest crosses in the country, that which stands, within the site of another Roman fort, in the church-yard at Bewcastle.

(*The Cheviots*)

In Northumberland north of the Wall, particularly on the Cheviots, there are great numbers of settlement sites and little forts; although some no doubt date from the pre-Roman Iron Age many must have been occupied during the Roman period; they are too numerous and too ill-explored to be treated with any thoroughness. Their greatest concentrations are along the line of the North Tyne and along the Till and its tributaries, especially the Glen and Breamish. Perhaps the most striking of all is the circular multi-ramparted camp of Greaves Ash, which has outlying earthworks and huts and other interesting internal features. Not much farther down the Breamish there are many round barrows round Prendwick, where also are the camps and hut sites of Chesters (2 miles east of Greaves Ash) Near Chesters in particular there are large round barrows on Ingram Hill, and there is a double-ramparted circular fort on Brough Law. Considerably farther north near the junction of Glen and Till there is another good circular fort on Yeavering Bell, south of Kirknewton. We have picked out only a few of the antiquities of the Cheviots; in general they may be regarded as a continuous series with those of southern Scotland.

XI. *SCOTLAND*

Lack of resources makes it impossible to treat Scotland even with the modest degree of detail which has been attempted for England and Wales. But in order to cover the whole of Great Britain in some fashion a general outline will be given of the principal types of monument to be found in different regions of the Northern Kingdom. These will be found mainly to represent (1) the settlement of the megalith-building peoples along the west coast from Galloway to Orkney and the subsequent spread of some of them to the Moray Firth region; (2) the arrival of the Beaker peoples along the east coasts and their spread across country; they, together with the ensuing Food-Vessel and Urn peoples (pp. 66, 67), not only built round barrows or cairns, but very often buried their dead in well-made rectangular 'short cists' measuring from 3 to 4 by about 2 feet, built with flat slabs and often roofed with a large coverstone; (3) the development also by these peoples of the stone circle for tombs or other sacred areas; (4) the Celtic invasions and the resulting astonishing scale of military building in the form of (*a*) rare large hill-forts or 'hill-towns' comparable to those of the south of England in scale, (*b*) the specially constructed type known as the Gallic Fort in which stone walls are bound with timber (*murus gallicus*), (*c*) forts which have long been described as 'vitrified', although recent experiment has shown that they

are in fact Gallic forts with their stone walls fused by the burning
of the timber, (d) small forts or 'castles', in the Lowlands, generally with two or more earthen ramparts, in other regions with
massive stone masonry (very many of these date from the Roman
period, when Scotland was still of course mainly independent
and 'prehistoric'), (e) brochs, the distinctive north Scottish
architectural development—a circular tower with rooms, stair-
cases and passage-ways in the width of the walls, (f) crannogs
constructed on semi-floating log platforms in lochs, (g) earth-
houses, subterranean refuges often of very large size and complex
plan.

The main geographical features of Scotland are quite simply
defined.   After the boundary of the Cheviots there are small
lowland regions round the lower Tweed and in southern
Galloway and the head of the Solway Firth; the Southern Uplands
stretch across from the North Sea coast between St. Abb's Head
and North Berwick south-west to the Galloway Hills.   Next
to the north follows the Midland Valley, the great lowland
wedge of Scotland that lies between the northern scarps of the
Lammermuirs, Moorfoots and Lowther Hills and the southern
edge of the Highlands, and which today has so large a share of
the population and industry of the country.   This lowland area
is of course partially broken up by various natural features, minor
hill-formations such as the Ochils and Pentlands, sea inlets, and
tracts of moorland.   The Highlands, which must be taken to
include the western islands that are geographically very much a
part of the mountain system, are cut across from south-west to
north-east (the main lie of the Scottish ranges) by the Great Glen.
North-East Scotland includes important coast plains, those of
Aberdeen and Banffshire, lands round the Moray Firth, Caithness;
the Orkney Islands are also a lowland area.

(South of the Clyde and Forth)

(a) *East.*—In this area across the English border, the chief
monuments are the innumerable small forts, often with double
ramparts and either round or irregular in plan, which must
often have been in use during the Roman occupation of England,
and which were for the most part, indeed, probably put up

against the Romans. They have their greatest concentrations in the valleys of the Tweed and its tributaries, in the middle and upper reaches of the Annan and in Berwickshire. There are, for example, 16 of these small forts within a small region of the Tweed valley near Peebles and 20 round about Moffat in the Annan area. This south-eastern territory also has some of the relatively rare larger hill-forts; perhaps the finest in the country at Traprain Law in East Lothian, and another of great interest in Burnswark in the Annan area, where a fine hill-fort lies between a pair of Roman siege-camps. Others of these large hill sites are Bonchester Hill, Roxburghshire, Eildon Hill near Melrose, White Melville and Cademuir Hill near Peebles and Kaimes Hill, Midlothian. Beaker and Food-Vessel burials are most frequent in Berwick and East Lothian. There are also isolated brochs near Stirling and Galashiels.

(b) *West*.—From the Annan westward to Galloway and the Clyde the most important and interesting new element is provided by the megalithic tombs. These belong to the so-called Clyde–Solway class which is characterized by parallel-sided megalithic galleries set in cairns that may be either long or round (p. 46), and which may have a semicircular courtyard at the entrance. There are several of these round the Nith and a number more between the Dee and Stranraer. The southern half of Arran is particularly rich in these galleries (including Carn Ban, a well-known example with long cairn and well-defined forecourt), and there are some three in southern Kintyre. Small forts are rather less plentiful here than farther east, although they occur in some numbers round Kirkcudbright and along the coast from Burrow Head to Glenluce, from the Mull of Galloway to Loch Ryan, and in Arran and southern Kintyre; their absence in the Galloway Hills is most noticeable. There is a larger hill-fort near Castle Douglas and several crannogs in Wigtownshire—notably a cluster of four in Dowalton Loch. Three brochs can be mentioned near Glenluce, Stranraer and Port Logan.

The line of the Clyde–Forth that demarcates our present region was followed by that second Roman frontier in Britain usually known as the Antonine Wall. A line of forts were first built here in A.D. 81 during Agricola's successful Scottish campaign, but after the retreat to the line of Hadrian's Wall they were re-established more strongly in about A.D. 140. With a fort about every 1½–2 miles the Antonine Wall girdles this narrow waist of Scotland from Bridgeness to Old Kilpatrick; the best identifiable forts (from east to west) are at Mumrills, Rough Castle, Castlecary, Bar Hill, Balmuildy and Old Kilpatrick.

(North of the Clyde and Forth—to the Esk and Ardnamurchan)

(a) *East.*—The eastern side of this central region has not many spectacular sites, although it was an area well settled from the Beaker period onwards. Beaker and Food-Vessel sites (round cairns and cists) are most numerous on either side of the Tay, but most sites worth visiting are of the Iron Age. There are, for examples, two important Gallic forts on the Ochils south of the Tay, both named Castle Law; one lies behind Abernethy, the second behind Forgandenny. There are two of the larger hill-forts in Angus, south of Brechin and near Inchbare, and four vitrified forts between Tay and Esk. This last region also contains several of the 'souterrains' or earth-houses. This whole area, and particularly the Tay valley, is notable for the sites of Roman forts, the finest being the multiple-ditched fort of Ardoch, north of Bridge of Allan.

(b) *West.*—This is the only Scottish region where Mesolithic sites will be mentioned; two caves near Oban, MacArthur's and Druim Vargie, are famous for the Azilian remains found there (cf. Victoria Cave, Settle, p. 259). As far as megaliths are concerned, the Clyde–Solway group already described south of the Clyde extends also north of it as far as Loch Etive. There is a considerable concentration on the island of Bute and on the Clyde near Dunoon; there are two on the south side of Loch Fyne (one with forecourt), then another small concentration across Loch Fyne in the Crinan region. This last region is, indeed, important enough to merit a special digression; in addition to megalithic tombs there are circles and lines of standing stones, a number of Bronze Age cists, some with carvings of exceptional interest, small forts and one vitrified fort. The most northerly of the Clyde–Solway megalithic gallery-graves are three on the south side of Loch Etive, while

the most westerly are two on the southern coast of the island
of Islay.

The distribution in this region of small forts is very similar;
there are many in Bute and round Loch Fyne, especially on the
southern side, while those already mentioned in Kintyre (p. 267)
continue right up the west coast of the peninsula and on in an
unbroken line northward to Etive, where there are a number,
together with one broch, on the small island of Lismore.
There are many more in east Islay between Port Ellen and
Ardtalla and also in the west of the island north of Portnahaven.
Mull has a sprinkling in the south- and north-west, and the latter
area also has two brochs. Finally the two small islands north-
west of Mull—Coll and Tiree—can show a great concentration
of these small forts.

Vitrified forts are not common but there is one in Bute, one
south of Loch Fyne, one (already mentioned) in the Crinan
area, one on Etive and two south of Loch Linnhe.

It will be noticed in all the western Highland regions the distribution of antiquities is almost entirely coastal or by sea inlets;
the mountains from the Grampians through Inverness and Ross
and Cromarty were virtually uninhabited in prehistoric times.

*(The North-Central Region—from Esk and Ardnamurchan to Loch
Broom and the Moray Firth, including the Hebrides)*

(a) *East.*—North-east Scotland from the Esk (Montrose) up
to the Moray Firth has lowland areas well populated in Bronze
and Iron Age times; the only area with monuments of Neolithic
character is round the Moray Firth itself. These are the group
of megalithic round cairns known as the 'Clava' group; they
seem to have been introduced by settlers pushing across or round
from the west coasts; they are typologically very late and must
many of them belong to the Bronze Age. The main concentrations (and they tend to be built in small clusters) are in
the Ness and Nairn valleys and the upper valley of the Spey
round Aviemore; they have been named after a well-known
group in the Clava estate near Culloden. In this Clava type
the round cairn commonly has both a containing peristalith and
a much larger outer ring of standing stones. In some there is

a passage through the inner peristalith to the central chamber, but in other and presumably later examples the passage has been omitted and the chamber is closed; the outer ring of standing stones naturally tends to become the main architectural feature, and it will be noticed that they are peculiar in that the stones on one side (often the south-west) are the largest, the heights dwindling towards the north. It is this latter characteristic which makes it perfectly clear that these Clava-type tombs are closely related to another distinctive type of monument found in the present region, though with a much more eastern distribution. These are the so-called Recumbent Stone Circles, some 70 of which are to be found in the triangle formed between the coasts and a line from the mouth of the Spey to Bervie Bay. This distinctive Aberdeen type of circle commonly has three rings with traces of a very low cairn at the centre. The outer ring (as in the Clava megaliths) generally dwindles in size from south to north, and the largest pair of uprights have fitted between them a huge recumbent slab which may weigh up to 20 tons. Some of these circles were frequented down to a late phase of the Bronze Age, but they belong initially to the Beaker period, and appear to be architecturally derived from the Clava tombs.

The Aberdeen and Moray Firth areas were exceptionally thickly settled by the Beaker invaders and can show a number of cairns and short cists. Another type of monument which is numerous in this region is the vitrified fort; they are most frequent round the Beauly Firth, but there is one example as far north as Dornoch Firth, three in the Nairn valley and one in the Findhorn. A very notable Iron Age site is the Gallic fort on the coast at Burghead on the south side of the entrance to the Moray Firth. There is a scatter of small forts through Aberdeen and a group of them in the Beauly valley. There are earth-houses near the river Don in the Alford neighbourhood.

(b) *West.*—This region of north-west Scotland is on the mainland almost entirely lacking in antiquities; the rich areas are the islands, Skye and the Hebrides, most particularly the south Hebridean islands of North and South Uist and Barra. As might be expected from its geographical position, the megaliths of this island region have elements derived from both north (Caithness passage-grave group) and south (Clyde–Solway gallery group); as for the covering cairns, the round form is commoner than the long. One of the very few of these tombs to have been properly explored, South Clettravel in North Uist, is an excellent example of passage-grave—galley-grave hybrid. A noteworthy example which comes closer to the passage-grave type is Rudh' an Dunain in Skye; this has a large round cairn with a peristalith and a forecourt with a recumbent slab at its centre; the polygonal chamber is approached through a passage and ante-chamber. Another well-known monument in this region is Callernish in the island of Lewis; here the small round cairn and rectangular chamber are far less spectacular than the peristalith, which is so far outside the cairn as to suggest an independent stone circle; avenues and stone rows radiate from it. Small forts are common on the north and south coasts of Skye, abundant in North Uist and down the west coast of South Uist, but rather less frequent in Harris and Lewis. We are also entering the fringes of the northern cradle of the broch; there are remains of some 44 in Skye and the Hebrides (most in northern Skye) and two on the mainland near Glenelg.

(North Scotland, the Orkneys and Shetlands)

This region is of course a direct continuation of the last. The area between Glenelg and Enard's Bay is blank, but in Sutherland, Caithness and the Orkneys we have perhaps the richest and most interesting regions in Scotland—and one indeed which contains many of the most celebrated sites in Britain. The Caithness group of megaliths (p. 46) are more numerous than the Clyde-Solway group; they often occur in clusters, while the southern ones are scattered. The chamber is usually a true passage-grave in which a narrow entrance way leads into the much larger chamber (p. 44). The cairns of some of these megaliths are in themselves most remarkable; they may be either short or long, but have more or less straight sides, while one or both of the ends may be recessed to form a semicircular court—it is this feature that gives the curious 'horned' plan. In the south-east part of the region the short horned cairn is found, though sparsely, as far south as Dornoch Firth, but the distinctive long form is not recorded beyond Morven on the

southern Caithness–Sutherland border. The concentration of
both long and short forms in Caithness itself is remarkable—
for instance 9 or 10 of them between Lochs Shurrery and Calder.
Here in Caithness, Warehouse Hill is a good centre—with fine
groups at Camster and on Sordale Hill and Cnoc Freiceadain.
There are further megalithic sites to the south in Easter Ross.
The other type of monument for which this most northern
region is celebrated is the broch—whose place of origin it is.
North and west of a line from Lochinver to Cromarty Firth
brochs are amazingly numerous along the rivers and coasts of
Sutherland and all over the tip of Caithness. Many are of
course so completely ruined as to be (without excavation) very
little more than overgrown hummocks, but it is most remarkable
that there should be evidence for at least 80 brochs in Sutherland
and 145 in Caithness. Ordinary small forts are correspondingly
rare in this region. There are several earth-houses on the southern
Caithness–Sutherland boundary, inland from Helmsdale.

The Orkneys must always have the strongest possible appeal
to those interested in prehistory. Now they seem remote, but
in prehistoric, more especially Neolithic, as in Viking, times,
they were an important point on the sea route that led from the
Atlantic coasts of Europe right over to Scandinavia. Most of
the islands have megalithic architecture to show; on the largest,
Mainland, the most famous and magnificent is Maeshowe
(p. 46), the stone circles on lake Stennis, and notably the Ring
of Brodgar, with its well-preserved encircling bank and ditch
(p. 63). On the west coast of Mainland, too, is Skara Brae,
the most complete prehistoric settlement in Britain (p. 64).
There are also 50 brochs on Mainland, including a fine excavated example on the north coast opposite the island of
Rousay. Rousay itself is extraordinarily full of archæological
interest, partly, perhaps, because its owner is enthusiastically
interested in the subject. Sites have been well excavated and
well preserved. The most imposing is the megalithic tomb
of Midhowe, whose immensely long gallery is divided into a
series of compartments or stalls by pairs of upright slabs projecting opposite one another from either wall. Many bodies
were found on stone slab benches in these stalls. Taiversoe
Tuack, which is unique in having a second storey quite clearly
present above the roof of a lower one, is another of the many

megaliths in this diminutive island. There are brochs, and one of them, fully excavated together with its surrounding cluster of huts, stands just above the sea looking across the sound to Mainland. Among the comparatively few monuments on Hoy one is of unusual interest; this is the Dwarfie Stane, a burial chamber which is cut out from an outcrop of solid rock.

There are interesting megaliths on others of the Orkneys— *e.g.* Quoyness on Sanday and a complex example with many cells on the Holm of Papa Westray; all the islands also have examples of broch architecture. As for the Shetlands, they have not many important megalithic sites recorded, but there are as many as 78 brochs, including one of the most famous of all, the Broch of Mousa, and also the carefully explored Bronze and Iron Age village of Jarlshof (p. 94). Here, not far from the Arctic Circle, we may be allowed to end this survey of the outstanding prehistoric monuments of Britain.

INDEX

Abbevillian, 12-13
Abernethy, 108
Acheulian, 12-15
Aesica brooch, 139
Agricola, 137-8, 142-3, 144
agriculture, 25-7, 28-9, 33-4, 48, 50, 55, 76, 86, 89-93, 94, 96-9, 101-2, 113, 116, 122, 126-7, 128, 139-42, 145-8, 164
Albinus, 144
All Cannings Cross, 104
Allectus, 147
Alpine race, 85
Alps, 73, 89-90, 95, 99, 105
amber, 70-4, 106, 118
anchor, 119
Angles, 150
Anglesey, 138
antiquarian societies, 155
Antiquaries of London, Society of, 157
Antonine Wall, 143-4
Antoninus Pius, 143-4
Arbor Low, 63
archæology, 151-79
archery, 34, 37, 49, 55, 57, 73
Arminghall, 63
'henge', 161
arrowheads, 22, 34, 37, 42, 49, 55, 57, 73
flint, barbed, 170
art, 9, 17-20, 21, 45, 105-6, 109-11, 117-118, 121-2, 124-5, 129-31
Celtic, 139, 146, 149
Arthur, 150
Aryan languages, 53
Atlantic sea-route, 29, 43, 45-7, 52, 67, 112, 120
Atrebates, 125-6
Aubrey, 152
Augustus, 132
Aurignacian, 17
Avebury, 4, 29, 57-63, 76, 153
axes, bronze, 68, 72, 78-83, 87-9, 93, 95-6, 100
copper, 45, 55
flint, stone, 19-22, 36-9, 48, 51, 55, 163

axes, iron, 122
and see battle-axes, hand-axes
Aylesford, 121
Azilian, 20-2, 24

Barrows, long, 40-3, 46-8
round, 40, 57, 59, 69, 82, 95, 97-8, 106, 110, 133, 170
Bath, 142
baths, 141-2, 145
Battersea, 111, 131
battle-axes, Battle-axe Folk, 53-4, 55, 59, 85, 97
beads, 36, 71, 73, 83, 84, 118, 163
beakers, Beaker Folk, 52-67, 69-73, 74-6, 82, 85, 134
Beech Bottom, 124
Belgæ, 120-34, 136, 137, 141, 151
Bigbury, 123
Birdlip, 111, 130
bits, 109, 111
Bleasdale, 82
Blenheim Park, 134
boars, *see* pigs
boats, canoes, 20-1, 29, 33, 36, 69-70, 87, 116-17
bone-work, 16, 18, 21-4, 36, 39, 83, 95, 103, 135
Boucher de Perthes, 155
Boudicca, 108, 138, 172
Bourton-on-the-Water, 134
Boyd Dawkins, 156
Bredon Hill, 114, 135
Brigantes, 129, 137-9, 144
British Museum, 160
Brittany, 6, 43-4, 52, 62-3, 70, 72, 78, 113, 119, 120, 121, 127, 129
brochs, 135, 138
bronze, 27-8, 51, 54-6, 62, 67-8, 70-4, 78-83, 87-9, 93-9, 100, 106, 109-11, 117, 121, 129-31, 133
Bronze Age, Early, 51 ff., 134
Middle, 76 ff., 86-8
Late, 85 ff., 100-1
brooches, 109, 121, 133, 139

Brough-on-Humber, 142
buckets, 93, 96, 103, 121
burials, Palæolithic, 14, 18-19
  Neolithic, 29, 39 ff.
  megalithic, 41-7, 63
  Bronze Age, 40, 56-9, 63-4, 66, 68-9,
    74-6, 82-3, 90, 95, 97-8
  Iron Age, 106, 110, 121, 127, 133
Bury Hill, 128
buttons, 55, 88

Cærleon, 143
Cæsar, 108, 109, 119, 121-8, 132-3, 137
Caistor-next-Norwich, 162
Camden, 152
camps, Neolithic, 29-33
  (forts), Iron Age, 107-8, 112-14, 119,
    123-4, 127-8, 135, 137, 143, 146, 171
Camulodunum, 132-3, 137, 138-9, 142,
    161, 172
canoes, see boats
Canterbury, 142
Cantii, 142
Caratacus, 137
Carausius, 147
Carn Brea, 30
carpentry, 21, 36, 96, 117-18, 122
carts, 27, 94, 116-18
Cassivellaunus, 123, 131
Castle-an-Dinas, 112
Castle Dore, 113
Castle Law, 108
cattle, oxen, 25-7, 29-34, 48, 54, 65, 67,
    76, 82, 84, 86, 90, 91-3, 94, 98, 102,
    116, 122, 132
cauldrons, 96, 100, 117
caves, 9, 15-18, 22, 93-4
Celtic art, 139, 146, 149
Celts, the, 54, 85-7, 89-91, 99, 101, 105-
    119, 120-1, 125, 133-4, 148-50
Channel Isles, 52, 78
chariots, 94, 106, 109, 122
Chester, 143-4
Chichester, 139
Christianity, 149-50
Chun Castle, 112
Churchill, Winston, 158
Chysauster, 113
circles, stone, 57-64, 77, 82, 134, 153
  wood, 63-4, 82, 134
Cissbury, 108

Clactonian, 12-14
Claudius, 137, 139
climate, 4, 7-8, 10-17, 19, 21-3, 25-6,
    89, 99, 101, 120
Clyde, 143-4
coal, 139
coins, 124-7, 129, 131, 133, 138, 149
Colchester, 132, 138-9, 142, 172
Colt Hoare, Sir R., 154
combs, weaving-, 103, 117, 135
Commius, 126-7, 131-2, 134, 137
Constantine, 147
Constantius, 147
Copernicus, 155
copper, 6, 27, 45, 51, 55, 62, 87, 99,
    139
coral, 109, 131
Coritani, 142
Cornovii, 142
Cornwall, 6, 30, 52, 72, 88, 91, 112-14,
    118, 135, 139
Cotswolds, 41-2, 47, 114, 119, 129-31,
    134, 142
Cranborne Chase, 156
Creswellian, 18-20
Crete, 72, 83
Crô-magnon Man, 18
Cunnington, W., 156
currency-bars, 124-5, 127
Cymbeline (Cunobelin), 132, 172

Daggers, bronze, 55, 57, 68, 72-3, 78-82
  copper, 55, 57
  flint, 55, 57
  iron, 109
Danebury, 128
Dartmoor, 6, 77
Darwin, Charles, 23, 155
Defoe, Daniel, 152
Denmark, 68-70, 77
Derbyshire, 139, 144
Desborough, 111, 130
Deverel-Rimbury, 90-3, 97-8, 101
dice, 118
Diocletian, 146-7
discovery in archæology, 159
distribution maps, 177
ditches, boundary-, 92-5
  (defensive dykes), 124, 127-8, 133,
    134
Dobuni, 129

dogs, 22, 30, 34, 90
Dolaucothy, 139
Dorchester, 142
Dorset, 5, 40, 90, 114, 118, 128-9, 142;
    and see Wessex
dress, 36, 55-6, 77-8, 88, 96-8, 103, 109
Druids, 62, 134, 138, 153
Durotriges, 129, 142

East Anglia, 9, 10, 20, 37, 63, 78, 90,
    108, 137, 139, 169, 173
Egypt, 28, 29, 68, 71-2, 83, 99
Ehenside Tarn, 30, 36
Elmswell, 139-40
enamel, 131, 133
enamelling, 139, 149
enclosures, cattle-, 92-3; *and see* camps,
    Neolithic fortified, 105; *and see*
    camps (forts)
eoliths, 8
Etruscans, 88, 106, 109
Exmoor, 6
experts, 174

Farnham, 22
Fens, 4, 78, 132, 169-70
fertility-cults, 17, 39, 58-9; *and see* magic,
    religion
fields, 29, 34, 77, 86, 91-2, 93, 98, 113
Finavon, 108
fire, 9, 16
firedogs, 124
fishing, 20-2, 33, 48, 65, 116-17
flint, flint-work, 8 ff., 19 ff., 33-4, 36 ff.,
    48, 51, 55 ff., 68, 73; *and see* tools
fogous, 113, 135
Folkton, 69
food-vessels, Food-Vessel Folk, 66-70,
    73-6, 82
forests, 4-5, 19-24, 25, 119, 122
forts, *see* camps
France, 4, 10, 17-18, 21-2, 29, 43, 46,
    67-8, 85-6, 88-90, 100-1, 106-7, 109-
    110, 111-13, 120
    (Gaul), 108, 113, 119, 120-3, 125-6,
    128-31, 132-4, 138, 147; *and see*
    Brittany
Frilford, 134

Gaul, *see* France
geology, 3, 5-9, 13-14, 17-19, 20-3

Germans, 85-6, 113, 120-1, 133, 150
Germany, 13, 48, 68, 85, 89-90, 105,
    120-1, 132, 147
Gibraltar skull, 155
glass, 118, 132
Glastonbury, 114-18, 129, 135
Gloucester, 142
gold, 55, 56, 62, 67-8, 71-4, 78, 94, 95-7,
    125-6, 133, 139
Gorsey Bigbury, 63
Goths, 148
Graig Lwyd, 37, 48, 163
Gravettian, 17-18
Great Chesters, 139
Greece, Greeks, 72-3, 83, 88, 96, 99, 101,
    105, 106, 110, 125, 135-6, 142
Greenwell, 156
Grime's Graves, 37-9
Grimspound, 77
Grunty Fen, 78

Hadrian, 138, 142
Hadrian's Wall, 138, 139, 143-5, 147-
    148
halberds, 55, 68, 73
Haldon, 30
Hallstatt, 99, 100-1, 105-6, 120, 128
hand-axes, 9-16
harpoons, fish-spears, 16, 19-21, 22
Heathery Burn, 93
Hebrides, 47
helmets, 106, 109, 110
Hembury, 135
Hetty Pegler's Tump, 41
Highland Zone, 137, 143, 146, 151, 168
hill-forts, *see* camps
Hittites, 99
hoes, 33, 77, 91
Holland, Low Countries, 48, 54, 86, 89,
    101, 120
Honorius, 148
horses, 16, 94, 109-10, 111, 122
Horsham, 22
Hounslow, 110
houses, huts, 22, 28, 30, 48-9, 55, 57, 65-6,
    77, 86, 93, 94-5, 101-2, 110-11, 113,
    116, 122, 128, 135, 141-6
Hunsbury, 119, 129
hunting, 13, 16-19, 21-4, 25-6, 34, 48, 65
    76, 82, 86, 102, 110
Huxley, T. E., 155

Ice Age, 7-8, 10-17, 19, 23, 25, 175
Iceni, 108, 129, 138-9
Ictis, 112
Illyrians, 85-6, 89-90
India, 12
Industrial Revolution, 27, 154
Industry, 27-8, 37, 48, 50, 72-4, 87, 99,
    122; *and see* bone-work, carpentry,
    flint-work, leather-work, metal-
    lurgy, mining, pottery, spinning,
    stone-work, weaving
interpretation in archæology, 175
invasion, 151
Ireland (Irish), 6, 20, 28-9, 44-6, 51-2,
    54, 56, 66-8, 70-2, 76, 78, 86, 88, 96,
    119, 135, 148-50; *and see* Scots
iron, 90, 95, 98-9, 100-1, 102-3, 109, 111,
    114-19, 120-2, 124, 132-3, 139
Iron Age, 62, 85-6, 99, 100 ff., 120 ff.
Italy, 88, 90, 105-6, *and see* Etruscans,
    Romans

Jarlshof, 94-5
jet, 62, 68, 73
Jutes, 150

Kent, 8, 47, 54, 90, 108, 120-3, 124, 126,
    129, 132, 137, 142, 147
Kent's Cavern, 15, 18
Kit's Coty House, 47
Knossos, 72, 83

Labour in excavation, 165
lake-dwellings, lake-villages, 30, 89-90,
    99, 114-18, 129, 135
language, 53-4, 86; *and see* speech
La Tène, 105-19, 120-2, 124, 129, 146,
    149
Latin, 142, 149
lead, 118, 139
leatherwork, 36
Leicester, 142
Leland, 152
Levalloisian, 13-15
Lexden, 133
Lincoln, 142
Little Woodbury, *see* Woodbury
Lockleys, Roman villa, 141
London, 132, 138, 142, 160

Loose Howe, 70
love, in archæology, 165
Low Countries, *see* Holland
lynchets, 91; *and see* fields
Lysons, Samuel, 154

Maeshowe, 46
Magdalenian, 18, 22
magic, 17, 27, 39, 40-7, 69-70, 73; *and see*
    art, circles, fertility-cults, religion
Maglemosian, 20-4
Maiden Castle, 40, 114, 128, 135, 137,
    142, 161, 171
Man, Isle of, 46
manure, 94
Marseilles, 106
Mass Observation, 158
Mauer, 13
Maximus, 148
Meare, 114, 129
Mediterranean, 28-9, 43, 50, 53-4, 55,
    68-9, 73, 94, 96, 106, 112, 120
Mediterranean race, 28-9, 48, 85
Medway, R., 137
megaliths, megalith-builders, -folk, 39-
    48, 62-4, 94, 134; *and see* circles,
    stone
Mendips, 139
Mesolithic, 19 ff., 25, 28, 48
metallurgy, 27, 45, 50, 51-2, 55, 66-8,
    70-3, 78-82, 87-9, 89-90, 93-4, 95-8,
    99, 100-1, 103, 112, 114, 117, 124,
    129; *and see* bronze, copper, gold,
    iron, lead, tin
microliths, 19-24
Midlands, 3-4, 7, 108, 119, 124, 129, 132
mining, flint-, 37-9, 48
    metal, 87, 112, 124, 139; *and see*
    metallurgy
mirrors, 109, 111, 129-30
Mold, 95
Mortimer, J. R., 156
Mousterian, 14-15
museums, 154-6

Neanderthal Man, 14-16, Gibraltar
    skull, 155
Nefertiti, 83
Neolithic, 25 ff., 51, 91
New Barn Down, 93

New Grange, 45-6
Noah, descendants of, 8-9
Nordic race, 53, 78, 85
Northumberland, 143

Oldbury, 124
Origin of Species, 155
Orkney Isles, 46, 54, 63-6
ornaments, 18-19, 27, 35-6, 55-7, 67-8, 70-4, 78, 82-3, 88-9, 93-4, 95-8, 103, 109-10, 131-3; *and see* amber, art, beads, bronze, brooches, gold, jet, pins, silver, torques
Overton Hill Sanctuary, 58

Palæolithic, 8 ff., 25
Palestine, 12
palstaves, 80
Parisi, 108-9, 119, 129
pastoralism, *see* cattle, pigs, sheep
Paul, St., 105
Paviland, 18
Peacock's Farm, 169-70, 171-2, 175
Peterborough (people), 48-50, 54, 66-7, 76
Picts, 148-50
pigs, 19, 34, 90, 110
Piltdown Man, 13
Pin Hole cave, 15, 18
pins, 88, 89, 95, 103
'pit-dwellings', 102, 104-5
Pitt-Rivers, 156, 174
Pleistocene, 7 ff.
ploughs, 91, 92, 102, 122, 141
Plumpton Plain, 86, 93
Polden Hill, 131
pollen analysis, 174
pottery, potting, 27-8, 162
  Neolithic, 34-6, 42, 47-9
  Bronze Age, 52, 56, 65, 68, 74, 82, 86, 93, 95, 97-8
  Iron Age, 103, 106, 110, 118, 122, 127, 128, 129, 132
  Roman, 146
  Samian, 138
Prince Consort, 154
Psychology, 158
purpose of archæology, 179
Pytheas, 112

Querns, 33, 102, 118

Rapiers, 80-2, 88
razors, 83, 100
religion, 17, 28, 39-50, 56-64, 68-70, 74, 82-3, 92, 97, 133-4, 146, 153, 155; *and see* barrows, burials, circles, Druids, fertility-cults, magic, megaliths
Remi, 126
Rhine, 145
Richborough, 147
Rillaton, 72
roads, *see* Roman roads
Rochester, 142
Roman army, 137-9, 143-5, 149
Roman civilization, Empire, 138, 142, 144, 146, 148-9
Roman conquest, 137-8
Roman roads, 138, 149
Romans, Rome, 91, 92, 105, 110, 111, 119, 120-3, 131-3, 136-51; *and see* Cæsar

St. Albans, 123, 132; *and see* Verulamium
St. Catharine's Hill, 127
St. Michael's Mount, 112
salt, 139
Samian pottery, 138
Saxons, 91, 147-50, 151
Scandinavia, 43, 69, 163; *and see* Denmark
Scotland, 5, 6, 22, 46, 51, 54, 55, 64, 67, 73, 76, 108, 135, 138-9, 143-5, 147-8; *and see* Hebrides, Orkney, Shetland
Scots (Irish), 148-50
sculpture, 146, 149
Scythians, 106
self-consciousness in man, 157
Severus, 144-5, 147
sheep, 29, 30, 65, 77, 78, 90, 93, 94, 102, 116
Shetland Isles, 94-5, 98
shields, 95, 109-10, 111, 131
ships, 27, 69-70, 119, 122-3, 126
Shropshire, 139, 142
sickles, 49, 89, 96, 100, 102, 134
Silbury Hill, 59
silver, 121, 133, 139
Skara Brae, 64-6, 77, 83, 95
skulls, 13-14, 18, 29, 40, 52, 85, 155
slings, 113, 128

social organization, 12-13, 27-8, 41, 43-4, 48, 54, 62, 65-7, 71-2, 76, 83, 87, 93, 95, 101, 105, 109-10, 114-18, 121, 124-5, 126, 128, 136

Society of Antiquaries, 153; *and see* Antiquaries of London

Spain, 29, 43, 45, 52, 54, 85

spam, 158

spearhead, bronze, typology of, 176-7

spearheads, spears, 78-82, 83, 88, 89, 93, 95, 100, 109, 128; *and see* harpoons

spear-throwers, 16

speech, 9; *and see* language, Aryan languages

spinning, 28, 96, 103; *and see* weaving

Stennis, 63

stone, stone-work, 12, 19, 33, 37, 55, 63, 65, 68, 69, 95; *and see* flint, querns, tools

Stone Age, *see* Palæolithic, Mesolithic, Neolithic

stone axes, analysis of, 163

Stonehenge, 4, 57, 59-61, 76, 134, 152-153

stratification, 167, 175

Stripple Stones, 63

Stukeley, 58, 62, 153

surveying, 168

Sussex, 5, 13, 29, 30, 37, 54, 86, 90, 92-3, 108, 124, 126, 129, 137, 139, 141

Sutton Hoo ship grave, 161, 173

Swanscombe Man, 14

Swarling, 121

swords, bronze, 88, 89-90, 93, 95, 100-1; *and see* rapiers

iron, 90, 99, 100, 106, 109, 111, 118, 128, 129

Tardenoisian, 22-4

Tasciovanus, 131

temples, Roman, 139, 142

Thames, 5, 10, 14, 70, 77, 90, 108, 119, 122, 126, 131

tin, 27, 52, 87, 99, 112, 118, 139

tool-making, 8-13, 28, 51, 99; *and see* tools, metallurgy

tools, bone, 12, 16, 18, 20-4, 36, 39, 57, 83, 95, 103, 117, 135

bronze, 28, 51, 55, 68, 70, 72, 78-82, 83, 87, 89, 93, 95-6, 98-9, 100

copper, 45, 52, 55

tools, flint, 8-9, (core, flake) 9-16, (blade) 16-21 *and* stone (Mesolithic), 19-20 (Neolithic and Bronze Age), 36-9, 49, 55, 57, 68, 70

iron, 100, 102, 103, 117, 118, 122, 124

torques, 78

Torrs, 111

towns, Roman, 138, 142-3, 145, 147-9

trade, 28, 37, 45, 48, 52, 55, 67, 70-2, 73, 84, 87-9, 95-6, 98-9, 103, 106, 111-12, 113-14, 118-19, 120, 129, 132-3

trial trenches, 168

Trinovantes, 123-4, 132

Trundle, 127

typology, 78-80, 176

Uffington White Horse, 42, 125

urban life, 27

urnfields, 97; *and see* Deverel-Rimbury

Urn Folk, 76-84, 86-7, 90, 98

urns, 74, 82, 96-8, 121, 127

Ussher, Archbishop, 155

Veneti, 113-14, 119, 121, 128

Verulamium, 131, 138, 142

villages, 26, 64-6, 94-5, 101, 103-4, 112, 141, 143, 146; *and see* lake-villages

villas, Roman, 141-2, 145-8

vitrified forts, 108

Wales, 6, 18, 22, 37, 42, 44, 48, 61, 64, 95, 100, 114, 135, 137-9, 143-4, 146, 148, 163

warfare, 81-2, 83, 106-8, 111-12, 113-14, 119, 120-1, 122-3, 126-8, 131-2, 134-9, 142-50

Wayland's Smithy, 42

weaving, 27, 36, 56, 77, 96, 103, 117 129, 135

Welwyn, 141

Wessex, 37, 52, 63, 64, 70-6, 90, 98, 101, 108, 114, 119, 127, 137, 141

Wessex culture, 62, 70 ff., 83, 163

wheat, identification of species, 164

Wheathampstead, 124

Whitehawk, 30

Wiltshire, 5, 29, 41, 57-63, 72, 100, 104, 128, 154, 156; *and see* Wessex

Winchester, 127
Windmill Hill (people), 29-36, 40, 44, 48, 52, 54, 91, 176
Witham, 110, 111
Woodbury, Little, 101-4, 107
Woodhenge, 63
Worlebury, 135

Yarnbury Castle, 128
York, 142-4, 147
Yorkshire, 4, 5, 29, 41, 55, 68, 69, 76-7, 89-90, 108-9, 129, 139-40, 148, 156

Zeus, 59

PRINTED IN GREAT BRITAIN BY
R. & R. CLARK, LTD., EDINBURGH